Praise for "Leadership in a Wiki World"

"Rod Collins is one of the most extraordinary graduates of our executive leadership seminars. He has combined the insights from his learning opportunities with his own fresh ideas and extensive executive experience to create stunning and sustainable business results. This book coaches you on how to achieve extraordinary performance with less effort, while making money and having more fun. How's that for a business book promise!"
　　　　- **Robert White,** former Chairman, ARC International,
　　　　and author of *Living an Extraordinary Life*

"*Leadership in a Wiki World* is a must-read for leaders who want to stay ahead of the rapid changes that are impacting the way we work. It's full of practical advice and tested techniques that will help anyone lead more effectively in the post-internet world"
　　　　- **Wendy Mack,** co-author of *Change at the Core:*
　　　　Unleash Your Team's Energy to Drive Results

"The 21st century has emerged in a very dramatic and surprising fashion. Unprecedented unemployment, economic turmoil and attacks on our native soil have us all probing for answers. Rod Collins' brilliant work *Leadership in a Wiki World* crisply explains, educates and presents managers with a road map for success in both business and life in our new millennium"
　　　　- **John Stypulkoski,** President, Vertical Resources

"This book is of critical importance to 21st century leaders who want to tap the creativity, collective intelligence, and commitment of people in their organizations. In the Work-Thru, Rod Collins gives us not only a practical process for accomplishing this goal, but an unequalled leadership development opportunity to boot! By embracing the role of Work-Thru facilitator, a leader gains a competency essential in a world that relies on networks and matrices rather than linear organization charts. And in demonstrating this competency the leader not only helps create powerful results, she builds trust throughout the organization."
　　　　- **Glenna Gerard,** Co-author, *Dialogue: Rediscover the*
　　　　Transforming Power of Conversation, and Creator of
　　　　the *Presence Walkabout*™ Programs

Leadership in a Wiki World

Leveraging Collective Knowledge
To Make the Leap
To Extraordinary Performance

Rod Collins

LEADERSHIP IN A WIKI WORLD:
Leveraging Collective Knowledge to Make the Leap to Extraordinary Performance

First published by Dog Ear Publishing
4010 W. 86th Street, Ste H
Indianapolis, IN 46268
www.dogearpublishing.net

dog ear
PUBLISHING

ISBN: 978-160844-466-3

This book is printed on acid-free paper.

First Edition
Printed in the United States of America

Library of Congress Cataloging-in-Publication Data

Collins, Rod.
Leadership in a wiki world: leveraging collective knowledge to make the leap to extraordinary performance / Rod Collins – 1st ed.
p. cm.
Includes bibliographical references

1. Leadership   2. Collective Knowledge   3. Organizational Change   I. Title

To my wife, Catherine,
for her constant support,
intuitive empathy,
and abundant kindness

CONTENTS

ACKNOWLEDGMENTS

Writing this book has been the culmination of an illuminative personal journey full of surprises, insights, learning, and growth. I have had the privilege of sharing this adventure with many remarkable people, some through their constant presence, others through our work together, and still others through the wisdom of their written words. However our paths have crossed, they have all influenced the ideas contained in this book. Any errors, of course, are my own responsibility.

I am very grateful to all my many friends and colleagues in the Blue Cross and Blue Shield organizations throughout the United States for their commitment and dedication in serving the millions of customers in the Federal Employee Program. Though there is not enough space to acknowledge each of them individually, I am forever enriched because they are the ones who first showed me the incredible power of collective knowledge and taught me that nobody is smarter than everybody.

Many thanks to the following people for investing hours in reading parts of the manuscript or discussing its underlying principles, providing feedback, and helping me think more clearly about the concepts in this book: Anne Murray Allen, Virginia Avrutin, Rose Marie Barbeau, Paul Bodor, Sandra Bond, Dennis Carrai, Rob Creekmore, Glenna Gerard, Dawna Jones, Seth Kahan, Wendy Mack, Stephanie Nestlerode, Jeanette Nyden, Fred Plumb, Brian Prentice, Don Prentice, Lew Rhodes, Ed Smith, Robert Tipton, Bob Tobias, and Linda Williamson. And special thanks go to Meghan Donohue for editing, and to Chris Clarke-Epstein and Jane Atkinson for inspiring the book's title.

I am also indebted to the many intellectual pioneers whose writings have opened me to the innovative ways of thinking and acting that are hastening the arrival of the wiki world: Ken Auletta, Rod A. Beckstrom, Josh Bernoff, Ori Brafman, Steven Cabana, James Champy, Ram Charan, Jim Collins, Thomas L. Friedman, Gary Hamel, Michael Hammer, Dee Hock, Jeff Howe, Jeff Jarvis, A. G. Lafley, Polly LaBarre, Charlene Li, Andrew Lih, Melanie Mitchell, Ronald E. Purser, Eric Raymond, Peter M. Senge, James Surowiecki, Don Tapscott, William C. Taylor, Margaret J. Wheatley, and Anthony D. Williams.

Finally, I am deeply thankful for the love and support of my wife, Catherine, our daughters Melissa and Meghan and their spouses, and our three wonderful grandsons who are true children of our new wiki world.

PREFACE

This book is about two ideas whose time has almost come. When they firmly take root, they will dramatically reshape the ways we work together, especially in large organizations. While these ideas have already begun to sprout, most of us underestimate their impact and remain largely unaware that they will inevitably end the world as we have known it. That's because we fail to recognize that the growing number of unprecedented events, especially in the first decade of our new century, is a harbinger of our passage into a radically different world with a completely new set of rules. Instead, we find ourselves befuddled and confused trying to come to terms with surprising realities that the old rules told us could never happen. For a long time most of us believed that terrorist attacks would never visit our soil, real estate values would always go up, and the smartest organizations would always be the ones led by the smartest people. Those beliefs have been shattered as we indelibly remember where we were on September 11th, have no idea when we will recover our lost home equity, and are incredulous how supposedly smart people brought us to the brink of an economic depression. As we enter the "teens," recent polls reveal that the majority of us feel negatively about the 21st century's nameless first decade. For so many, it has been a time of great turmoil and disruption.

However, the nameless decade has also been a time of rapid technological development and unprecedented strides in human capacity. Cells phones, e-mail, the Internet, social networking, open source, and an online encyclopedia created by the masses were unimaginable a mere 20 years ago. Yet, it is these unprecedented events that will be the true game-changers and they will have a far greater influence on defining our future than the disruptive consequences of failed beliefs. That's because the game-changers are manifestations of the two ideas whose time has almost come.

The first of these ideas is: *When human organizations have the processes to leverage collective knowledge, nobody is smarter or faster than everybody.* We see this concept reflected in the workings of new business enterprises, such as Google, Linux, and Wikipedia, each one built upon the groundbreaking principle that the smartest organizations are those with the capacity to quickly access the wisdom of the crowd and the ability to leverage the resulting collective knowledge into a level of performance so extraordinary that it wrecks all our beliefs about the ways large groups get things done.

Linux and Wikipedia are redefining the standards for how we lead nonprofit and volunteer organizations as they challenge the conventional wisdom that organizational excellence comes from efficiently leveraging the individual knowledge of heroic leaders and star performers. Google, on the other hand, is disrupting the established practices for how we manage corporate enterprises. While its meteoric rise is often associated with the quality of its remarkable search engine, the real story behind Google's extraordinary success is its revolutionary capacity to organize collective knowledge into an efficient operating model. Unlike the organizational design in most other businesses, the methodology that Google uses to rank the Web's content is not built to amplify the knowledge of individual experts. Instead, PageRank is a process that quickly collates the collective knowledge of the masses to guide the order of its search results. Given that it is the preferred choice for over two-thirds of Web surfers, it's clear that Google has leveraged its discovery that nobody is smarter or faster than everybody into a profitable business model. It's this discovery that is making so many traditional companies very nervous, and with good reason. Once Google fully understands that search is an application and that aggregating collective knowledge is the game-changer, they are likely to migrate their formidable skills and talents into unsuspecting complacent industries, creating innovative operating models that will displace longstanding business platforms in the new decade as quickly as they dethroned the popular search engines of the last decade.

While it may take a little time for us to get comfortable with the notion that collective wisdom usually trumps conventional wisdom, our growing familiarity with the Internet will make it a little easier to accept this first revolutionary concept. It's the second idea that will be much more troublesome because it goes against the grain of the most fundamental belief for how we organize the efforts of large numbers of people: *In the smartest and fastest organizations, leaders do not have the authority to issue orders or to expect compliance.* In other words, when organizations learn how to leverage collective knowledge, they don't need bosses to get things done.

Most of us cannot conceive of an organization without bosses. We believe that companies would quickly slide into chaos if someone were not in charge. However, Linux, Wikipedia, and Google are extraordinarily successful precisely because their leaders have very limited authority. Linus Torvalds and Jimmy Wales don't give orders or make assignments in their open sourced operating platforms. The volunteers of Linux and Wikipedia decide where they'll devote their efforts and are responsible for organizing their own work. And Google arranges its organization to make it impossible for its leaders to behave like traditional bosses. With 50 – 100 direct reports and workers having the right to self-direct 20 percent of their time, managers are forced to learn new ways of leading where the ability to get things done comes from the power to connect and collaborate rather than the authority to be in charge and in control.

This second idea is so troublesome because it revolutionizes the practice of leadership, especially in the large organizations. For more than a century, leaders have been bosses, and the authority to issue orders and to expect compliance has been their defining attribute. While some have been more participative and others have been more autocratic, everyone inside a traditional organization understands that, regardless of style, the boss is in charge. However, as more businesses discover that their survival depends on their capacity to leverage collective knowledge, they will quickly realize that their continued reliance on a cadre of supervisors is the greatest impediment to meeting the new demands for innovation and speed in fast moving markets. When nobody is smarter or faster than everybody, you don't need bosses editing or overruling collective wisdom.

However, diminishing the bosses does not mean that organizations do not need leaders. In fact, in the new economy of the emerging Digital Age, leaders are more important than ever. That's because collective knowledge needs to be processed and aggregated. Someone needs to guide the creation of our common ground and the shaping of our shared understanding, whether through electronic learning platforms, such as PageRank, or through large group collaboration sessions, such as the Work-Thrus that will be described later in this book. The leaders of these smarter and faster organizations will exert a different type of influence where they are the facilitators of the discovery processes that shape the decisions rather than the controllers who take charge and make the decisions. Thus, we are learning that the key to successfully managing in fast changing times is to focus more on making discoveries and less on making decisions. When you make the right discoveries, it turns out that the right decisions are likely to follow. If businesses want to make sure that their organizations are designed for innovation, they can't let decision-makers short-circuit the discoveries resident in their collective knowledge. That's why, in the new economy, leaders are facilitators who do not have the authority to issue orders or expect compliance.

These two ideas will inevitably revolutionize the practice of management and will completely redefine the challenge of organizing the work of large numbers of people. In the Digital Age, the business of business has more to do with mass collaboration than mass production. And, as we will discover throughout this book, you can't use mass production practices to successfully lead or manage in a mass collaboration world. As difficult as it may be for some of us to comprehend, the world as we have known it really is about to end, and should you find this hard to believe, ask yourself this question: If you had to wager on which company will be around at the end of the next decade would you bet on General Motors or Google?

There's a reason that the time for these two ideas is emerging now, and it has more to do with the times than it does the ideas. These two concepts could never take hold in world where hierarchies and mechanistic models continue to define our social organizations. The fact that these ideas are beginning to sprout now can only mean that the world that we have known for the last 150 years is clearly fading away. We are rapidly exiting the Industrial Age and entering the new and very different Digital Age. The defining characteristic of this new age is that its breakthrough technologies have made networks far more powerful than hierarchies. That's why facilitative leaders leveraging collective knowledge in collaborative communities will inevitably displace authoritative bosses and their hierarchical bureaucracies.

In the chapters ahead, you will become acquainted with the new rules of a very different business world. We call it the wiki world because the defining attribute that will separate the winners from the losers in the new economy will be the capacity to keep pace with the speed of accelerating change that is now a permanent fixture of our global business environment.

There are different ways that you can approach the subsequent chapters, depending upon which of the following three groups best describes your relationship with digital technology. The first group is the *digital natives*. These technology aficionados were generally born after 1975 and have spent the entirety of their young lives in the new wiki world. For them, working with digital technology is second nature, and much like a language, the networked thinking that is the foundation of the Web is hard-wired into their brains. As a consequence, they can't relate to the fundamentals of hierarchical thinking and don't adapt well to traditional organizations.

The second group is the *digital immigrants* who, like the digital natives, are very conversant in digital technology. However, unlike the digital natives, the new technology is not hard-wired into their natural thinking. Thus, rather than being second nature, their relationship with digital technology is more like a second language. That's because most of the digital immigrants were born before 1975 and were originally reared in the hierarchical and mechanical thinking of the Industrial Age. This is not to imply that the digital immigrants are more comfortable with the old ways of thinking. Quite the contrary, it's highly likely that they prefer the new ways, but much like the person who has become very fluent in a second language, they have become highly adept at mentally transitioning from the original tongue that remains their first frame of reference.

The third group is the *digital strangers*. The people in this last group were all born before 1975 and may or may not be familiar with digital technology. Those who are unfamiliar never touch a computer, would never purchase an mp3 player, and see their cell phones as nothing more than convenient telephones. They are also likely to have their secretaries print out their e-mails and dictate responses that their assistants will handle. On the other hand, there are those digital strangers who consider themselves computer savvy. They e-mail, surf the Web, and know how to use Microsoft Office. Yet, they are nevertheless digital strangers because they see the computer as a highly sophisticated machine and the Internet as the world's best reference library. They don't participate in social networking nor do they consider the Internet to be a place where people gather to build online communities and create knowledge.

In approaching the subsequent chapters, the digital strangers will benefit most if they read the chapters in their regular order. On the other hand, those who are digital natives or digital immigrants might consider beginning with Chapter 1, skipping to Chapter 4, and returning to Chapters 2 and 3 after completing the remaining chapters. Chapter 2 presents an overview of traditional hierarchical management and explains why its underlying assumptions and beliefs are unsustainable in the Digital Age. Chapter 3 provides a summary overview of the new leadership responsibilities of Digital Age businesses and makes the evolutionary connections between the old and the new management models for leaders who have been schooled in traditional management.

Finally, please note that Chapter 7 departs from the usual narrative and presents a step-by-step description of the principles, practices, and procedures for leading Work-Thru sessions. Work-Thru is an innovative and powerful meeting format that provides companies with quick access to their collective knowledge. Depending upon your preference, you may choose to read this chapter in its regular order or come back and read it at the end. However you choose to approach the chapters, I hope that you will find much value in these pages and will commit to discovering and applying the incredible power of collective knowledge to make the leap to extraordinary performance.

Rod Collins
rodcollins@wiki-management.com
www.wiki-management.com
Aurora, Colorado

Part One

A NEW MINDSET

Chapter 1

THE INEVITABLE REVOLUTION

There's little that can be said with certainty about the future except this: sometime over the next decade your company will be challenged to change in a way for which there is no precedent.

- Gary Hamel
The Future of Management[1]

A popular image that has connected with many executives is Jim Collins' notion of "getting the right people on the bus."[2] In his best-selling study of businesses that made the leap from good to great, Collins found that, unlike most companies' usual practice of figuring out what to do and then finding the people to do it, the leaders who guided these extraordinary organizations did the opposite. Instead, Collins discovered, "they first got the right people on the bus and then figured out where to drive it."[3] Given the increasing uncertainty and complexity in today's markets, it is not surprising that perplexed executives would latch onto the notion that many of their problems would be solved if only they had the right people.

But what if having the right people is not enough? While "getting the right people on the bus" is important, isn't it just as important to be on the right bus? After all, you can gather all the right people you need and you can even determine the right direction that you need to take, but if you're on the wrong bus, you're not going to get to where you need to be going. Worse yet, you won't be able to keep the right people even if you are able to recruit them because once they figure out that yours is the wrong bus, they won't stay for very long.

If you want to attract and retain the right people, then you need to be on the right bus. And if you want to be on the right bus, you will need to look at technology in a completely different way. That's because the difference between the right bus and the wrong bus is all about technology, but not in the ways that might first come to mind.

THE POWER OF A SOCIOECONOMIC REVOLUTION

When we think of technology, we think of tools and gadgets. We marvel at the amazing breakthroughs in electronics and robotics. What comes to mind is the progressive stream of inventions over thousands of years from the very first wheel to the latest iPhone. For most of us, technology is about things. It's about the modern machines that make life easier, faster and more convenient. However, there is another dimension of technology – one that is often overlooked because it has nothing to do with things. This other dimension is about people and the ways that people work together.

The history of technology is an iterative journey. It's a journey between people and their things and between developments in physical technology and advances in social technology. There are milestones on this journey that mark the breakthrough moments when great leaps in physical technology dramatically reshape social technology. These landmarks proclaim the revolutionary transitions between the socioeconomic eras that shape our day-to-day experience and form the social mindsets that define the framework of our political, family, and work lives. And so, throughout the history of civilization, these occasions have marked our passage from the Stone Age to the Agrarian Age, and then to the Industrial Age.

As our iterative journey continues, most of us are well aware that, with the convergence of personal computers, the World Wide Web, and fiber optics, we are witnessing a significant revolution in physical technology. However, very few of us realize that we are once again at one of those rare historical milestones where a great leap in physical technology generates an inevitable revolution in social technology. And just because most of us don't see it coming doesn't mean it isn't happening. Whether we realize it or not, today's emerging Digital Age will reshape the prevailing social mindset, and as a result, it will also dramatically change the work we do and the way we work.

It is difficult for us to comprehend just how quickly and how thoroughly the world of work is about to change. Nevertheless, we are at a tipping point in the evolution of large business organizations where traditional corporations and their executives now find themselves in an unprecedented business reality for which they are totally unprepared. The signs are all around us, but we miss them because we see the world through a social lens that is rapidly losing relevance.

Have you noticed the recent sudden acceleration in the pace of change across all industries? Have you seen that there is more on the "corporate plate" than ever before? Have you recognized that the methods and practices that have always predictably delivered results are not so predictable anymore? Have you found that twentysome-things are refusing to adapt to your corporate ways and that you can't keep them for more than 12 – 18 months before they head for the door? Finally, have you noticed in your most private moments – the ones that you don't share with others – that you are not quite as sure of what you are doing as you once were?

These are all signs that the world of work is already changing and changing fast. To help us understand just how dramatically a socioe-conomic revolution changes the world of work, let's look back to the time before the Industrial Revolution and engage together in a little mind experiment.

Imagine that we step into a time machine and that our destination is to travel back to central Pennsylvania in the early 1700's. The trip begins smoothly enough. However, along our way back in time, we encounter the most severe turbulence that any of us has ever experi-enced. After some very frightful moments, our vehicle manages to land on the gentle slopes of the early 18th century commonwealth. As we all breathe a sigh of relief, the captain informs us that she has good news and bad news. The good news is that despite the obvious mal-function in our time machine, we have managed to land safely. The bad news is that we cannot travel back to the 21st century and that we are now permanent residents of this 18th century agricultural paradise.

As we alight from the vehicle, how many of us will easily find work in our current chosen professions? In the Agrarian Age there were not many executives, managers, analysts, or technical specialists. There were no pilots, telemarketers, computer programmers, or even professional athletes. Most of today's jobs are products of the Indus-trial Age and simply did not exist in the Agrarian Age.

We find ourselves today in a similar position as we transition into the Digital Age. If you've walked through the airport terminal in Den-ver, you may have seen the thoughtful ad for the business school at the University of Denver that proclaims "The top 10 jobs of 2015 don't exist today." That is the power of a socioeconomic revolution.

A CENTURY-OLD SOCIAL TECHNOLOGY

When we think of technology we usually focus on physical technology because, over the last 100 years, that's where we have seen countless incremental changes. We have come a long way from the Model T Ford to the Toyota Prius and from rotary "party line" telephones to wireless cell phones. The history of the 20th century has been about the steady stream of inventions and progressive improvements in machines and their ability to make our lives easier and more convenient. If you've ever visited the Carousal of Progress at Disney World, you have a sense for all the improvements to lifestyle and quality of life brought about by the continual enhancements in physical technology throughout the last century.

Remarkably, however, we have hardly seen any incremental change in our social technology. For more than a century, the social technology of work, especially in large organizations, has remained essentially unchanged. The hierarchical management model that was used to run the first large assembly lines is still used today to manage 21st century organizations.

Some of you may protest, "That's not true! What about participative management?" Unfortunately, while the luminaries of worker involvement did indeed spark a human relations movement in the later part of the 20th century, to be candid, their influence on management practices has been superficial at best. Sure managers today are more benevolent when compared to the draconian habits of the early Industrial Age bosses. However, when it comes to implementing the insights of the human relations movement, management's efforts have been far more about style than substance. Today's managers may spend more time soliciting input from their workers, but at the end of the day, the managers are still the bosses, the workers are still subordinates, and these professionals are still expected to do as they are told.

It turns out that while executives have been very willing to adjust the style of management to accommodate prevailing social trends, they have been most unwilling to modify the organizational structures that reinforce the manager's authority to assign work and to assure workers' compliance with management's directives. However, the lip service paid to the values of participative management over the last half of the 20th century may not be sustainable into our 21st century world because of three sudden developments that are rapidly ushering in the Digital Age.

THREE DEVELOPMENTS

The first of these developments is the incredible accelerating pace of change that has overtaken every industry over the last two decades. The unprecedented speed of market evolution is dramatically altering the business landscape. In the recording industry, for example, throughout most of the 20th century market change was about vinyl records going from 78 rpm's to 45 rpm's to 33 rpm's. However since the late 1970's, we have witnessed the obsolescence of vinyl records, the coming and going of eight-track and cassette tapes, the advent of the compact disc, and now we have the ability to bypass records, tapes, and discs altogether to directly store digital music onto our computers or mp3 players.

While executives across all industries readily acknowledge that the world is moving faster, what they don't fully comprehend is that the increment of time for market change is now shorter than the increment of time for moving information up and down a chain of command. This means that the social technology of the command-and-control organization cannot keep pace with the speed of change in today's faster moving markets.

The second development is that the Internet has created the unprecedented capacity for mass collaboration. Don Tapscott and Anthony D. Williams, in their insightful book *Wikinomics*, describe how this new phenomenon of mass collaboration will profoundly change the world of business as we know it.[4] It is the Internet that is the breakthrough milestone – that great leap in physical technology – that is driving the passage from the Industrial Age to the Digital Age.

The groundbreaking contribution of the Web is that it is a revolutionary new medium where individuals anywhere in the world can speak to one another without going through a central organization. For the first time in history, we have the capability for large numbers of geographically dispersed individuals to effectively and directly work together in real time – and they can do it faster, smarter, and cheaper. Who would have believed just 20 years ago that you could build a successful computer operating system using only volunteers working without a plan, without assigned tasks, and even without pay – and that the product that these volunteers put together would be so good that an established industry giant like IBM would abandon its own efforts at proprietary offerings to become part of the voluntary community of workers? Yet that is the incredible story of Linux and the emerging power of mass collaboration.

The third development is the ascendance of knowledge networks and the decline of facilities and machines as critical economic assets, resulting in a radical transformation of both the primary means for creating economic value and the fundamental economic value proposition across all businesses. We last saw such a change in the transition from the Agrarian Age to the Industrial Age when the fundamental economic value proposition shifted from self-sufficient farming to mass production and when machines became the means of production, replacing land, which had been the means of subsistence. As we now transition into the Digital Age, mass collaboration is replacing mass production as the fundamental economic value proposition and economic success is no longer about machines or owning the means of production. It's now about networks and having access to the means of collaboration.

This shift from mass production to mass collaboration means that corporations no longer enjoy the luxury of owning all the critical economic assets. It is the workers, and not the corporations, who own the knowledge in the networks. And it is the workers who now own the primary means for creating economic value. This new reality was dramatically demonstrated on September 11, 2001.

The corporate headquarters of Empire Blue Cross Blue Shield was located in the north tower of the World Trade Center. While nine of its employees and two consultants lost their lives on that tragic day, over 1,900 workers survived the terrorist attacks. Empire lost over 250 computer servers, over 2,000 desktop computers, and over 480,000 square feet of office space when the north tower collapsed.[5] In a single instant, Empire had lost its headquarters facility and all of its equipment. Yet remarkably within three days Empire was fully operational. While the company had lost its machines, Empire was fortunate that almost all of its workers survived and its data had been backed up to another site on a regular basis. With its people safe and its data secured, Empire had the essentials it needed to be quickly back in business. Within in a matter of hours, the company was able to locate alternative facilities and make the computer hardware arrangements to once again begin processing health insurance claims.

The New York state examiner's report on the recovery efforts of Empire Blue Cross Blue Shield cited three contributing factors for the company's very effective response to the terrorist disaster. First, Empire's disaster recovery plan, especially its regular back up of electronic data, securely preserved the company's critical business information. Second, Empire's continuous quality improvement program created a business environment where all employees understood the operations of the whole company and were aware of how their individual functions impacted other departments and the company as a whole. As a result, despite the catastrophic disruption of their working arrangements, when the employees began reporting to their temporary locations, they understood the specific effects of the disaster and what needed to be done. But perhaps, most importantly, the continuous quality improvement program encouraged employees to act independently and move projects to completion. This proved to be crucial on September 11th between 8:46 a.m. when the first plane crashed into the north tower and 10:28 a.m. when the tower collapsed.

Despite the chaos and confusion in those first moments after the attack, middle managers at other Empire locations did not hesitate to make critical decisions when they were unable to contact senior management. Their quick thinking and their bold initiative in making important decisions that were usually beyond their normal authority were essential contributions to the data preservation that enabled Empire's resilience.

Finally, the state examiner singled out the employees as a key factor for Empire's extraordinary recovery. The report states:

> Empire has a very stable workforce that has repeatedly shown its commitment to the company. The dedication, responsibility and hard work of all of the individuals who work at Empire were clearly contributing factors. Notwithstanding the trauma employees had been through, many World Trade Center employees reported to work at other sites within hours of the disaster, and many more by the next morning. Empire's workforce deserves much of the credit for the rapid and efficient recovery.[6]

Unfortunately, most managers today are not aware that the new means for creating economic value belongs to the workers and, thus, they continue to regard human resources as corporate assets available at their discretion. This helps to explain why today's twentysomethings are refusing to adapt to the ways of hierarchical management. Unlike previous generations of college graduates, today's younger workers understand that knowledge is a key economic asset, are discovering that they own it, and are bolting from traditional organizations in unprecedented numbers to find working arrangements more suitable to the way they see the world.

Traditional managers underestimate the impact of their inability to retain younger workers because they believe that it is just a matter of time before these dilettantes come to terms with the "real world" and, like prodigal children, find their way back to the corporate fold. However, what is more likely to happen is that it will not be long before these managers awaken to the fact that it is they who need to come to terms with new realities and abandon outdated management practices because no 21st century business can survive for very long if it cuts itself off from the means of collaboration.

THE INEVITABLE REVOLUTION IN SOCIAL TECHNOLOGY

It is the physical technology of the Internet and its groundbreaking capacity for mass collaboration that will change the work we do and the way we work and bring about the inevitable revolution in social technology. How do we know this? Because this is exactly what happened at the start of the Industrial Revolution when the physical technology of the assembly line and its then new capacity for mass production brought about an inevitable revolution in the social technology of its time.

Before mass production, all business was small business and the average size of the typical enterprise was four workers.[7] You might be surprised to learn that before the Industrial Revolution, there were no bosses and there were no subordinates – there were only workers. The arrangement of supervisors and subordinates into hierarchical organizations is part of the social technology that emerged with the Industrial Revolution when for the first time business needed to come to grips with the challenge of organizing the work of large numbers of people. In its time, mass production brought about a great leap in the efficiency of work because it made centralization more efficient, but only if businesses had the ability to effectively organize large numbers.

Today we are witnessing the next great leap in the efficiency of work as the new breakthrough technology of mass collaboration makes decentralization more efficient. Accordingly, mass collaboration will define the Digital Age in the same way that mass production defined the Industrial Age. This means that every company needs to be asking itself, "How will mass collaboration reshape my business?"

And when it answers that question, it will quickly learn that you can't manage mass collaboration businesses using mass production practices.

When the central challenges of business are continual innovation and keeping up with an unrelenting pace of change, your organization better be built for knowledge and speed. Thus, the dominant management model for Digital Age companies will not be the usual "bus" of a command-and-control discipline whose prime values are order and authority, but rather an emerging new "bus," which I call wiki-management, whose core values of knowledge and speed will redefine the social technology for managing large organizations.

Getting on the right bus for a new age will not be easy for seasoned executives whose entire work lives have been spent inside traditional organizations. This is because wiki-management is a complete mindset shift that challenges every assumption about how we work, especially in large businesses. In the new management model, collective learning replaces central planning as the basis for smart strategy and self-organization succeeds hierarchical organization as the new foundation for execution advantage. The exercise of power is no longer about being in charge; it's now about being connected. This means that management's primary work is no longer defined by the longstanding tasks of planning, organizing, directing, coordinating, and controlling.

As we will learn in the subsequent chapters, when business survival depends on how well you are connected to the means of collaboration, management's new primary responsibilities are customer values, collective learning, shared understanding, focused measures, and collaborative community. These are unfamiliar concepts to many managers who are used to being in charge and know little about being connected. However, now that the fundamental management task is about making decentralization efficient, organizing the work of large numbers of people is a completely different challenge from what we have been used to.

For well over a hundred years, the assembly line and its hierarchical architecture have served as the prototypical model for managing multitudes of workers. From the very beginning, the Industrial Age was boss-driven and dominated by giants whose names remain familiar today: Carnegie, Rockefeller, and Ford. These "captains of industry" built huge centralized organizations based upon the principles of vertical integration. Control was paramount to the Industrial Age corporation and vertical integration provided organizations with maximum control. Vertical integration also provided the solid foundation upon which to build the command-and-control structures that defined the twentieth century corporation and reinforced the role of the bosses and the tasks they assigned as the focus of work.

The Digital Age is quite different. First it is customer-driven. Keeping the bosses happy is no longer enough. Today we are working for the customers, and more and more these shoppers are likely to be knowledge workers. This means that somebody else's knowledge workers are your customers. These educated consumers have high expectations, much information and many choices. They are far more demanding than the bosses would ever dare to be, and they will readily exercise their options when their expectations are not met. That is why the days of working for the bosses and "just stick to your job" are over. Today, we are indeed working for the customers and keeping them happy is the job. The question is no longer "Who's the boss?" It's now "Who's the customer?"

This shift from boss-driven to customer-driven is radically changing our understanding of the purpose of a business. Most of us learned in Business 101 that the purpose of a firm is to increase shareholder wealth. This was the unquestioned assumption of the Industrial Age that made perfect sense for a time when an elite group of shareholders owned the means of production. But what is the purpose of a company in the Digital Age? Michael Hammer asserts that today "the mission of a business is to create value for its customers."[8] This dramatic conversion in work's purpose is another example of how the social technology revolution is significantly changing our ways of thinking and our ways of managing.

In today's business environment, the successful companies will be those who are continually adapting to changing customer values and who understand that the creation of shareholder wealth is no longer a direct objective but rather a reward for keeping the customer satisfied. This is not to say that turning a profit is not important. Quite the contrary, revenue growth is more important than ever because so many of the workers/customers own stock. This is to say that companies focused on shareholder wealth will run the risk of concentrating on short-term bottom line results at the expense of long-term customer value, thus jeopardizing continual profits as we all have witnessed in the recent financial meltdown. In contrast, companies that continually keep their eye on customer values and how they are changing are more likely to grow their markets and promote sustainable profits.

THE MANAGEMENT GAP

Managing at the new pace of change in the Digital Age requires more nimble and flexible organizations based upon network models that are more decentralized by design. Joint ventures and business partnerships of allied but independently owned organizations that can quickly and seamlessly configure themselves to deliver what's most important to customers are better poised for success in changing markets. Because managers in these innovative arrangements often do not have command authority over many of the people who are essential to business success, they find themselves in a most challenging conundrum: How do you manage when you have no practical authority over many geographically dispersed workers in fast-changing markets?

Unfortunately because too many managers refuse to acknowledge the market shift from bosses to customers, they fail to recognize the conundrum and create a severe management gap for their companies as they continue to act out an obsolete management discipline. They remain largely unaware of the new management challenge because they continue to view the world through the social lens of a mechanistic mindset that believes that traditional organization charts still accurately reflect the work we do and the way we work.

The organization chart is the embodiment of the fundamental assumptions of management commonly shared, until recently, by successive generations of both managers and workers. For a long time, we have firmly believed that, if anything is to get done, someone needs to be in charge, and that the smartest organization is the one with the smartest individuals. Command-and-control management assumes that an organization's intelligence fundamentally resides in a select number of star performers who are able to leverage their expertise through the power to direct and control the work of others. Most organizations put their trust in stars and heroes. They are convinced that a single highly intelligent individual can make the difference between success and failure.

For well over a hundred years, we have all shared a social lens that believed in the need for bosses, the power of individual heroes, and the preeminence of specialized knowledge. Most of us believe in organization charts because, whether we realize it or not, we operate from an unquestioned mindset that assumes that projects are best handled when we break them into discrete parts, divide the labor, and then reassemble the finished work under the direction of a central leader. We believe in organization charts because most of us accept that that's just the way it is. But is it? The twentysomethings don't presume so. To their way of thinking, bosses aren't all that necessary, heroes are overrated, and the hoarding of knowledge makes absolutely no sense. This is because the twentysomethings are the first generation to come of age in the Digital Age and the first generation to embrace an entirely different social mindset from the many generations raised in the 20th century.

The millennials don't relate to a world where human activity is broken up into parts and then put back together again. For them the world is, always has been, and always will be an interconnected network. This is why the twentysomethings are bolting from hierarchical organizations and why they don't believe in organization charts. They aren't adapting to the ways of thinking and the ways of acting in traditional organizations because they choose not to, rather they don't adapt because, quite simply, they can't. There is nothing in their mental DNA that will allow them to buy into a mechanistic mindset, as did so many previous generations. The only social lens that they have ever known is the network mindset and to them the world is a network, not a machine. For this reason, as they move through their 20's, 30's, and 40's, they are likely to dramatically change every industry they touch as they propagate the market with their very different values.

Every generation born for the foreseeable future will share the new network mindset that already defines the world of today's twentysomethings. This is another reason why a revolution in social technology is inevitable. Thus, getting on the right bus means that executives must learn let go of organization charts, embrace new and unfamiliar responsibilities, and come to terms with a very different set of assumptions about managing in the new economy if they are to successfully meet the challenge of the management conundrum.

When you are organized for knowledge and speed, you quickly discover that if anything is to get done, everyone needs a shared understanding, and that the smartest organization is the one that has quick access to its collective knowledge. When the pace of change is continually accelerating, it becomes painfully clear that no single individual, or even a small group of experts, is smart enough to process all that is happening in real-time. If you want to manage successfully in the world of mass collaboration, you inevitably learn that nobody is smarter than everybody and that collective wisdom is more valuable than conventional wisdom. After all, it was the conventional wisdom of an elite few that created the recent financial meltdown. If we had had the foresight and the capacity to tap into the collective knowledge of all of the managers and workers in the financial services industry, it is doubtful that their collective wisdom would have reinforced the conventional wisdom that extending zero-down, low document mortgages to high-risk borrowers would make for a winning strategy.

The most untapped resource in corporate America today is the collective intelligence of an organization's own workers. What is amazing is that accessing this abundant reservoir requires no investment in dollars because it is already paid for. What it does require is the development of innovative collective learning processes that employ a radically different social technology when we bring people together inside organizations. Given the ever-widening gap between the advances in 21st century systems technology and the stagnation of a century-old social technology, it's just a matter of time before all of us will be asking the question that is causing so many twentysomethings to turn their backs on traditional companies today: "Why, when we are able to quickly collaborate in cyberspace with all kinds of people from all over the globe, is it so hard to get anything done whenever we get together in the same room"?

Two of the most important developments in the new social technology of management that will help to fill the management gap are the emergence of business processes as the new focus of work and the identification of organizational learning and mass collaboration as critical core competencies for 21st century business. These two developments are responses to management's urgent need to adapt to a very different business world.

BUSINESS PROCESSES

The importance of organizing work around business processes was first identified by Michael Hammer and James Champy in *Reengineering the Corporation*.[9] Unfortunately, the essence of Hammer and Champy's groundbreaking thinking became lost as command-and-control managers seized upon one aspect of reengineering – cost-effectiveness - such that the very term reengineering itself became synonymous with cost cutting. Thus, in the hands of command-and-control managers, reengineering was distorted into a quick fix to control costs, and like most quick fixes, did not yield lasting positive results.

The true insight in Hammer and Champy's work has nothing to do with cutting costs but rather with a shift in the focus of work, especially as service industries were becoming more and more prevalent. Throughout the 20th century, work was task-oriented. Rather than performing all the tasks related to the production of the automobile, each individual in Henry Ford's factory was assigned a specific task under the direction of a clear singular boss and was trained in the most efficient methods for the performance of that task. This task orientation has continued to define the fabric of organizational work as most companies still organize themselves into functional departments where only a few individuals are responsible for central planning, where information is compartmentalized and shared on a "need to know basis," and where the corporate mantra is "Do your job and stick to your job." In task-orientated companies, workers work for the boss, focus on tasks, and contribute to the completion of activities.

By contrast, in the process-oriented organization, workers work for the customers, focus on processes, and contribute to the achievement of results. Process-orientation is a complete paradigm shift from the task-orientation that has long defined the way work is done in most companies. When a business is working for the customers, everyone understands that value is more about delivering results than completing tasks. All of us can think of an example when we as customers encountered an individual in a business who wanted us to appreciate that she did her job right – that is, completed her tasks correctly – even though others' failures to complete their tasks meant that we did not get the result we expected. In the process-oriented organization, there is a shared understanding that the accomplishment of individual tasks and activities is meaningless if customers do not receive what they reasonably expect. Results only happen when the complete end-to-end set of activities are all cohesively performed, that is, when the entire process works. In the process-oriented company, no one ever utters the statement, "That's not my job." When the focus of work is the performance of processes, doing what's necessary to make sure that customers get results is everyone's responsibility.

ORGANIZATIONAL LEARNING

In response to the corporate struggle to adapt to the new demands of accelerated change, Peter Senge has identified learning as a critical core competency for meeting the challenges of a faster paced and more complex business world. In his seminal work, *The Fifth Discipline*, Senge makes the case that most companies are short-lived because they suffer from fatal learning disabilities.[10] Senge's observation is particularly relevant to today's dynamic business realities because, in fast changing times, whether or not an organization has a competent learning capacity may very well determine whether or not a company survives.

Businesses can no longer afford to impose top-down corporate views that distort or are completely out of touch with reality. By the time the errors are realized, it may be simply too late to act. Accordingly, learning organizations encourage work cultures of reflection and inquiry where anyone can challenge existing assumptions and where workers are expected to drive innovation. Learning organizations recognize that success in a demanding, rapidly changing market calls for employees who are internally committed and focused on understanding and keeping up with what the customer wants rather than distracted by what the boss thinks. This is in stark contrast to the command-and-control organization where the vision of an elite few is the mandate of the many, consistently reinforced by an externally directed reward and punishment control structure.

The leaders of learning organizations fully appreciate that nobody is smarter than everybody. They understand that, when cross-functional teams engage in effective dialogue, they are capable of discovering significant learnings about important business issues and building a powerful shared vision that produces an almost intuitive alignment among differing, and sometimes geographically dispersed, business units. When individuals through team learning are aligned with a shared vision, they are far more likely to work to support each other in their efforts to deliver customer value. Without alignment, groups in organizations often act at cross-purposes in disconnected silos.

Genuine team learning requires a different kind of discourse from the limited conversational norms of command-and-control organizations. Specifically, the debate and defensiveness of traditional organizations must be replaced with dialogue and inquiry. Success in the 21st century marketplace will belong to those companies who are skilled at achieving value-added, win-win, synergistic solutions, rather than the hollow win-lose political victories so common in hierarchical organizations.

Senge identifies systems thinking as the cornerstone of management practice in the learning organization. Leaders who engage in systems thinking recognize that the apparent reactive solution is often no solution at all, but rather a mere short-term fix that serves only to postpone and exacerbate the root problem. In fast-paced markets where customers demand real and consistent value, companies that rely on short-term, shortsighted quick fixes will find themselves losing their place in the market – or going out of business altogether. We need look no further than the recent examples of Enron and World-Com or of Bear Stearns and Lehman Brothers for proof of the fatal consequences of shortsighted thinking in fast-changing times. The complex business problems of the 21st century will require proactive and thoughtful solutions based on a firm understanding of the organization's fundamental business processes and widely distributed knowledge about how the parts of a business interrelate.

When markets shift from boss-driven to customer-driven, managers can no longer assume that everything they need to know is inside their organizations as was often true in the Industrial Age. In today's Digital Age, much of what managers need to know to succeed lies outside the organization in continually changing markets. Accessing this knowledge means that managers need to reach out into the market to understand the minds of their customers and they need to partner with the workers in learning about and understanding changing customer values by leading real-time learning processes.

MASS COLLABORATION

Another new critical core competency for managing in the Digital Age is mass collaboration. Because effective large organizations are less likely to be hierarchical bureaucracies, mass collaboration is redefining the challenge of managing large numbers of people. The most effective managers of the Digital Age will be those who have the skills and the emotional intelligence to lead collaborative communities.

With the new capabilities of 21st century technology, the work of large numbers of people no longer needs to be centrally managed. In fact, the new businesses of the Digital Age, such as eBay, Google, or Wikipedia, are more likely to be decentralized organizations where workers and customers anywhere in the world share common platforms to collaborate in cyberspace. While some may question the scholarly precision of Wikipedia in comparison to traditional ency-clopedias, there is little doubt that Wikipedia has shifted the paradigm for the business of reference materials, and it is probably safe to assume that, in the relatively near future, Wikipedia will improve its quality control issues and surpass both the effectiveness and efficiency of traditional encyclopedias.

Today's new decentralized organizations will create pressure for hierarchical companies to become more flexible and nimble if they hope to compete in the new economy. As it becomes more common for managers to be accountable for initiatives where they have no direct reporting relationship with many of the key staff on the project team, managing by control is not an option. When critical staff work for another company in the business alliance or work in another country on the other side of the globe, collaboration based on a shared understanding becomes a necessity for getting the job done, and this requires a substantial shift in management skills and compe-tencies.

A NEW MANAGEMENT MINDSET

Process-orientation and the new core competencies of organiza-tional learning and mass collaboration do not align well with com-mand-and-control management. The exercise of the control mechanism, which is at the heart of traditional hierarchical manage-ment, inevitably drives a focus on bosses and tasks despite corporate rhetoric about the value of the customer and the importance of learn-ing and working as a team. Managing cross-functional processes and facilitating collective learning will require real and substantial growth on the part of managers to adopt entirely new ways of thinking, behaving, and managing.

To demonstrate this point, let us once again return to our mind experiment – only this time, imagine that we are all top executives who travel 10 years into the future to Dublin, Ireland. As we land on the rolling hills of the Emerald Isle in the year 2020, the captain once again informs us that, because of a malfunction in the time machine, we cannot return to the first decade of the 21st century. However, she also notifies us that she has radioed ahead and a group of executive recruiters will be meeting the vehicle to help us secure work in our new time and place. As we consider our predicament, each of us feels fairly confident that, despite the 10-year difference, all of us should be able to find work as executives. After all, management is management and we all experts at running large organizations.

As we alight from our time machine, we are divided into smaller groups and your particular group is greeted by an executive recruiter who takes you to one corner of a very large room for your interviews. As you are waiting your turn, you are able to overhear the recruiter's conversation with one of your fellow executives. In response to the recruiter's inquiry about her executive qualifications, your colleague proudly relates stories of her ability to take charge, to effectively exert authority over people, and to get workers to do what needs to be done. After she finishes, you notice that the recruiter appears puzzled as she comments, "But I thought you said you were a top executive? The skills that you are describing are suitable for placing you as a manager of a small store or perhaps a prison guard – but not an executive in a large organization." As the recruiter sees the confusion on your colleague's face, she goes on to explain, "A lot has changed in the last 10 years. In today's large corporations, we are looking for executives who are highly skilled facilitators and great consensus builders. Do you have any experience as an executive facilitator or examples of where you were able to use consensus management as a competitive advantage?"

As your colleague sits silently, you can see that she suddenly realizes that she may only be 10 years into the future, but she is in a completely different world. She is now clearly living in the Digital Age and it is quite obvious that the rules of the game have definitely changed. It is only then that she is able to see beyond her own mental boundaries as she suddenly discovers that, when it comes to managing in the new wiki world, she is most certainly on the wrong bus.

As we enter these first days of a new age, we are indeed at a tipping point in the evolution of management where traditional executives find themselves in an unprecedented business reality for which they are totally unprepared. We are viscerally experiencing the pervasive uncertainty of these unprecedented times in the recent global financial crisis. However, despite the worst financial meltdown since the Great Depression, the current economic crisis will surely pass and normalcy in the capital markets will eventually return. What will not return, however, are the traditional ways that we have used to manage businesses, especially large businesses. We can no longer afford the top-down mandates of the elite few who created the financial meltdown, especially now that we have both the physical and the social technology to manage very differently and far more effectively. In truth, the current financial crisis is actually a symptom of a much deeper management crisis that will continue to play itself out until the social technology of a new and completely different management mindset is firmly in place. This means that the single greatest threat to the survival of many businesses over the next decade may very well be their own managers. For proof, we need to look no further than the long list of stalwart companies who have been done in by the myopic decision-making of an elite few: Enron, WorldCom, Arthur Andersen, Bears Stearns, Lehman Brothers, AIG, Fannie Mae, Freddie Mac, Citigroup, Countrywide, Washington Mutual, General Motors, and Chrysler.

RESETTING THE "3 M's"

Managing innovation is now the central business issue across all industries. The new economy of the Digital Age is all about change – continuous unrelenting change. If business leaders want to survive the current management crisis and learn to successfully manage at the new pace of change, they will need to "change buses" and embrace a very different mindset by completely resetting their management principles, processes, and practices in three critical areas. I call this transformation the "Resetting of the 3 M's": resetting the managers, resetting the meetings, and resetting the measures.

Resetting the managers means transitioning the leader's role from "boss" to "facilitator." Resetting the meetings is about transforming business gatherings from political debating jousts to channels of collective learning by including more people in open conversations. And resetting the measures is accomplished by replacing disjointed metrics habits with a focused measurement discipline that collectively identifies the most important drivers of success and aligns key cross-functional goals.

Resetting the "3 M's" will call for an extraordinary level of leadership courage. Unfortunately, given the accelerating pace of change of this new economy, there isn't much time to change buses. However, for those leaders who are ready to take the leap, there are companies whose different ways of thinking and acting are better aligned with the 21st century's new network mindset. It turns out that wiki-management is not new. In fact, several of the model companies in this book had the foresight to recognize the power of collaboration well before the Internet and have been practicing this alternative management approach for more than 50 years. What is new is that, rather than being the exception, wiki-management will become the norm by the end of the next decade.

This book describes the principles, processes and the practices of this new management discipline for anyone working in a business who is ready to accept and acknowledge that companies can't succeed using mass production methods in a mass collaboration world. It is based upon my own experiences as the leader of a $19 billion business alliance of 39 independent companies where I had bottom line accountability for an enterprise involving thousands of workers over whom I had no practical authority.

This book also describes the practices of the many wiki-management organizations that served as models as I actively explored the business literature to discover the new ways of thinking and acting necessary to meet the redefined challenge of organizing the work of large numbers of people.

The chapters that follow describe the various dimensions of the significant power shift brought about by the Internet and its capacity for mass collaboration and how this shift is substantively transforming the roles and responsibilities of managers in the new economy. You will learn that the wiki-management revolution has as much to do with how we reach consensus offline as it does with how we collaborate online. And as you read on, you will discover a whole new business world where leaders are facilitators, workers are highly involved in shaping strategic thinking, and business processes are designed around what's most important to customers.

In the course of my research, I was surprised to discover that the traditional command-and-control management model is not formally taught. There are no business school courses that provide an overview of the century-old social technology. Rather, hierarchical management is a mindset that is passed on from generation to generation of managers through the informal socialization habits of corporate cultures. Accordingly, as is the case with most mindsets, managers are largely unaware of why they do the things they do. They just know that's the way it's always been done and assume that that's just the way it is.

Because behavior change is as much about letting go of old ways as it is about learning new habits, we need to first become aware of why managers do the things they do. In the next chapter we will take a short detour from the main theme of the book and provide a quick synopsis of the origins and the thinking behind the principles, processes, and practices of command-and-control management. Hopefully, by raising our awareness of the roots of a century-old management technology, we will better understand why it worked for so long, but more importantly, why it will no longer work in a wiki world.

Chapter 2

ORDER AND AUTHORITY

"Scientific Management" (and its successor, "Industrial Engineering") is the one American philosophy that has swept the world – more so even than the Constitution and the Federalist Papers.

- Peter Drucker
Management Challenges for the 21stt Century[1]

So often, in making behavior changes, it's not the learning of new practices that presents the greatest challenge, but rather the letting go of old habits that proves to be most difficult. This is because old behaviors are so second nature that we don't have to think about them – we do them automatically, often unconsciously. Letting go of traditional management practices will be very difficult because the assumptions and beliefs of hierarchical management have become so deeply ingrained over the 150-year life of the modern corporation.

If you were to peruse the catalogues of most university business schools, you are not likely to find a course entitled "Command-and-Control Management." A deeply ingrained paradigm doesn't need to be taught. In fact, the curriculum of most business schools is focused either on strategic analysis or technical expertise, such as marketing, finance, or information systems. This may explain why so many MBA graduates, especially those from the top tier schools, end up working as management consultants rather than as corporate executives. Neither are there training programs inside corporations that specifically teach an overview of the hierarchical management discipline. There may be courses that focus on an aspect of command-and-control, such as performance management, but there are no comprehensive corporate programs on the overall traditional model. Even the American Management Association (AMA), which provides extensive national training programs, does not offer a specific course on command-and-control management. Quite the contrary, the curricula of the leading management and leadership training organizations such as the AMA, the Center for Creative Leadership (CCL), and Franklin-Covey are focused on how not to be command-and-control managers!

Nevertheless, despite the millions of dollars spent in these training programs and despite the absence of any formal training in the traditional model, the practices of hierarchical management remain deeply embedded in the corporate "DNA" of most organizations. Even considering its historical success throughout the 20th century, the staying power of command-and-control management is nothing short of incredible when you consider all the literature and evidence that supports alternative approaches and all the money that organizations invest in training on the latest trends in humanistic management practices. It just begs the question: If nobody likes command-and-control management, then why is it so commonly practiced?

THREE EARLY BUSINESS THINKERS

To begin to answer this question, let's go back to the early 1900's when the Industrial Age was enveloping the Western world. While the origins of the command-and-control model can be traced back to military practice, the development, evolution, and adaptation of this model to the newly emerging concept of the corporation were heavily influenced by three business thinkers whose work and ideas were the drivers for the productivity expansion that accelerated the Industrial Age.

Frederick W. Taylor developed the philosophy that guided the evolution of the modern corporation throughout the 20th century. Taylor advocated a systematic quantitative approach, known as scientific management, which was designed to greatly improve the efficiency and productivity of workers. An engineer by training, Taylor believed that there was one right way to do each job and that it was management's responsibility, by applying scientific methods such as time and motion studies, to discover the best way to perform each task and to develop the appropriate standard methods for workers to follow. Taylor held workers in low regard, believing that they were incapable of understanding how best to carry out even the simplest of tasks and that they required close supervision if work was to be done right.

The class distinction between managers and staff that continues to this day in hierarchical organizations traces its roots to Taylor's philosophy. He drew a sharp divide between managers and workers, with managers being responsible for applying scientific principles in the planning and engineering of work, while workers needed only to concern themselves with performing their assigned tasks. The rapid and broad acceptance of scientific management practices led to the establishment of the many rules and canons that eventually evolved into the modern policies and procedures manuals that continue to give precedence to management protocol over individual judgment.

Taylor's philosophy took root in the new emerging American corporations because it immediately resulted in tremendous productivity gains and because everyone was making money. Increased production obviously drove increased profits for the corporate owners, but equally important – even though scientific management treated workers as nothing more than machines who needed to be made efficient – these workers were realizing higher and more stable wages than when they worked as independent craftsmen or on the farm.

The relatively higher wages necessary to induce worker compliance with imposed work standards laid the foundation for the expansion of the middle class throughout the 20th century. While many have deplored Taylor and his methods – indeed, "Taylorism" has come to be a pejorative term – scientific management did result in a productivity explosion that consistently improved the standard of living.

Henry Ford provided the engine that drove the modern corporation. Prior to the 20th century, goods were produced by individual craftsmen on an item-by-item basis. Ford completely revolutionized manufacturing with his development of the assembly line, which quickly became the most advanced application of Taylor's philosophy at the time. The construction of automobiles was engineered into a sequence of discrete activities, with each worker assigned a specific task at a specific location as products moved along a conveyor belt. By forcing workers to toil at a set pace on a single task, the assembly line dramatically increased worker output. It wasn't long before Henry Ford's mass production concept, which was quickly adopted by other automobile makers, became the standard for all manufacturing industries. The resulting growth in the production capacity of American factories is often credited with creating and fueling the modern consumer culture.

With Taylor's philosophy firmly taking hold in the factories of the early 20th century, the stage was set for the formulation of the new discipline of corporate management. Up until this time, with the exception of the military, work was generally organized around smaller numbers of people. The farm was a family enterprise and those who engaged in the crafts or the professions worked either as individual practitioners or in small local firms. For the most part, there were no large business organizations. Only governments and churches had the need to organize large numbers of people around a common cause. Typically, this was accomplished through centralized hierarchical social structures with clear definitions of stratified power and authority.

With the emergence of the concept of the corporation in the expansion of the railroads in the late 19th century and the development of large factories in the early 20th century, for the first time in history there was a need for businesses to organize large numbers of workers. Until this time, administering the business and doing the work were generally performed by the same people. However, when a new socioeconomic age is born, it changes the work we do and the way we work. This was evident as the Industrial Age took root. The advent of scientific management and the invention of the assembly line created the need to separate the administration from the technical performance of the business.

While Frederick Taylor is the first to draw the distinction between management and staff, it is the Frenchman Henri Fayol who first recognizes management as a separate and distinct discipline. Fayol lays the theoretical foundation for the application of command-and-control as the framework for this new discipline by codifying the five fundamental responsibilities of management: planning, organizing, directing, coordinating, and controlling. Fayol also articulates the guiding principles for effectively managing the command-and-control organization, many of which we will recognize from our own organizational experiences. These include the principle of division of labor where Fayol reinforces Taylor's thinking that efficient production is only possible if work is divided into specialized tasks. The principle of authority and responsibility specifies that authority is the manager's right to command others to do a job and that with this authority comes the manager's responsibility to get the job done. The principles of unity of command and unity of direction postulate that each person has only one supervisor and that there should only be one manager for a particular set of objectives. Lastly, the scalar principle calls for a ranking of authority and clear communication protocols among the various organizational members. This principle means that certain decisions can only be made by certain levels and that when communicating vertically within an organization, the chain of command must always be respected.

THE FIVE ASSUMPTIONS OF INDUSTRIAL AGE MANAGEMENT

If you were to shadow the typical manager in a traditional organization, you would find that just about everything that he does fits into one of Fayol's five fundamental responsibilities. Work plans and timelines, job descriptions and organization charts, directives and assignments, meetings and conference calls, status reports and performance appraisals – these are the activities that make up a typical manager's day. Command-and-control managers believe that if they did not plan, organize, direct, coordinate, and control, then they would be shirking their responsibilities. That is why good people – as most of these managers are – engage in what often appears to be calculated, controlling, and coercive behavior. Their sometimes officious and difficult ways are more often than not motivated by a well intentioned, but misguided, sense of duty and responsibility.

How did these otherwise good people get this notion? We know that they didn't learn these behaviors in business schools or in leadership courses. And how is it that most managers arrive at their sense of what it means to be responsible? To answer these questions, we need to understand the five assumptions of Industrial Age management that would guide the development of the concept of the modern corporation and solidify the mindset that would define the manager's sense of responsibility and shape managerial behavior for well over a century.

THE FIRST ASSUMPTION: CENTRALIZATION

Centralized design of production creates and expands markets. This first assumption promotes the notion that the key to effectiveness and efficiency is centralization. The more parts of the production process that can be brought under one roof and sequenced under the principles of scientific management, then the greater the number of affordably priced products that can be put to market. This was the formula for the creation of new markets for the parade of household machines that produced the modern consumer culture. The immense success of this formula reinforced the idea that building centralized capacity enabled managers to predictably create markets by directly shaping consumer behavior. In other words, managers in the early 20th century developed the sense that the capability to do mass production meant that they were in charge of the markets. Thus, Henry Ford was very comfortable making the statement that buyers could have their cars in any color that they wanted as long as it was black! This notion that the bosses were in charge prescribed the first responsibility of traditional management, *planning*.

Planning is the determination of business strategy to shape the corporation's growth and success by defining goals for future performance and by allocating the tasks and resources needed to achieve the goals. Traditionally, the responsibilities for assessing the market environment, forecasting future trends, and designing centralized capacity to achieve business objectives have been the exclusive tasks of a company's top executives.

The assumption that centralized design of production creates and expands markets reinforced the belief that business planning was directly analogous to blueprint design. Just as a well-designed architectural blueprint results in a well-constructed building, a well-designed business plan results in predictable market success. And as the architect's blueprints must be prepared in great detail so that all the construction specialists will perform their parts consistently, so too top management needs to produce detailed business plans to assure that corporate strategic goals are translated into department goals so that all of the functional specialists will perform their parts correctly.

Over time, as the class distinction between managers and workers became internalized and as planning became the domain and the responsibility of management, the belief evolved within corporations that those with the loftiest titles are responsible for shaping the future of the organization. Another belief that took hold is the notion that the "cream rises to the top," and thus, the smartest people make their way into the top management positions. This, in turn, resulted in an ascription of intelligence, whereby how smart somebody is treated is defined by the position that he holds. Thus, most individuals behave as if the top managers are the smartest people in the organization and that their thoughts and ideas hold more weight than others. This leads to a troublesome dynamic, especially in today's fast changing Digital Age, in that oftentimes managers are more interested in appearing smart – to maintain this institutional belief – than they are in learning. This notion of ascribed intelligence coupled with the definition of planning as a management responsibility fosters the consummate bureaucratic practice that managers need to sign off on most

anything before it can be done. But more importantly, it also fosters
the belief that not to do so would be irresponsible.

THE SECOND ASSUMPTION: FUNCTIONAL EXPERTS

Functional experts drive performance. The arrival of the assembly
line with its sequencing of tasks and its specialized division of labor
reconstructed the workplace into a world of specialists. Output production measures were established to assure individuals were proficient at their assigned jobs. The idea was that, if all the workers
mastered their specific tasks, then productivity would be dramatically
increased. And for the most part, this is exactly what happened as
industries flourished. This explains why the primary focus of work in
the Industrial Age became the performance of tasks and the corporate
mantra became "Do your job and stick to your job."

There were several consequences to the emergence of this new
task-orientation. First, the most efficient way to structure the many
tasks needed to complete the production process was to group similar
tasks into discrete functional departments. Second, the workers in
each of these areas would be under the direction of functional supervisors who would be experts in the performance of all the tasks contained in the function. This was another version of the "cream rises to
the top." The know-how of these functional experts would be leveraged across all the workers in the department as a way of assuring
that everyone performed efficiently according to the prescribed right
ways. These protocols became the foundation for the third consequence, the eventual crafting of policies and procedures manuals that
are, in essence, the vehicles for codifying the right ways for performing all the tasks within a department or a company. Finally, over time,
as the functional experts came to be viewed and treated as the drivers
of excellent performance, the concept of the "star performer" was
born.

Even today, most managers believe that the organization with the
smartest individuals is the smartest company and the most likely to
succeed. The roots of this thinking go back to the early days of the
Industrial Age when the knowledge of the functional experts, their
stewardship of the right ways, and their close supervision of the workers' tasks did seem to assure that the factories performed like well-
oiled machines. Thus, just as a machine needs to be properly designed
and built so that the different parts are well coordinated, the need to

array the functional experts led to the second responsibility of command-and-control management, *organizing*.

Organizing is the design and structuring of tasks and roles to accomplish a company's goals and objectives. As newly forming corporations brought more people under one roof or into one enterprise, managers needed to design social structures to assure that the divided activities of various functional departments were coordinated and integrated into a cohesive and efficient whole. Thus, the two basic tasks of the organizing responsibility became the division of labor and the definition of the relationships among the individuals and departments within the organization.

The early practices of organizing were heavily influenced by the prevalent engineering discipline that was the driving force behind the rapid progress of the early 20th century. Thus, organizations were viewed as machines that were made up of different parts that needed to be connected and configured in the right way to operate effectively. The continuing and pervasive influence of engineering on organizational design can be seen well into the 1990's when, even as James Champy and Michael Hammer are urging the transformation of organizations from a focus on tasks to a focus on processes, they label this effort as the reengineering of the corporation.

The overarching influence of engineering and its mechanical model is further seen as organizations came to be perceived as closed systems. This helps to explain why organization charts, with their boxes and lines, resemble mechanical schematics. Thus, as practiced throughout the Industrial Age, organizing is essentially the social engineering of people and their work into closed systems. Consistent with the machine model, the parts were the tasks and activities located in functional departments and the connections were the arrangements of the departments into hierarchical relationships where roles are clearly defined with differing levels of authority, responsibility, and accountability.

According to this thinking, the key to making sure that the corporation worked well was to make sure that the lines of authority were properly designed and reinforced in the day-to-day workings of the company. This is why command-and-control organizations are structured around order and authority. Bosses are invested with significant power in their abilities to hire and fire, enforce their commands, and control rewards for performance. In command-and-control organizations, people, by design, work for the boss. Bosses are an ever present and unquestioned reality in the day-to-day lives of workers. In fact, for most people, one's boss is the single most authority with whom the typical worker interacts on a regular basis.

The roles and relationships of the corporation are ascribed to provide clarity around who does what work and who is the boss of whom. The thinking is that through the correct configuration of order and authority, the integrated work of functional experts drives performance. This is why when performance fails, the first action of management is often to reorganize. If the corporate machine isn't working, it must mean that the parts are not properly configured. When managers reorganize to turn around poor business performance, they do so because they believe that's what it means to be a responsible leader.

THE THIRD ASSUMPTION: TAKE-CHARGE MANAGERS

Authoritative take-charge managers are essential for achieving results. The central role in the command-and-control organization is the boss. Based on the military model, bosses are arrayed into a hierarchy with supervisors reporting to managers who, in turn, report to officers, with everyone ultimately under the authority of the Chief Executive Officer. These bosses issue directives and their subordinates are expected to carry out those commands. Authority, flowing down from the top of the organization, insures the orderly transfer of strategic objectives formulated by senior executives into tactical activities performed by the workers.

Compliance with supervisory directives is a basic expectation that is commonly reinforced in the traditional organization through the performance appraisal process. While the exercise of supervisory authority became less autocratic by the end the 20th century in comparison with the draconian practices of its early days, this basic expectation remained unchanged. In those earlier days, the workers had no voice in the work to be done. Taylor's scientific management was quite explicit that workers were incapable of designing effective and efficient work. However, as workers became more intelligent, especially after the influence of the GI Bill on the number of college graduates entering the workforce after World War II, managers did relent some from Taylor's assumption and began to seek input from workers. Nevertheless, while there may have been a greater voice for the workers, there was little change in the fundamental authority structure of the organization. Thus, the participation of the workers was merely a consultative resource to management because, at the end of the day, the boss was still the boss and the basic expectation that subordinates carry out their assignments remained unchanged.

This expectation reflects the core belief of command-and-control management that, at every level of the organization, somebody has to be in charge with clear unquestioned authority or the organization risks falling into chaos. According to this belief, the key to maintaining order and achieving consistent results is to hire authoritative take-charge managers. This thinking gave rise to the third responsibility of management, *directing*.

Directing is the prime responsibility in hierarchical management. It is the authority to issue orders and to assure compliance with those orders. Directing is so essential to the traditional mindset that most managers believe that nothing would get done if they did not have the ability to command and exert their will. This explains why order and authority are the central values of command-and-control management. The orderly arrangement of work and the exercise of managerial authority are seen as the fuel that drives the corporate engine. Without this fuel, the engine would sit idle.

The belief that directing is the prime responsibility has shaped both the selection and the behavior of those we choose to lead our organizations. Accordingly, we want our leaders to be proficient in the exercise of power and authority. There may be differing views about what that proficiency looks like, but few people inside organizations question the need for somebody to be in charge. This explains why having executive presence is so often seen as the ability to demonstrate skillful dominance through the power to influence and persuade others to the executive's point of view.

Traditional thinking also fosters the expectation that effective managers, especially top executives, need to be the smartest people in the room. This way when they exert their will throughout the organization, what they are directing workers to do will be good for the company. Over time this perception has shaped the profile of what we look for when hiring executive leaders: smart, confident, take-charge individuals who can effectively persuade large numbers of people to their way of thinking. This profile has served as the backdrop for executive recruiting in the command-and-control company. Thus, when managers act like bosses and appear to be autocratic and domineering in exerting their will to get things done, keep in mind that they are probably behaving this way because they believe that taking charge is what everybody expects of them and that not to do so would be irresponsible.

THE FOURTH ASSUMPTION: NEGOTIATING

Negotiating is the key to balancing interests and solving problems in business processes. The task-orientation and the functional department structure of the command-and-control organization result in an inevitable fragmentation of the complete set of activities necessary to perform business processes. However, traditional management theory holds that this should not be a problem if top management has properly designed and organized the correct sequence of activities and if everyone performs his tasks as assigned. In the unexpected event that issues arise among the functional departments, the managers are to meet and negotiate the balancing of their interests and the resolution of any problems so that the intended design of the work is carried out.

As a practical matter, issues and problems tend to happen more than expected. This is because the task-orientation and the functional organization of traditional companies causes workers to focus more on the performance of their individual tasks and on keeping their functional bosses happy than on whether or not value is delivered to the customer. For the typical corporate worker, life at the office is an experience that happens more inside a department than inside a company. This often leads to an overly competitive environment where not only is the business competing in the marketplace, but the functional departments are also vigorously competing against each other for status and limited resources within the corporation. In some companies, this internal sparring is promoted and encouraged on the theory that a little competition brings out the best in everyone. However, more often than not, internal competition does nothing more than create an environment where managers are prone to work against each other as they get caught up in internal political battles. Even in the friendliest corporate environments, the division of the work of business processes into relatively independent functional departments leads to some level of tension and confusion when the tasks of the different departments don't seem to come together. Inevitably, the different departments have different points of view, different interests, and different ways of operating that may not be immediately compatible. This circumstance creates the need for the fourth responsibility of traditional management, *coordinating*.

Coordinating is a prerequisite for effective execution. All parts of the business processes need to come together if products are to be available for market. Making sure that all the activities are performed in the proper sequence to produce quality products on time is what coordinating is all about. The work of coordination generally happens in meetings where functionaries gather to agree on work plans, timelines, what is to be done, and who is to do what. As a rule, managers spend more time in meetings than in any other activity. For many, if not most managers, their calendars are completely booked – and sometimes double-booked – with one business gathering after another such that their workdays are just a continual progression of meetings. The need to coordinate and the need to monitor tasks are the two main reasons managers spend so much time in meetings in the command-and-control organization.

Most corporate meetings follow the committee-style format with a chairman, an agenda, and usually handouts or other audio-visual materials. There are often presentations that precede discussions where the merits of different points of view and positions are weighed, debated, and evaluated in reaching a resolution to a problem. Throughout these discussions, managers are typically focused on what's important to their functional areas and making sure that any decisions or problem solutions do not jeopardize their department's interests. Because so often the departments represented in these meetings are hierarchical equals, the work of coordination becomes a negotiation of different interest groups in search of mutually acceptable solutions. As is often the case in negotiations, agreements reached are compromises, which while workable, are likely to be least-common-denominator resolutions. Nevertheless, because they are workable, products are produced and sold, everyone accepts that realistically they did the best they could, and most importantly, the bottom line is delivered.

Over time, effective negotiating has become the key management competency for effective coordination. The thinking is that, if all the participants in the meeting are effectively representing their interests, then the resulting negotiated decision will be the one that best balances the interests and best solves the problem. The reason why so many managers in meetings are advocates for their department's interests is because they feel that it is their responsibility to represent their group and that the best way to serve the company is to negotiate well on behalf of their department.

THE FIFTH ASSUMPTION: MONITORING

Monitoring all the tasks assures the accomplishment of activities. This final assumption is the second reason managers spend so much time in meetings. After the plan is clear, the work is organized, the orders have been given, and the tasks have been coordinated, the only thing left is the execution of the activities. Because managers are held accountable for the accomplishment of these activities, they feel intense pressure to be sure that all the tasks are performed as expected. Understanding that "the devil is in the details," managers know only too well that the failure to perform even one task correctly could jeopardize the accomplishment of an activity. Because managers are expected "to be on top of things," they often set up extensive reporting requirements to track the progress of all tasks.

The advent and the rapid development of computer technology in the second half of the 20th century greatly expanded the reporting capabilities and options available for management reporting. Today there are many ways that managers can customize the tracking of task performance. These reporting requirements are discussed between managers and subordinates as well as across departments in periodic status meetings where the progress of the tasks is reviewed. The need to be sure that all the tasks are on track leads to the fifth and final responsibility of traditional management, *controlling*.

Controlling is making sure that work is going according to plan, that unintended consequences or unforeseen problems are identified and handled, and that desired objectives are met. The primary vehicle for control is reporting. That is why most traditional organizations define the connection between the subordinate and his supervisor as a reporting relationship. Reporting takes many forms and shapes: formal and informal, written and spoken, quantitative and qualitative, fact and opinion. After the assignments are made, supervisors expect workers to input appropriate data into computerized reporting systems and to bring any important developments or unusual occurrences to their attention. In fact, the reporting of pertinent information on the status of various business activities is what makes up most of the conversations between supervisors and subordinates. Whether formal or informal, bosses expect workers to keep them posted on all relevant information.

Significant amounts of corporate time and resources are devoted to controlling. Formal reporting includes budgets, financial statements, production metrics, schedules, Gantt charts, and quality control indices. These periodic reports may be prepared and reviewed on a quarterly, monthly, weekly, or, in some instances, even a daily basis. They may be reviewed individually or collectively, depending on the manager's preference. These data summaries are important vehicles to make sure that managers have everything that they need to stay on top of work performance and to be fully prepared to respond when the managers have to report to their bosses. Appearing smart is an important value in command-and-control organizations, and these reports go a long way to helping managers maintain that image.

In addition, throughout the typical work day, there are numerous informal communications where subordinates are checking-in with their supervisors by e-mail, phone, or in meetings to report breaking news, developing events, or any unusual occurrences they come across. The reporting expectation is clearly socialized into the hierarchical organization, and workers fully understand that, when it comes to keeping the boss informed, there should be no surprises.

The exercise of control varies in practice from manager to manager. Some managers delegate more than others with the expectation that they are kept abreast of only the most important developments. Other managers want to be continually informed about all details, want to closely monitor all developments, and be involved in all decisions. This latter approach is often pejoratively called micromanagement and is a prevalent habit in the command-and-control organization.

Of the five fundamental management responsibilities, controlling is the one that workers most encounter in their day-to-day interactions with their supervisors. If managers delegate and exercise a relatively lower level of control, the workers generally have a better and more fulfilling work experience. On the other hand, micromanaging supervisors can make for difficult days as they are constantly looking over the workers' shoulders and insisting that everything must be run by them before anything can proceed. Whether they micromanage or not, all managers in hierarchical organizations practice some level of control over the people who report to them and everyone understands that not meeting the supervisor's reporting expectations can be a career-limiting move.

After directing, controlling is the next most important management responsibility as practiced by traditional managers. The two responsibilities of directing and controlling are viewed by many managers as their keys to execution effectiveness. They put a high value on being in charge and feel that, if they are not in control, then they can't execute. Managers monitor all the tasks because they feel it is their responsibility to be on top of everything to make sure that things get done.

A CENTURY-OLD MINDSET

The advent of a new socioeconomic era changes our world and the way we see the world. This was as true at the onset of the Industrial Age as it is today with the emerging Digital Age. Throughout the many centuries of the Agrarian Age, the family had long been the locus of work. The home was the workplace where farmers and craftsmen toiled together with their spouses and children. During the Agrarian Age, life on the farm was about the land. Everyday language, through stories and parables, reflected a mindset where the land was the dominant metaphor for social life. In this land mindset, life and work were viewed as part of the cycle of the seasons and the job of the farmer was to understand and respect nature's laws and its sometimes unpredictable ways. For the farmer, work was about planting and harvesting and responsibility was about aligning with and respecting the land. Farmers had no notion that work was about taking charge or being in control. They were very clear that the laws of nature were in command.

The Industrial Age radically altered society's mindset with the machine replacing the land as the dominant metaphor defining social life. As the workers moved into the factories, work was no longer about tilling the land. It was now about running and making machines. It wasn't long before the world was viewed through the prism of the new machine mindset where workers were viewed as parts of the factory and where their primary value was in running the factory's machines efficiently to leverage the power of mass production. As this mindset took hold, managers viewed themselves as the corporate machine operators who through their superior skills and intelligence could control the machines and its people.

In the command-and-control organization, the most important people are the bosses. From the beginning, they were seen as the engineers whose actions would ultimately determine the success or failure of these new corporate machines. Accordingly, command-and-control organizations were structured around order and authority to assure that the bosses had all the tools they needed to issue orders and to assure that those orders were carried out. While the bosses were the engineers, the tasks and activities they assigned were viewed as the framework of the corporate machine and the workers were seen as a part of that framework. As a result, workers were not viewed as individual contributors, but rather as parts of the collective production process. Workers were seen as replaceable parts of the machine, and over time, command-and-control management came to treat people as if they were living machines to be directed and controlled by management.

One consequence of the machine mindset is the "inside-out" approach to organizational work. Traditional managers often assume that everything that is needed to be successful *out* in the marketplace is contained *inside* the organization. In the early days of the Industrial Age, this assumption was reinforced by the fact that the bosses were the drivers of an emerging consumer culture, with people eager and ready to purchase whatever the corporations put on the market. That's why corporate cultures are so often inwardly focused on what's important to the bosses.

Working inside-out reinforces the notion that bosses are more important than customers. In fact, in inside-out organizations, there is no real value attached to the customers as they are often viewed merely as a market mechanism for the transaction of products into profits. This explains why traditional organizations often define the domain of management as inside the corporation.

Another consequence of the machine mindset is the belief that we can manage our world by separating things into parts and then arranging the parts in the right way to optimize efficiency. It is this belief that provided the groundwork for the development of both scientific management and the assembly line. More importantly, this belief also promoted the notion that the world is both linear and predictable and that by understanding the objective nature of linear relationships, we could use this knowledge to predictably control the world around us. In the resulting machine mindset, the world came to be seen as a well-ordered machine following predictable natural laws.

Mindsets are born from assumptions that are often true when first formulated. As the assumptions continually verify themselves through repeated successes, over time they become unquestioned and eventually fade into the background, often becoming unconscious. What remains is the accepted ways of thinking and acting and everybody's understanding that that's just the way it is. For well over a century, the machine mindset has dominated corporate management because, whether managers were aware of them or not, the five fundamental assumptions behind it worked for all that time. Throughout the 20th century, centralized design of production did create and expand markets, functional experts did drive performance, authoritative take-charge managers did achieve results, negotiating was the key to balancing interests and solving problems, and monitoring all the tasks did assure the accomplishment of activities. Thus, these five assumptions defined the fundamental responsibilities of management, shaped how managers think and behave, and solidified what has become a century-old mindset.

The Industrial Age and its machine mindset, in its time, changed the work we do and the way we work. It created entirely new occupations as factory workers, managers, accountants, and industrial engineers began to populate the factories and the early corporations. It created new ways to organize work where effectiveness and efficiency were catapulted by highly engineered mass production processes controlled by a managerial elite. Workers were no longer farmers or craftsmen working on all the elements of their trade, they were now functionaries working on specific tasks assigned by bosses.

Command-and-control management thrived throughout the 20th century because the machine mindset became socialized across the society-at-large, because bosses were accepted as an important and central role in day-to-day work life, because work really was about the functioning of machines, and because the bosses owned the two critical assets at the time: capital and the machines. The bosses were indeed in charge and, through the exercise of authority in centralized organizations, they were able to command and control large numbers of people to efficiently produce affordable goods that sold successfully in the market. Command-and-control management was generally accepted because it worked so well. Despite its shortcomings, how could anyone argue with its success? Thus, the hierarchical management model, with its mechanistic linear thinking, its propensity for order and authority, and its inside-out approach has become so pervasive and so acculturated that most people, whether they like it or not, assume that there are no other alternatives. That is the power of a mindset.

Managers, despite all their rhetoric today about empowerment and employee involvement, continue to lead from order and authority because, deep down, they believe that is their job – and not to do so would be irresponsible. Until recently, the reason why everybody does command-and-control, even though nobody likes it, is because we see the world through the machine mindset, and from this perspective, that's just the way it is.

But is it? Just as the Industrial Age radically changed the mindset of the Agrarian Age, might not the Digital Age alter the mindset of the Industrial Age? The land mindset did not last forever – is it reasonable to expect the machine mindset to continue to last as the Digital Age settles in? Is a new mindset already emerging and perhaps our current ways of thinking cause us to miss the signs? These are important questions that we will address in the next chapter as we begin to explore new ways of thinking and acting. However, before you turn the page, be prepared because everything you have believed about the way we work and the work we do is about to dramatically change.

Chapter 3

KNOWLEDGE AND SPEED

[W]hat the flattening of the world means is that we are now connecting all the knowledge centers on the planet into a single global network, which – if politics and terrorism do not get in the way – could usher in an amazing era of prosperity, innovation, and collaboration, by companies, communities, and individuals.

- Thomas L. Friedman
The World Is Flat[1]

Mindsets are our pathways to understanding how the world works and how we fit into the world. They are products of common assumptions, values, and beliefs that shape the ways of thinking and the ways of acting among large groups of people. Mindsets are useful social tools for processing the uncertainty and the ambiguity of the world around us so that we may have a shared point of reference around which we can organize a shared reality. This shared reality becomes the context in which we develop the ideas, concepts, and perceptions that become the mental models for social and economic relationships. While these mental models help us to cope with reality and to make sense of our world, the assumptions, values, and beliefs underlying our mindsets can become so strongly held that we collectively become unaware that mindsets are also mental boundaries that limit and constrain our thinking.

The notions, perceptions, and understandings that we share in common shape what we collectively see and, and equally important, what we collectively don't see. These mental boundaries are often reflected in our language. For example, in English, there is only one word for snow while Eskimo languages have many different words to describe different types of the white stuff. For Eskimos, snow is a significant part of their daily lives and so their language reflects that they able to perceive what those of us in more temperate climates fail to see. This shows that what we see often depends upon what our mindset trains us to recognize. In other words, what you see is what you get. If an Eskimo were to ask of an American what type of snow she sees, the American might be puzzled and say snow is snow – that's it. To which the Eskimo would probably shake her head and think that, when it comes to snow, Americans just don't get it! Whenever we find ourselves thinking, "They just don't get it," we are experiencing a difference of mindsets.

Mindsets are not forever. They are held only as long as their underlying assumptions, values, and beliefs work and continue to be shared. New mindsets emerge when knowledge breakthroughs, new technologies, or political transformations disrupt the generally accepted assumptions, values, or beliefs. That is exactly what happened when the Industrial Age's machine mindset displaced the Agrarian Age's land mindset.

New mindsets are usually not immediately well received because they challenge our notions of the way the world works and how we fit in. Those who have vested interests in the old mindset can be counted on to vigorously resist any challenge to their understanding of the world and their position in that world.

We are our ways of thinking and our ways of acting, and these often define our identities. Thus, letting go of one's mindset can feel like losing one's sense of identity. No wonder new mindsets meet such resistance – those invested in the old mindset are defending a threat to their identities. This means that we can surely expect those whose identities are fully connected to hierarchical bureaucracies will rigorously fight any attempts to explore the possibilities of self-organized working arrangements. Nevertheless, with the recent emergence of the Digital Age and its newfound capacity for mass collaboration, we may not have a choice. None of us will be able to stop the rapid ascendance of a new mindset that is already seriously challenging the long-accepted assumptions about how we work in organizations.

The assumptions that define our day-to-day reality are not absolute. They work as long as the prevailing knowledge, technology and politics remain relatively constant. If a change in any of these three occurs, our perceptions may need to be adjusted. However, when changes occur in all three areas, new assumptions emerge to create the conditions for a new socioeconomic era. When this happens, the prevailing mindset gives way to a new mindset with a new dominant metaphor. This is where we find ourselves today as the network replaces the machine as the dominant metaphor for the Digital Age.

SHIFTS IN KNOWLEDGE, TECHNOLOGY AND POLITICS

The prevailing knowledge for the last 300 years has been physics. Beginning in the late 20th century, the prevailing knowledge has begun shifting to biology. The mapping of the human genome marks the first significant event in this shift. The great inventions and developments of the Industrial Age, for the most part, have been applications of physics and engineering. In the Digital Age, the great discoveries and developments will be in applications of biology and the emerging complexity sciences. These discoveries and developments will deeply enhance our knowledge and understanding of organic and evolutionary processes and will challenge the notions that the world is a machine, that order only comes from planning and organizing, and that business factors are linear and controllable.

The prevailing technology in business throughout the Industrial Age has been mass production. It is no wonder that both *Fortune* and *The Economist* named Henry Ford the businessperson of the 20th century because it is his assembly line that catapulted the mass production revolution. While we might be tempted to see the computer as the breakthrough that would change the prevailing technology, both mainframe computers and the early PC's were simply more sophisticated machines to automate and improve the efficiency of mass production. Most of today's corporate computer systems are really just highly efficient automated assembly lines. Instead, the new prevailing technology in the Digital Age will be mass collaboration, and the catalyst for this technology is a derivative of the computer, the Internet.

For the first time in history, the Internet allows large numbers of people to communicate and collaborate directly with each other without using a centralized organization or medium. This is opening new possibilities for how we organize work. Linux and Craigslist are examples of decentralized enterprises that work by creating common platforms in which individuals can self-organize their contributions and collaborate their efforts into cohesive products that are highly valued by customers. These new self-organizing decentralized organizations are demonstrating that not only does mass collaboration work well, but most times it allows them to work smarter, faster, and less expensively than their centralized counterparts. These new innovative organizations are challenging the notions that take-charge leaders are essential for achieving results, that work is organized best when directed by the bosses, and that all the tasks need to be monitored closely to assure the completion of activities.

The prevailing politics of business organizations during the 20th century has been centered on the bosses. Power belongs to those who own the critical economic assets, and in the Industrial Age, the critical assets were capital and plant, property, and equipment. Because the bosses owned the money and the machines, they controlled the means of production. This enabled the bosses to design organizations structured around solidifying their own power and authority. Even though workers would often organize themselves into unions in response to the corporate bosses' uses or abuses of their significant power, the negotiated settlements and management concessions at the end of work actions didn't alter the economic reality that the bosses still owned the critical economic assets. That would not change until the onset of the Digital Age dramatically shifted the critical economic assets.

In the new economy, machines have become commodities. Remember the example of Empire Blue Cross Blue Shield in Chapter 1. Empire lost its building and its machines in the terrorist attacks on the World Trade Center, but the employees and their knowledge survived. Empire quickly and easily replaced the building and the machines and, incredibly, was open for business in only three days. Today the critical economic assets are capital and knowledge, and whoever owns the knowledge owns the means of collaboration. While the bosses still have custody of the capital, it is the workers who now own the means for creating economic value.

This is a major shift in corporate politics. Whereas, in the Industrial Age, the worker needed the corporation more than the corporation needed the worker, today the inverse is becoming more common. With the critical economic assets now distributed between the bosses and the workers, organizations will find it increasingly difficult to maintain the traditional hierarchical politics. Corporations will discover that their survival may very well depend upon their ability to shift their organizational norms from a politics of control to a politics of partnership. Whether corporations like it or not, the stark reality is that the workers own the knowledge, they will increasingly have more options about whom they work for, and they have been and will continue to exercise those options.

Another significant shift in the politics of business is the increasing power of the customer. No longer can corporations view customers as transaction mechanisms between products and profits. The Internet has transformed passive purchasers into knowledgeable consumers and has leveled the playing field. For example, thirty years ago, new car dealers had far more leverage in sales negotiations when they controlled the knowledge of the actual costs of cars. Today, it is not unusual for the customer to have more knowledge about the retailer's costs than the salesman. In the Digital Age, customers are more knowledgeable and demanding, and just as they have learned with their workers, corporations are recognizing that they need the customers more than the customers need them.

These shifts in the prevailing knowledge, technology, and politics brought about by the birth of the Digital Age are challenging and disrupting the fundamental assumptions of Industrial Age management. Because of these trends, assumptions that have worked and that have been rock solid for well over a hundred years appear to be crumbling. More and more businesses are discovering that it is no longer true that centralized design of production creates and expands markets, nor do functional experts necessarily drive performance. New enterprises, such as Google or Wikipedia, are proving that authoritative take-charge leaders are not essential for achieving results. Business leaders are discovering that negotiating does not always bring the necessary closure to the balancing of interests needed to manage at the pace of change and often creates more problems than it solves. Finally, in these fast changing times, there is more information than can be humanly monitored, and attempting to centrally track all the related tasks only seems to slow things down and guarantee that activities will not be accomplished well or on time.

As leaders discover that the assumptions of command-and-control management no longer work in today's faster paced business environment, they will inevitably have to question whether or not the primary responsibilities of planning, organizing, directing, coordinating, and controlling are the key tasks of management going forward. And if these are no longer the right tasks, then what are the primary responsibilities of management in the Digital Age? To understand their roles and responsibilities in the new economy, managers will need to embrace the new network mindset, which is based on a new set of assumptions arising from the recent shifts in knowledge, technology, and business politics.

THE FIRST ASSUMPTION: ITERATIVE ALIGNMENT

Iterative alignment of products with customer values creates and expands markets. This first assumption challenges the traditional belief behind the inside-out approach that centralized planning is the key driver to strategic market success. In today's economy, the corporate bosses no longer dictate the markets. If organizations want to succeed in the new economy, they better understand that they work for the customers, not the bosses. Newer businesses that have originated in the Digital Age, without any historical ties to the Industrial Age, understand this lesson well.

For example, when eBay wanted to introduce its own proprietary payment system, Billpoint, as a transaction payment option, its customers objected. They were quite satisfied using PayPal for their eBay purchases and had no interest in using an unknown and unproven system for their sensitive payment information. Furthermore, it was important to eBay's customers that there be one standard for purchase transactions and PayPal was their overwhelming preference. PayPal had earned the customers' trust when it came to paying for their merchandise and they didn't care whether eBay owned PayPal or not. As far as the customers were concerned, eBay in conjunction with PayPal met their value set for a safe, reliable electronic market. eBay, clearly understanding that they work for the customers, abandoned management's plans for its own homegrown payment system and adopted PayPal as its payment standard. Ultimately, eBay reworked its strategy by acquiring PayPal and setting it up as an independent subsidiary to assure that the financial operating model that is so highly valued by the customers remains intact.[2]

eBay's actions demonstrate the "outside-in" approach to organizational management, where companies design their strategies and operations by starting with what's important to the customer. If customer values are at odds with management thinking, then management adjusts its thinking or chooses a different customer with similar values. In today's market reality, managers working outside-in understand that they do not get to tell customers what to value. Also, these companies know that, in fast changing times, customer value sets are not necessarily stable. Companies need to remain in constant touch with their customers to anticipate any modifications in consumer values so they can continually align their strategies, operations, and products to keep pace with changing markets. Outside-in organizations understand that managing at the new pace of change means that they cannot rely solely on the knowledge of their inside experts. The domain of management is now both inside and outside the corporation.

The traditional inside-out organization believes everything it needs to succeed should be contained within its walls, hence the penchant for vertical integration. Its managers assume that they are market experts and that their knowledge is unquestionable, especially when they engage in strategic planning. The outside-in organization, on the other hand, understands that, when you are working for the customer, you will never have everything you need to succeed within your walls. They assume that market reality is subject to accelerating change and that management's first job is to continually align its strategies and its products with what's most important to customers. This new assumption defines the first responsibility of wiki-management: *customer values*.

Having a clear unfiltered sense of what is most important to customers is the starting point for wiki-management. Most traditional organizations today are ill equipped to meet the challenges of this first responsibility because most companies don't face reality very well. Unfortunately, the typical company is more interested in defining a more comfortable scenario in accordance with its own preconceived understandings than it is in discovering the oftentimes brutal realities of fast changing markets.

Working through the complexities of market reality is no longer a solo or an elite group endeavor. The traditional corporate practice of relying upon a single CEO or a small group of top executives to interpret what customers want has become untenable and very perilous. The simple fact is, unlike in the Industrial Age, no single individual or small elite group can process the amount of change happening in markets today in real-time. To successfully and continually keep up with evolving customer values requires uncensored dialogue processes that can quickly and clearly discover the essential business factors in fast changing markets. These processes are non-existent in most companies today. Adopting these new processes will be challenging for traditional companies because it means abandoning corporate "party lines" and the hierarchical politics of censorship that are so prevalent in command-and-control organizations.

However, the Digital Age will give companies no choice because the perceptions of executives inside an organization do not necessarily reflect the reality outside in the market. In fast changing times, market reality can be very harsh and often it is not what management wants to hear. But whether management likes it or not, market reality is what it is, and management's only choice is to get real. This will mean developing new competencies for quickly processing what's happening outside the corporation. In the Digital Age, only those corporations that proactively understand and accept market reality on its own terms can expect to have any hope of developing strategies and operations that will work. Going forward, the key to long term success is no longer about long-range planning; it's now about staying in tune with what's happening in continually changing markets and having the competency and the flexibility to continually align products with what's most important to the customers.

THE SECOND ASSUMPTION: CROSS-FUNCTIONAL LEARNING

Cross-functional team learning drives performance. The command-and-control organization believes that the best way to organize work is to distribute the workers into separate functional departments and to have the smartest people at the top of the organization divide the labor among the departments. The traditional way of working relies very heavily on the individual intelligence of functional experts and star performers. According to this way of thinking, if the various functional specialists do their jobs correctly and as instructed, everything will work when the functional parts are put back together at the end of the project or process.

The second assumption of wiki-management challenges this way of thinking. As noted above, no one individual is smart enough to keep up with the amount of change happening in markets today. In the future, the only way that companies can reasonably expect to work through the ever present ambiguities of fast changing times is to have the capability and the business processes to immediately access the collective knowledge of all the people affiliated with the organization. If you want to manage successfully at the pace of change, then you must accept the reality that, when the world is moving fast, nobody is smarter or faster than everybody.

The Industrial Age organization is structured around order and authority and is designed to assure its take-charge leaders and star performers have the necessary power and authority to exert their individual prowess. This promotes the cult of the individual hero and reinforces the belief that companies are smart when they are able to leverage the talents of their smartest individuals. The Digital Age organization, with its focus on knowledge and speed, views the smart company very differently. To be successful in the new economy, organizations need to be designed to promote real-time collective learning and shared understanding to enable all individuals to effectively self-organize their work at the pace of the market. The network mindset believes that companies are smart when they leverage the collective knowledge of everyone. Thus, success in continually changing markets requires companies to develop sophisticated competencies as learning organizations.

While much has been written about the importance of organizational learning and many managers acknowledge the need for this new competency, few understand what it means to be a learning organization. And even fewer know what to do on a practical day-to-day basis in the workplace.

The paradigm of learning for most managers is the individual achiever model that is so familiar from their many years of formal education. In their attempts to move their companies to become learning organizations, many corporations are establishing internal corporate training programs or affiliating with independent professional leadership training groups to demonstrate the value that management places on learning. Unfortunately, these well-intentioned managers are operating from the wrong paradigm! Becoming a learning organization is not about having smarter individuals – that was the Industrial Age mindset. It's about having a smarter collective organization and it's about having core organizational processes for facilitating and iterating large group learning in short periods of time. Being a learning organization means having real-time access to the collective knowledge of your organization and the ability to use the power of collective wisdom to help discover and understand what is happening in the market.

Leveraging collective knowledge means the focus of work needs to shift from functional experts to cross-functional teams. It also means that organizations can no longer assume that everything they need to know is already known by the brightest people inside their organization. In fast changing times, the smartest people aren't experts, they're learners. The smart companies in the Digital Age will be the learning organizations that are able to use their cross-functional intelligence as the foundation for their strategic and operational performance. The need to be competent in processing the collective knowledge of cross-functional teams leads to the second responsibility of wiki-management: *collective learning*.

In the Digital Age, conversation will replace the assembly line as the catalyst that drives the corporation. When we moved from the

Agrarian Age into the Industrial Age, better machines dramatically boosted productivity through the technology of mass production. As we now move into the Digital Age, better conversations will dramatically boost productivity through the technology of mass collaboration. Going forward, it will be management's job to assure that effective conversations are an organizational core competency, especially among large groups of people.

While the Internet is opening new possibilities for expanding and improving our social networking, we often find that these electronic chats work best after a face-to-face relationship has been established. The basic foundation for effective conversations is the face-to-face meeting with its full context of both verbal and non-verbal content. However, the face-to-face meeting of cross-functional teams can be very challenging, especially if the team is large.

The best conversations are dialogues where individuals focus on deeply listening to each other and on building on each other's ideas to create innovative solutions or breakthrough thinking. Learning is more likely to emerge from collaborative dialogues than it is from advocacy debates. However, because dialogue rarely happens naturally in small group discussions and almost never happens in large group meetings, important business conversations, especially those involving large cross-functional teams, will need to be facilitated if the necessary learning is to happen in real time. This is management's new responsibility, and as we will learn in Chapter 7, the effective performance of this responsibility will require a dramatic transformation in the way meetings are conducted inside organizations.

THE THIRD ASSUMPTION: SELF-ORGANIZING TEAMS

Self-organizing teams operating from a shared understanding are essential for achieving results. This assumption reflects the fact that, in large organizations today, an increasing amount of the work is actually self-organized. Even though many managers continue to maintain the illusion that they are directing the performance of all activities and that their direct involvement is critical to achieving results, the present reality is that the world of work is so complex that no one person nor one group of people can organize everybody's work. This is because the nature of complexity has morphed with the advent of the Digital Age.

In the Industrial Age, complexity was focused on configuring the many details. Managing complexity was viewed as the central engineering of the many parts of an activity, an organization, or a machine into a functioning whole. This centralized approach works when reality is static and fixed and when the basic complexity issue is about structuring a multitude of details, as is true in most manufacturing production. For example, the effective production of dishwashers does work properly when the many detailed parts are arranged in the right configuration as designed by the managers.

The digital world has brought about a new reality. Because the nature of work today is more about knowledge and services than about manufacturing, the world of work is no longer static and fixed. The accelerating pace of change of the new economy creates markets that are dynamic and continually evolving. This, in turn, has transformed the basic complexity issue. The essential task for managing complexity today is not so much about organizing the details into a predetermined process as it is about continually adapting and aligning business processes to changing market realities.

When the world of work is dynamic and changing, work cannot be centrally organized in any meaningful way. Keeping pace with changing markets means that work is done best when self-organized by intelligent workers. However, as more and more work by necessity becomes self-organized, command-and-control management practices are ill equipped to derive the full benefits of self-organization. Taking full advantage of workers' intelligence requires two attributes: knowledge and understanding. Today's workers, unlike the workers of the early Industrial Age, are capable of self-organizing because they are far more educated and far more knowledgeable. However, while the workers have the necessary knowledge for self-organizing, what they often lack is the level of understanding necessary to fully leverage their knowledge. This defines the third responsibility of wiki-management: *shared understanding*.

Consistent performance is the key to sustained business success. Therefore, it is not surprising to find that consistency is a fundamental, if not the most fundamental, operating value for managers. This explains why control has been so important to Industrial Age managers. In command-and-control management, control is the driver of consistency. Historically, the practice of control has provided managers with the necessary information to know whether or not all activities are coming together as planned or whether they need to reorganize the activities to achieve consistent results. However, given the dynamic and changing nature of the Digital Age, managers are discovering that control, which worked so well when the pace of change was much slower, is not quite the driver of consistency that it once was.

The new driver of consistency in the network mindset is shared understanding. The most important attribute of this understanding is that it is shared. Shared understanding cannot be mandated. That is why so many corporate mission statements become nothing more than empty placards. Shared understanding is real only when it is built from the thoughts and voices of everyone in the organization and when everyone is free to give voice to her thoughts. It is the interplay of the thoughts and the voices of knowledgeable workers in cross-functional learning that produces true shared understanding. When the knowledge owned by the workers is combined with a shared understanding of customer values, company values, and the operating framework to connect those values, then all the workers are able to make real-time decisions in the face of continued change. Having built the initial shared understanding together, the workers will have first-hand knowledge of who needs to be involved if they are to deliver consistent results. The evolution of shared understanding through real-time conversations of knowledgeable workers is not only the new driver of consistency in fast changing times, it is also the key to handling the new basic complexity issue of adapting and aligning business processes to continually changing market realities. If managers are involving diverse cross-functional teams in facilitated learning processes to fully grasp the dynamics of their new market realities, they are well on the way to laying the foundation for the shared understanding needed today to drive consistent business results.

THE FOURTH ASSUMPTION: THE FEW DRIVERS

Focusing on the few drivers assures the accomplishment of activities. Because control is at the core of command-and-control management, the prevailing theory is that the key to managing the delivery of a complex set of activities is to monitor all the details. This thinking has promoted the belief and the expectation that it's the manager's responsibility to "be on top of everything." Thus, managers and staff spend large amounts of their efforts in time-consuming rituals of control with staff producing voluminous reports so that managers can have access to every project detail even though many of the reports are left unread because they simply don't have the time to pour over all the details. This behavior is becoming problematic because, in their zeal to be on top of things, micromanaging bosses wind up continually slowing things down. This is not an effective management strategy when the market values knowledge and speed.

Unfortunately, because customers are often more demanding than bosses, the standards and expectations for delivering on the details have never been higher. This creates a real conundrum for today's managers: How do they move fast and at the same time make sure that all the details are right? The solution is to recognize that it is no longer true that the best way to assure the delivery of details in large organizations is for the managers to monitor all the tasks. In fact, as the pace of change continues to accelerate, we can be sure that micromanagement will become a management strategy for guaranteed failure. The successful delivery of details in fast changing time calls for a new management strategy, and this defines the fourth responsibility of wiki-management: *focused measures.*

All measures are not the same. Some measures are more important than others. In fact, in any project or activity, there are usually four or five measures that are the key indicators of ultimate success or failure. These gauge the few drivers that directly influence or directly correlate with the majority of the remaining measures.

The challenge for organizations is to identify the true four or five drivers – you just can't arbitrarily pick any small set of measures. The identification of the few drivers is not as easy as it may appear and often is best accomplished through a cross-functional learning process. When they are correctly identified, these measures provide a potent focus for managing complexity for both managers and staff. This focus enables managers to direct their attention to the most important things and it also allows staff to make meaningful connections between their individual tasks and the most important drivers of success.

What makes finding the few drivers difficult is that most companies have so many measures. Progress is sometimes a two-edged sword. While the computer has made a huge contribution to the efficiency of mass production with its ability to perform a multitude of routine tasks in literally microseconds, its ability to quickly measure everything has been both a blessing and a curse. An unintended consequence of the development of computer technology is information overload that, ironically, results in many managers today becoming information illiterate. This illiteracy shows up in the tendency for managers to treat all measures the same, and manifests itself as a pervasive fear or anxiety, especially in micromanagers, because they never know which detail may come back to bite them. Thus, these micromanagers need to measure everything and they've never met a measure that they didn't love!

The importance of focused measures is that they are a powerful tool for bringing clarity to the ambiguity and uncertainty created by fast changing times. The focused measurement of the true business drivers provides the frame of reference that makes self-organization effective. In the accelerating pace of change of the Digital Age, focusing on the few drivers is what assures the accomplishment of all the activities.

THE FIFTH ASSUMPTION: CONSENSUS BUILDING

Consensus building is the key to integrating interests and to avoiding problems in business processes. When you work for the customer, you find out very quickly that they can be very demanding. They have high expectations and even higher standards. They can be unforgiving and they don't care about your industry standards. If one industry can provide a service, such as 24/7 availability, then customers come to expect this level of service from all industries. In the new world of competition, large organizations are competing globally across industries, not nationally within an industry, and companies have to "get it right the first time" or customers will search the globe for someone who will. Globalization means customers have more options and they will exercise their options to find the company with the best quality products at the best price.

If you want to succeed in this new world of competition, your organization needs to be built around knowledge and speed. You have to assemble the necessary knowledge "to get it right" and you have to have the speed to produce high quality results "the first time." Expanding knowledge and increasing speed means that companies cannot afford to limit themselves to the resources within their organizations. Corporations will need to be able to quickly partner their strengths and competencies with the complementary strengths and competencies of other organizations or they may miss critical business opportunities.

In the old world of competition, corporations vertically integrated to bring all business processes inside their organizations. They relied upon negotiation and compromise among their managers to balance the internal interests of different departments and to solve what were viewed as the inevitable problems that arise when functional business structures are used to manage complex details. In the Industrial Age, markets tolerated the reduced quality and the poor speed that result from internal managerial compromises because competition was limited to key players within particular industries and everyone accepted industry practice as that's just the way it is. In the Digital Age, that's all changing. Competition is not limited and customers no longer accept bureaucratic constraints as the way it is.

In the new world of competition, balancing interests is not enough because when you balance interests, you are focused primarily on your own local concerns and not with the common good. As a result, the inevitable compromises among individuals focused primarily on their own agenda lead to least-common-denominator agreements that are less than the best the corporation can do. These compromises usually produce problems that need to be solved through further negotiations that take up a great deal of time, further diminishing product quality and slowing down the company's speed to market.

While negotiating works well to handle the issues of order and authority in command-and-control organizations, negotiating is not an effective vehicle when management needs to organize around knowledge and speed. In markets where excellence is defined as producing high quality fast, interests need to be integrated around the common good and not balanced around local interests, and the blending of interests needs to prevent and not create problems. This is especially important when independent organizations in business alliances need to quickly leverage their complementary strengths. Traditional negotiation habits need to be replaced by consensus building practices if corporations want to produce best solutions rather than least-common-denominator compromises. Furthermore, for consensus building to produce the quality necessary for best solutions, everyone working in the organization needs to be involved in the consensus. Thus, the fifth responsibility of wiki-management is *collaborative community*.

Mass collaboration, like its predecessor mass production, will dramatically increase the productivity and efficiency of work. But whereas the driver of mass production's surge was the assembly line, the catalyst for mass collaboration's productivity and efficiency growth will be open conversations. Just as the assembly line was a revolutionary departure from the craftsman's model for building products, open conversations will be a paradigm shift from the top-down communications of the command-and-control organization. This means that 21st century companies can no longer be structured as hierarchical bureaucracies. When open conversations are the catalyst for business effectiveness, organizations have to be collaborative communities.

Conversations inside hierarchical organizations are limited at their best and dysfunctional at their worst. This is because traditional managers, even benevolent managers, work to control conversations and communications. Typically, workers are not free to openly disagree with their supervisors in meetings, they can't initiate conversations outside their chain of command without their supervisor's permission, and they learn quickly what they can and cannot talk about. Managers, subtly or not so subtly, try to shape the thinking and the voices of their workers. However, as the Digital Age settles in, managers will discover that not only are their attempts to control conversations futile, but they are actually counterproductive. This is because the Internet has irrevocably changed both the nature and the possibilities of conversations.

With the proliferation of the Web, no authority – whether government or corporate – will be able to effectively control conversations or communications in the future. The Internet provides a background of transparency that is already reshaping social discourse now that everyone can talk directly with any one else in the digital world. The Internet also opens up new possibilities for how we work together. For example, tight immigration laws will no longer be barriers to companies in their search to hire highly skilled knowledge workers who are in short supply within their borders. Thanks to the innovative technology of the Web, these companies can now hire foreign workers to work online and reduce costs at the same time through overhead savings.

The Internet is also opening up new and innovative possibilities for how companies approach research and development. Businesses no longer need to limit themselves to a relatively small number of staff scientists working in house when they can potentially access the knowledge of all the scientists in the world through the power of mass collaboration.

When the market values knowledge and speed, mass collaboration demonstrates that nothing is as powerful and as fast as getting everybody together "in the same room at the same time" in open conversations. With the arrival of the Internet and other modern communication technologies, we are no longer limited to the four walls of physical conference rooms for bringing people together. Today, we have the ability to gather large groups of geographically dispersed individuals into a collaborative community in which they can work together in real time. What is missing from most organizations are the skills and processes to take advantage of the full potential of mass collaboration. Whether it's through the Internet, or in conference calls, or even in large group meetings in conference rooms, most executive leaders today are essentially incompetent when it comes to their ability to tap in real time into the knowledge that lies within their organizational reach. As a result, they lack the ability to quickly build the broad-based consensus necessary to realize the powerful benefits of collaborative communities.

Those leaders who develop these new competencies will provide their organizations with a tremendous competitive advantage because mass collaboration enables a company to work smarter and faster than its competition. When organizational success depends on knowledge and speed, working smarter and faster is what it is all about.

For leaders to become skilled at the new responsibility for building collaborative community, they need to become experts at facilitating and building consensus through effective dialogue among large numbers of people. This is a dramatic skills shift for leaders because in the traditional leadership model, when it comes to managing large numbers of people, the focus has been on top-down control rather than on facilitating peer-to-peer consensus. As we will learn in the later chapters, in a wiki world, leaders have to change the way they bring people together in meetings and they have to change the way they lead those meetings. That's because, in the Digital Age, the primary management task is no longer about the efficient use of machines; it's about the efficient use of networks.

WIKI-MANAGEMENT AND THE NETWORK MINDSET

The primary responsibilities of wiki-management are customer values, collective learning, shared understanding, focused measures, and collaborative community. These responsibilities reflect the new ways of thinking and the new ways of acting that better align with the emerging network mindset of the Digital Age. With the rapid expansion of the Internet, our world is fast becoming interconnected and boundaryless. In this new world, the attributes of autonomy and independence, which were so valued by command-and-control managers, are now viewed as obstacles to growth. Managerial sovereignty, well-defined boundaries and vertical integration that focus on a pursuit of separateness make no sense when the world is a network. When your social lens is the network mindset, you appreciate that learning and knowledge are only advanced when we build iteratively on each other's intelligence to understand how the parts work in relationship to the whole.

Thinking more holistically is essential for succeeding in today's new global economy. In the later decades of the Industrial Age, a global strategy meant that a corporation was multi-national with separate and independent business units scattered among different nations around the globe. Today, globalization is more likely to mean that workers on opposite ends of the world are able to take advantage of the time differences to work together 24/7 on the same project. The capacity generated by the Internet and other electronic technological advances to easily navigate across the traditional boundaries of time and space call into question the relevance of organizational charts and functional compartmentalization. Globalization is rapidly becoming the context for all businesses as all parts of the world are now connected in a real-time network.

Another attribute of the network mindset's new way of thinking is that it sees the world as fast-forward. That's why one of the defining attributes of wiki-management is speed. The term "wiki" is derived from the Hawaiian word for "quick" or "fast." A wiki is a Web site that allows large numbers of people to create and edit the content of a single Web page. Wikis are an effective technology for reaching a speedy and credible consensus from the collective contributions of all interested participants in the Web discussion. From the mid-1990's, when this innovative application was first originated, until early 2001, nobody outside of the small community of obsessive technologists had ever heard of a wiki. That all changed in January 2001, when the struggling start-up online encyclopedia Nupedia reformulated its business model by adapting the wiki technology and renamed itself Wikipedia. Within one year, the online encyclopedia grew from a handful of items to over 15,000 articles, and today Wikipedia boasts more than 2 million entries. In turning a niche IT application into a popular social technology, Wikipedia became one of the pioneers in the creation of the new Web, or what has come to be known as Web 2.0. The original Web was more or less a reference vehicle that brought an astonishing amount of information to our computer screens. The new Web is so much more. Now it is an interactive global town hall where anyone is welcome to gather in an open conversation and help build a consensus around how we will self-organize our work.

Wikis and other forms of Web-based social networking are opening up new possibilities and expectations for how quickly we work together that go beyond what we can do online. Don Tapscott and Anthony D. Williams wisely observe, "A wiki is more than just software for enabling people to edit Web sites. It is a metaphor for a new era of collaboration and participation."[3]

This is why the Internet – today's great leap in physical technology – is driving an inevitable revolution in the social technology of how we work together both online and offline. Given this understanding, a new management alternative that is designed for knowledge and speed and whose foundations are collective learning and self-organized work is aptly called wiki-management.

Another attribute of the new network mindset is innovation. This means that new technologies, such as the iPod, can become mainstream and radically restructure an industry overnight. In the machine mindset, progress was measured in the steady pace of periodic inventions and the improvement of existing products. The label "new and improved" was the way corporations signaled a change in the market. When innovation is the hallmark of market reality, products don't have time to be improved. Instead, they are discarded and replaced by new innovations. Why would you want a new and improved portable CD player when you can have an iPod?

The increased need for innovation across all industries is the clearest sign of the accelerated pace of change in the Digital Age. Command-and-control, with its machine mindset, is ill equipped to manage innovation. Thus, it is not surprising that a 2006 survey of 2,000 companies by the American Management Association found the biggest challenge facing corporations is creating disciplined processes for innovation.[4] The inability of many companies or even whole industries to appreciate the need for innovation was particularly troubling to the late Peter Drucker who, in one of his final interviews, poignantly observed, "If you don't understand innovation, you don't understand business."[5]

If Drucker is right, then the majority of businesses today practicing traditional hierarchical management don't understand business in the Digital Age. The context of management is no longer the maintenance of steady state; it's now the advancement of change and innovation. If companies hope to succeed in this new business context, they will need to shake loose from the practices of yesterday's machine mindset and embrace the new network mindset.

While this new world of speed, innovation, and change is far less predictable than the old steady-state world, it doesn't have to be less manageable. It just has to be managed very differently. The traditional disciplines of command-and-control management will not get the job done. Success in the new network world will require corporations to create systematic processes for organizing innovation. This means transforming the ways organizations harvest knowledge. Historically, corporations have relied upon the knowledge of an elite corps of senior executives, complemented by high-powered consultants, to navigate markets. However, one of the most important developments of the networked world is that knowledge is now diffused among the knowledge workers throughout the organization. This means that today the best knowledge is often with those workers who are much closer to the customers and the workings of the business processes.

Creating systematic processes for organizing innovation means quickly accessing and integrating the full spectrum of knowledge spread across the organization. This challenge is beyond the present competencies of command-and-control managers. The rapid assembly of the collective knowledge spread throughout an organization is messy, and the best ideas today do not necessarily come from those with the loftiest titles. Effective innovation processes are likely to be offensive to those who highly value order and authority. Meeting the challenge of creating disciplined processes for innovation means that organizations will have to abandon the highly structured practices of command-and-control and embrace the new chaordic processes of wiki-management. This is not as easy as it sounds because when you are used to the order and authority of the machine mindset, the messiness and the collegiality of the network mindset don't make sense. Nevertheless, the sudden appearance of the wiki world means there isn't a choice anymore.

When the primary values for building organizations shift from order and authority to knowledge and speed, the roles and responsibilities of leaders are completely redefined. Today's executives need to be skillful facilitators. This means that they can't be invested in moving groups toward a particular outcome or to a particular point of view. As facilitators, their new role is to bring together the full breadth of diverse thinking within a context of cross-functional team learning so that everyone together may discover the best outcome that emerges from their collective wisdom and then build the foundations for a shared understanding that will guide mass collaboration throughout the organization. The effective organization of large numbers of workers can no longer be accomplished through executive fiat, especially if the competition has the advantage of quickly accessing its collective wisdom. If traditional companies want to remain competitive in the new economy, they will need to quickly discover the new business wisdom of the wiki world: The power to collaborate is greater than the power to control.

Acting on this wisdom will call for a substantial transformation in organizational design and in executive core competencies. As we discussed in Chapter 1, moving from command-and-control to wiki-management will require a complete resetting of their organizational principles, processes, and practices in three important areas. Companies will need to reset the managers, reset the meetings, and reset the measures. In the chapters ahead, we will explore the resetting of the 3 M's in detail and we will provide practical examples of how leaders are adopting the five new responsibilities of wiki-management and leveraging the power of collective knowledge to make the leap to extraordinary performance.

Part Two

RESETTING
THE MANAGERS

Chapter 4

FROM BEING IN CHARGE TO BEING CONNECTED

As a leader, enhancing the architecture of participation means imposing limits on your ego – overcoming the know-it-all style of leadership that seems to be the default mode in most companies. You can think big without having to think of everything yourself.

- William C. Taylor & Polly La Barre
Mavericks at Work[1]

Before the late 19th century, there were no bosses and there were no subordinates in business enterprises. There were only workers. Prior to the Industrial Age, all business was small business and the average size of the typical working group was four workers.[2] Granted, all workers were not necessarily equal – there were mentors and apprentices. However, these were not permanent power arrangements, but rather temporary learning relationships. In the businesses of the Agrarian Age, there were no supervisors who issued orders and expected compliance. A worker's authority was earned through professional competence rather than ascribed by the power of his position. In the realm of business, the notion that authority is derived from one's role rather than one's practice only comes about with the emergence of the modern corporation and its need to organize the work of large numbers of people. Bosses are actually creations of the Industrial Age, and are thus, a relatively recent phenomenon in the history of work.

Shifting the locus of work from the farm and the craftsman's shop to the assembly line created the need for overseers who would design the intricate processes of the factories, organize the activities of the workers, and make sure that everything was working as designed. As these overseers became the indispensable critical agents of the budding corporate enterprises, it was generally accepted that, for these large organizations to leverage the efficiencies of the assembly line, the overseers needed to have the authority to issue orders and the means to assure that workers would comply with those orders. Accordingly, the early Industrial Age enterprises met the new challenge of organizing large numbers of workers by arranging the activities of the corporation into a hierarchical structure of overseers and subordinates where the authority to command became the foundation for the practice of leadership. Thus, the central role in the command-and-control organization was and continues to be the boss.

In hierarchical organizations, people, by design, work for the boss. Ingrained in the machine mindset of command-and-control leaders is the assumption that the exercise of hierarchical authority is the key to business effectiveness. This assumption reflects the core belief, shared by managers and workers alike, that somebody has to be in charge with clear unquestioned authority or nothing will get done. In command-and-control organizations, leaders are bosses, and despite their relatively recent appearance in the world of work, most of us cannot conceive of an organization without bosses.

Given the significant power and authority bestowed upon the leaders, the typical command-and-control organization has looked to promote the smartest and the most effective individuals to executive positions and to rely on their native intelligence to set the direction for the company. Thus, another deeply ingrained belief among hierarchical organizations is that the smartest business is the one with the smartest bosses. This belief has significantly shaped the profile of what we look for in the people we select to lead large organizations.

In recruiting for key leadership positions, organizations invariably search for highly intelligent, take-charge, charismatic individuals who can effectively persuade large numbers of people to their way of thinking. These highly confident and often larger-than-life characters generally fall into two categories, the heroic leader and the celebrity leader. The heroic leader is typically the smart individual who is the great problem solver with a track record for rescuing organizations from the grip of desperate circumstances, whereas the celebrity leader is the confident star whose charismatic intelligence and inspirational presence lifts organizations to new heights and motivates people to extraordinary action. Both of these types represent popular profiles of the effective boss where leadership is seen as a combination of individual talent and force of personality. When it comes to selecting it key leaders, hierarchical organizations believe in stars and heroes.

CELEBRITY LEADERS

The profile used for recruiting corporate leaders is influenced to some extent by the stereotypes continually reinforced by the mainstream media. The leader as the preeminent boss who either saves the day through the skillful use of his powerful personality or who brings the company down through the corrupt misuse of his authority is how the corporate executive is commonly portrayed in countless television and movie scripts, as well as in numerous articles in both the business and the popular press. Whether we agree with these stereotypes or not, continual exposure to the media messages of the popular culture is bound to influence our perceptions and our expectations of corporate leaders. Thus, the challenge in recruiting celebrity leaders for the top spots is often viewed as the savvy to know the difference between the skillful strong personality and the self-serving miscreant.

The media loves stars because they make for great entertainment. And so, the media is especially fond of celebrity leaders precisely because they are larger-than-life and charismatic. Their strong egos and the inevitable foibles that go along with them are often the fodder that pumps the entertainment well. Whether these celebrity leaders are good or bad bosses isn't as important as whether or not the conflicts and the controversies that surround their exercise of power have entertainment value. However, while celebrity leaders may be the darlings of the media, they can be overbearing and difficult to work with as the acting out of their egos often creates a great deal of consternation and confusion for those who have to travel with the star on the path to success. This point was poignantly and personally brought home for me in a weeklong management training course that I had the opportunity to attend several years ago.

At one point in the training, the class was divided into two groups and assigned to separate conference rooms where each group would be videotaped as they performed a common assignment. Each group was given the same list and was instructed to rank the various items in order of their importance to the accomplishment of a prescribed mission. When both groups had completed the task, we reassembled in the main training room to view the videotapes. We weren't long into the playing of the first tape before the laughter began. The individual who had been designated the leader in the first group immediately started taking charge, and without much success, attempted to control the performance of the task. It was clear that the other members of the group had their own ideas and resisted the leader's efforts to control the outcome. As we continued viewing the tape, the numerous dysfunctional interchanges and the jockeying for dominance by the different members of the group played out like a "Saturday Night Live" skit as the class, by this time, was doubled over with laughter. Amazingly, despite the conflicts among the members and the thwarted attempts of the leader to exert his presumed authority, the group somehow managed to complete the task while providing the entire class with a videotaped record that was a truly entertaining experience.

When the laughter subsided and the class had settled down, the instructor played the second videotape. The leader of the second group opened the discussion by making a suggestion on the process the team might use to complete the task. After several modifications by the group members, they quickly reached consensus on the approach that they would use to fulfill their assignment. As the class quietly watched the tape, this second group proceeded to employ their agreed-upon method and collaboratively began to rank the items. When the group was about half way through the list, the instructor walked up to the front of the room, paused the videotape, turned to the class, and asked, "What do you think?" After a couple of seconds, one person responded, "B-o-o-oring!" The instructor then turned to one of the members of this second group and asked him, "How were you feeling as you were working on this task?" He responded, "I was feeling pretty good. I wish our meetings back at the office went as smoothly. We were working well together. People were engaged and listening to each other, and we were getting the job done." The instructor then turned to one of the members of the entertaining first group and asked him, "How were you feeling when your group was working on the task?" He replied, "I know it was funny to watch us, but I was feeling awful while we were working on this. And our group did remind me of how things are back at the office. People were competing, not listening to each other, and talking over one another. I didn't like it." After a thoughtful pause, the instructor looked at the class and said, "I think we're watching an important management lesson here. Good management is not very entertaining to the outside observer, but it feels good for the participants. Likewise, when management isn't working well, it's often more entertaining to the outside observer than it is for the participants."

Good management, unfortunately, doesn't make it to the media, especially to the popular media, because it has no entertainment value. The media prefers conflict and competition mixed in with a little dysfunctionality. *The Apprentice*, for example, would probably not be a top-rated show if, week after week, we watched the participants discover new ways to achieve harmony and collaboration. People tune in to see who's bickering with whom and to find out who's getting "fired" this week. While *The Apprentice* is indeed entertaining, it isn't entirely representative of the way businesses, especially well-run businesses, work. And while Donald Trump may be an example of a skilled and accomplished celebrity leader, the show's portrayal of his star power and his conventional take-charge approach reinforces a stereotype that may have worked in the past, but is probably not the best model for what we should be looking for in the future leaders of our mass collaboration enterprises.

HEROIC LEADERS

The archetype for executive leadership and the most common profile for recruiting top talent in command-and-control organizations is the heroic leader. Most corporations want dedicated, intelligent, take-charge individuals guiding their enterprises. These talented leaders are very enticing because they usually have track records of outstanding success. With their unique blend of native intelligence, business acumen, polished style, and persuasive personalities, heroic leaders are often able to accomplish the impossible when called upon to propel organizations from mediocrity to excellence. Their single-minded discipline and never-say-die attitudes can inspire and motivate large numbers of workers to improbable heights of success. The steady hand of a confident take-charge heroic leader at the helm in turbulent waters provides great comfort to board members navigating companies through difficult times. Command-and-control organizations firmly believe that individual performers drive corporate success and the consummate performer is the heroic leader.

One of the most visible and heralded performances of outstanding heroic leadership in recent years was the remarkable revival of the Chrysler Corporation in the 1980's after Lee Iacocca assumed the top job. In the summer of 1978, Chrysler was in very serious trouble and on the verge of going out of business. In a fortunate stroke of timing for the ailing automaker, Iacocca had recently been fired as president of the Ford Motor Company. Despite posting a $2 billion profit, Iacocca was let go after a clash of personalities with Henry Ford II over the future direction of product development at the number two carmaker. Iacocca's track record for producing consistent results, most notably the very popular Ford Mustang, was well known throughout the automotive industry. Chrysler was in desperate circumstances and they needed a savior. So they aggressively courted Iacocca who agreed to become Chrysler's CEO in November 1978.

It didn't take long for Iacocca to realize that Chrysler was in far worse shape than he had anticipated. Ever the gifted problem solver and decision maker, Iacocca immediately took charge and put in place a three-pronged strategy to resurrect the dying corporation: 1) downsizing the company to reduce expenses and lower the break-even point, 2) securing congressional approval of $1.5 billion in federal loan guarantees, and 3) introducing the new product ideas that had been rejected by Ford. In a typical display of heroism, Iacocca galvanized Chrysler's workers by sharing in the sacrifice and reducing his own salary to $1.00 per year until the turnaround was accomplished. Iacocca's strategic moves wildly exceeded the Chrysler board's expectations as the recovering automaker's new products, the K-cars and the very popular minivan, became instant hits with car buyers and quickly turned the company's fortunes around. In 1983, a full seven years ahead of schedule, Chrysler completely paid back its federally guaranteed loans. And, in 1984, the company posted annual profits of $2.4 billion, more than the previous sixty years combined.

Heroic leadership works, which explains why so many companies use the profile of the heroic leader to guide their searches when recruiting for executive talent. However, heroic leadership doesn't work all the time. Unfortunately, not all confident take-charge, charismatic leaders are effective. In fact, there are probably as many failures among the bosses who fit this profile as there are successes. Until recently, the missteps of heroic leaders have not been fatal because the relatively stable pace of change of the Industrial Age usually provided sufficient time for corporations to replace the failed executive with another more successful heroic leader.

However, while incredible turnarounds are possible and do happen for some heroic leaders for short periods of time, corporate greatness is about staying-power and decades of continual success. Although highly effective heroic leaders are indeed good leaders, they don't necessarily leave behind great companies. That's why succession planning is becoming a critical business issue in today's dynamic markets. The troubling question that many companies have to confront, especially in fast-changing times, is: What happens to the organization when the hero moves on? Far too often, the company is so dependent on the dominant thinking and the powerful personality of the heroic leader that there is an enormous vacuum once the leader is gone.

Look at what happened to Chrysler after Lee Iacocca retired. A series of poor management decisions and an unsuccessful merger with Daimler-Benz diminished many of the remarkable accomplishments of the 1980's. Unable to sustain itself after regaining its independence, Chrysler was recently forced into another merger – this time with Fiat – to avoid certain bankruptcy. Even though Chrysler has found a life-line for the moment, it still remains to be seen whether its leaders can ultimately preserve this mass production enterprise in a mass collaboration world.

Great companies in the Digital Age will be those who have the capacity to adapt to continually changing markets and the ability to periodically reinvent themselves. When the pace of change is accelerating, greatness is more about smart organizations than it is about smart individuals. Thus, celebrity leaders and heroic leaders will likely become less and less effective as the requirements for business success shift to collective learning and mass collaboration. This does not mean that leaders are not important. Quite the contrary, in fast-changing times, leaders are more important than ever. However, effective leadership in the wiki-management organizations of the Digital Age is very different from the past practices of command-and-control management and will necessitate a new profile when we recruit for leaders in mass collaboration enterprises.

GREAT LEADERS

Fortunately, there are alternatives to celebrity and heroic leaders as we recently learned from the work of Jim Collins and his team of dedicated researchers. In his bestselling book *Good to Great*, Collins highlights the findings of his team's extensive research into the question of whether a good company can become a great company.[3] The idea for this research evolved from a chance conversation Collins had at a dinner meeting following the publication of his previous work, *Built to Last*, which he co-authored with Jerry I. Porras.[4] In *Built to Last*, Collins and Porras had summarized the successful habits of great companies, defined as those public companies that had sustained consistent business success for more than 50 years. At one point during the dinner meeting, one of Collins' colleagues causally commented that all the successful companies identified in *Built to Last* had been great almost from the very start, and that, while he was impressed with the analysis of these model companies, he wondered about the usefulness of the insights from these accomplished firms for the vast majority of companies who may be good, but not necessarily great. In other words, is it possible for a good company to become a great company or is the potential for business greatness something that is more or less determined at the birth of the firm?

This casual inquiry intrigued Collins and soon became his next mission as he assembled a team of talented professionals to set out on a research journey to find the empirical answer to this important question. Collins and his researchers painstakingly analyzed the business results of over 1,400 companies selected from the Fortune 500 list from 1965 – 1995. They methodically searched for companies that shared the following profile: "fifteen-year cumulative stock returns at or below the general stock market, punctuated by a transition point, then cumulative returns at least three times the market over the next fifteen years."[5] Their search identified 11 companies that met the criteria for good-to-great organizations. While they found this transition to be very rare – less than one percent of the companies analyzed made the leap – nevertheless, the empirical research revealed that it is possible for a good company to become a great company. Unfortunately this research also seems to show that the vast majority of good companies never become great companies, causing Collins to observe that perhaps "good is the enemy of great."[6]

As the research team began to dig deeply into the habits and the practices of the good-to-great companies, they were surprised and unprepared for a universal and unusual observation that cut across all 11 organizations, regardless of industry. They found that every one of the subject companies shared a type of leadership that defied conventional wisdom. The leaders of good-to-great companies, whom they eventually labeled "Level 5 leaders," consistently displayed a paradoxical blend of personal humility and professional will.[7] The evidence of willful behavior was anticipated, but what caught the researchers off guard was the pervasive consistency of humility among all the good-to-great leaders. Their behavior was in stark contrast to the largess and egotistical displays that we have come to accept in both celebrity and heroic leaders. These great leaders were not your usual stars and heroes.

Collins uses the very effective analogy of the "window" and the "mirror" to capture the essence of the unconventional behavior of these great leaders. He notes that when things in the company are going well, Level 5 leaders "look out the window" and credit other people or factors outside themselves for the company's success. However, when things go poorly, they "look in the mirror" and take full responsibility for their business circumstances. These great leaders behave very differently from the typical celebrity and heroic leaders who often take credit for others' ideas in good times and are quick to find someone or something else to blame in tough times.

The universal presence of this unexpected humility across all the Level 5 leaders captivated the researchers who, despite Collins' insistence that they disregard the executives in their identification of good-to-great habits, passionately persisted in pushing back. They continued to argue that the unusually consistent humility was a factor that simply could not be ignored. In the end, Collins acquiesced to the researchers, not because of the passion of their conviction, but because the research supported the conclusion. Thus, the significance of the identification of this blend of personal humility and professional will, and perhaps the most important contribution from Collins' breakthrough research, is that we now have an empirical alternative profile for effective leadership to consider when recruiting top talent.

The humility that the researchers observed in these great leaders should not be confused with either weakness or meekness. These exceptional leaders shared a fearless professional will to do whatever was in the best interests of their companies, and they were very capable of making the tough choices to do the right thing. Although it may seem counterintuitive, it is this combination of personal humility and professional will that enables these great leaders to be far stronger and far more effective than their celebrity and heroic leader counterparts. While the strong egos of the stars and the heroes go into high gear in service of themselves in difficult times, the great leaders understand from the start that everything is not about them, which frees them to focus the full force of their talents in service of the company when the company needs it the most.

Great leaders don't assume that they are the smartest people in the room, nor do they need to be. When facing difficult circumstances, their unique combination of humility and will becomes a potent source of courage for these great leaders to put aside any illusions and deal with reality on its own terms. Their strength and their power are firmly rooted in their capacity to bring together the best thinking and the unique talents of everyone in service of the company. Thus, their effectiveness is not derived from a strong ego or their abilities to take charge and persuade or coerce others to their way of thinking, but rather from a courageous sense of integrity that enables them to realistically assess themselves, their colleagues, and their circumstances to bring out the best in everyone so that together they can make the best of the circumstances.

The profile of the great leader as portrayed in Collins' description of the Level 5 leaders is very different from the common profile used by most companies to recruit their top executives. As a result, most recruiters and most hiring executives are not prepared for recognizing, and therefore, often turn away the best executive talent.

Companies gravitate to celebrity and heroic leaders because so often they are good leaders who do get the job done. However, what separates the good companies from the great companies is that great companies succeed over the tenure of multiple generations of leadership, whereas good companies often stumble after the good leader moves on. Unfortunately, celebrity leaders invest too much of their own and their companies' energy on their enormous needs to be the star and their constant preoccupation with looking good. Their gargantuan egos and their insatiable needs for their own adulation leave little room for the recognition and the development of potential successors. Heroic leaders, on the other hand, are constrained by their deep-seated belief that they are truly far smarter and far more capable than the people around them. Operating from this illusion, they are often overly focused on being right and on demonstrating the full extent of their intelligence. Their inflated pride in their skills as problem-solvers and decision-makers often serves to diminish the talents of their supporting cast as they far too easily dismiss alternative opinions and consistently edit the thinking and the contributions of their subordinates. What celebrity leaders and heroic leaders have in common is that, on some level, they believe that the success or failure of the company is all about them. Unfortunately, most executive recruiters and hiring managers seem to share and reinforce this misguided belief.

While Collins' research provides important insights into the characteristics and the behavior of great leaders, the Level 5 leaders in the good-to-great companies were still bosses. They may have been good bosses – even the best bosses – but they were bosses all the same. They occupied positions of power, and while they used their power wisely, they still pulled the levers of order and authority in hierarchical organizations. In a way, great leaders are a special breed of heroic leaders because they too are smart people who are able to propel their organizations from mediocrity to excellence. However, the power of their intelligence has much more to do with their emotional intelligence than with the usual attributes of academic intelligence so highly prized in traditional heroic leaders. Thus, their egos do not get in the way of their intelligence, which explains why they are far more effective bosses.

Nevertheless, Collins' research does not dispel the generally accepted notion that a single intelligent and talented hero can lead organizations to greatness – nor did it need to. After all, the timeframe for the focus of the good-to-great research is 1965 – 1995, arguably the last three decades of the Industrial Age. So it makes sense that in their search for good-to-great companies, Collins and his researchers would discover the profile of the most effective leaders in hierarchical organizations. That being said, there's every reason to believe that the great leaders are far better predisposed to manage the transition of their companies from mass production businesses to mass collaboration enterprises than either celebrity or heroic leaders.

The combination of personal humility and professional will that typifies the great leaders allows them to more easily abandon yesterday's assumptions and embrace the realities of fast-changing times more effectively than leaders whose sense of professional identity is firmly rooted in the established ways of their past accomplishments. Accordingly, great leaders surround themselves with other great leaders whose opinions and ideas are solicited and valued, and who are invited and encouraged to push back on the leader, all in the best interests of the company. The great leader's receptiveness to the intelligence and the talents of his team fosters a culture of leadership where other individuals are fully able to step into the top job when the CEO moves on. Succession planning is usually not an issue when organizations are lead by great leaders.

An example of effective succession from one great leader to another is the transition of the leadership of IBM from Lou Gerstner to Sam Palmisano. While Gerstner may appear to have been a heroic leader brought in to turn around a failing and once great company,

Gerstner's behavior and results clearly demonstrate that he was truly a great leader who led much more than a turnaround. He led a restoration to greatness, for IBM today is once again a great company. When Gerstner passed the baton to Palmisano, there was no vacuum. In fact, IBM is a stronger company today than it was when Gerstner retired. And there is probably no one prouder of that than Gerstner himself who, early in his tenure, abandoned plans to fragment IBM and instead made it his mission to rekindle the fire of the once great company by reconnecting with customers and cultivating a culture of great leaders. By successfully transforming its social technology and embracing the innovative principles, processes, and practices of wiki-management, IBM is an example of how a successful hierarchical bureaucracy can become a collaborative community competitively poised to take full advantage of the new efficiencies of mass collaboration. More importantly, by having the courage to revolutionize its core management model, IBM assures that they will remain a great company well into the Digital Age.

THE LEADER'S NEW ROLE

The first step in making the transition from hierarchical organization to wiki-management is to reset the role of the managers. In the Digital Age, the most effective leaders are facilitators, not bosses. Given today's accelerated pace of change, heroes and stars attempting to centrally direct the work of large numbers of people are no match for self-organizing teams of knowledge workers who can work faster, smarter, and less expensively thanks to the new tools of mass collaboration. If companies want to succeed in the new economy, they will need to abandon the long-accepted notion that a single intelligent and talented individual can lead organizations to greatness, and they will have to divest their managers of their traditional authority to issue orders and to expect compliance.

Today the central challenge of organizing large numbers of workers is about leveraging networks, accessing collective knowledge, and realizing the efficiencies of mass collaboration. This means that collective learning and self-organized work replace central planning and hierarchical organization as the foundation for effective strategy and execution. But more importantly, it means that the role of the business leader is no longer to act as a boss. Wiki-management leaders don't fit the mold of a Donald Trump or a Lee Iacocca. They behave more like the late Bill Gore, the legendary yet humble founder of the maker of Gore-Tex, or Linus Torvalds, the innovative unassuming catalyst behind Linux. Digital Age leaders are facilitators who are responsible for managing the architecture for mass collaboration by creating collective learning processes, building quick consensus, cultivating shared understanding, and keeping the company focused on the few drivers that guide self-organizing teams of workers to consistently deliver customer value in fast-changing markets. In the new social technology, the true measure of a leader has more to do with mobilizing human capacity than with motivating individuals.

When the market requires leaders to be facilitators, organizations have to be diligent in removing executive ego from the practice of management. That's why adopting wiki-management inevitably leads to eliminating the long established practice of the supervisor-subordinate relationship. There is no room for the command performances of celebrity and heroic leaders when the system is the star and the workers are the true heroes of mass collaboration. In the wiki-management organization, the central role is the knowledge worker and not the boss. In fact, those companies who successfully transform their management practices will eventually discover that there is no need for bosses because the days of leading by taking charge are over. Indeed the Digital Age is changing the work we do and the way we work, and perhaps no group of people will feel this more than executive leaders.

FROM CONTENT TO CONTEXT

The advent of the Digital Age marks the end of the era of the bosses. The efficiencies of mass collaboration are dependent upon workers having the tools that they need to self-organize their work. Thus, workers don't need leaders to tell them what to do or how to do it. Instead, they need their leaders to facilitate the creation of collective knowledge and the building of corporate-wide shared understanding that serve as the necessary framework around which the workers can self-organize their activities. Workers do not need supervisors overseeing the content of their work because today's average knowledge worker knows the content of his job better than his supervisor. Thus, the continual involvement of bosses in the content of work only gets in the way and slows things down. In the wiki-management organization, the leader's primary responsibility is no longer the content, but rather the context of work.

When the key tasks of management were planning, organizing, commanding, coordinating, and controlling, it made sense that the leader's role was to focus on the content of the work. In managing traditional organizations, the leader's role was to maintain stability and to assure that everything went according to plan. However, in managing the complex business alliances of the new economy, the key tasks of management are now customer values, collective learning, shared understanding, focused measures, and collaborative community. Thus, the leader's role is no longer about maintaining stability, but rather assuring that the organization has the wherewithal to quickly adapt and reposition itself as the context of markets evolve. Shifting the leader's role from managing content to managing context is a fundamental – some might say radical – transformation of the concept of business leadership.

Managing context requires a different set of competencies and a higher level of emotional intelligence than are needed to manage content. It's relatively easy to give orders and to require people to do things according to your way of thinking, especially when you have the power to withhold raises or even fire workers if they don't comply. It's more challenging to have the ability to quickly access collective thinking, to build shared understanding, and then to trust people's self-organization to get the job done. It's much easier to be convinced of your own intelligence and to impose your point of view on others than it is to trust the collective intelligence of the group or to detach yourself from your own opinions while you facilitate a consensus point of view. And it's more comfortable to believe in the illusion that a single intelligent and talented individual can lead organizations to greatness than it is to accept the reality that nobody is smarter than everybody and that the great leaders in the new economy are those who have the capacity to facilitate and to follow the collective wisdom of the knowledge workers and the customers.

Organizations that are built for knowledge and speed can't afford the hindrances of the egos of heroes and stars. They cannot allow a good idea to be stopped by a single boss, or the value of a suggestion to be weighted by the position of the speaker, nor can they tolerate a glacial bureaucracy that fails to meet evolving customer expectations or is too slow to recognize that customer values have shifted. That is why it is so important to eliminate the sovereignty of the supervisors.

Making the transition from managing the content to managing the context means adopting a new organizational architecture where the workers are responsible for results, where colleagues are accountable to each other, and where everyone is clear that they work for the customer. This means that work is process-oriented and not task-oriented, that people are evaluated by many colleagues rather than by a single supervisor, and that workers have the understanding and the tools they need to make independent judgments on behalf of the customer.

The management architecture necessary to realize the efficiencies of mass collaboration is very different from the organizational structure that successfully leveraged the machines of mass production. This is because the social technology of an organization needs to align with its physical technology to realize the full efficiencies of work. When the physical technology was the machines of mass production, the social technology for running large businesses could be built around the hierarchical chain of command and the functional division of labor depicted in conventional organization charts, and the role of the leader could be based upon the model of the engineer who centrally designs, directs, and controls all the activities. But now that the foundational physical technology is the networks of mass collaboration, the social technology for organizing the work of the large enterprise needs to be reset if organizations expect to successfully compete in the new economy. You can't realize the efficiencies of the revolutionary physical technology of mass collaboration using the century-old social technology of mass production. When the world is about leveraging the networks, chains of command, the functional division of labor, and organization charts are meaningless and counterproductive.

THE POWER OF BEING CONNECTED

The resetting of the leader's role will be particularly challenging because adopting the wiki-management model means changing the ways in which power works within organizations. Over the years the notion of power has received a bad reputation. While the social psychologists define power, achievement, and affiliation as the three fundamental orientations in human social relationships, most of us are much more comfortable with calling ourselves achievement-oriented or affiliation-oriented than we are with owning up to being power-oriented. If someone strives to be successful at an art or a craft, we think of him as wanting to be accomplished. If a person is good at making friends, we call him popular. But if someone is driven by a need to be continually in charge of things, we often describe him as power hungry. Most of us tend to think of power in a negative light. That's because most of our experiences with power are inside hierarchical organizations where power is equated with control.

The notion of power is actually neutral; it is neither good nor bad. Whether we experience power as positive or negative often reflects the quality of our relationships. That's because power is always interpersonal and only exists within the context of relationships. In hierarchical organizations, power is generally ascribed by position, with those few in higher positions having more authority than the many in lower positions. Thus, most of us perceive the exercise of authority as about being in charge and having power *over* people.

The Digital Age is completely reshaping the ways power is exercised inside large organizations. The late psychologist Abraham Maslow observed that the most effective leaders invest in power *with* rather than power over people. Our early experiences with mass collaboration are demonstrating that Maslow's observation holds true for organizations as well. Wikipedia, Craigslist, Linux, eBay, and Google are not primarily interested in control or having power over people. These 21st century businesses understand that, in today's fast-paced world, the best companies are those who build platforms to share power with people. By building decentralized structures via the Internet to tap into the collective intelligence of the many, these mass collaboration enterprises are able to redefine whole industries and easily dominate their mass production counterparts. Traditional businesses cannot compete with the power of self-organized communities because their hierarchical structures limit the interpersonal power of the many in a way that rarely happens on the Internet.

Wiki-management leaders understand that power with people is much more effective than power over people, especially when organizations have to be built for knowledge and speed to remain competitive. This means that the basis for power for executive leaders needs to shift from being in charge to being connected. Executive power no longer comes from dominating the thinking or directing the work of others; it now comes from integrating the best of everyone's ideas and leveraging platforms of mass collaboration. In contrast to traditional hierarchies, which limit the interpersonal influence of the many through the ascription of authority, the power structures of Digital Age companies amplify the opportunities for the development of relationships across all the people within an organizational network. The more connections there are, the quicker a business can access its collective wisdom.

In the world of mass collaboration, power does not come from amassing control, but rather from building a broad-based shared understanding. When shared understanding is the driver of business success, being in charge is meaningless because an effective shared understanding can never be mandated. Shared understanding is something that has to be facilitated and created by consensus. Thus, the quality of a company's shared understanding is directly related to the quality of its connections with both its customers and its workers. When the basis of power for executive leaders is derived from being connected, then leaders are facilitators not bosses and power loses its bad reputation.

A NEW LEADERSHIP PARADIGM

Despite the upheaval of the emerging Digital Age, it is possible for 20th century corporations to be sustainable businesses well into the 21st century, but not if their managers persist in following a 19th century management model. Whether or not the corporate giants of the late 20th century are part of the new economy will be strongly influenced by their wherewithal to reset their management practices in time to compete with the new wiki-management enterprises of the emerging Digital Age. When you look around at the new businesses being spawned by the Digital Revolution, such as eBay, Google or Linux, there's little question that the leader's new role is to facilitate productive collaboration among the knowledge workers.

Thus, the long-term survival of traditional businesses may very well hinge on whether or not they can transition the practice of executive leadership. As we discuss the manager's new responsibilities in the coming chapters, we will learn that the executive facilitator is a completely different leadership paradigm from the executive boss. Unless the executive bosses become or are replaced with executive facilitators, hierarchical managers preserving their perches of order and authority will severely handicap traditional organizations in a new economy that values knowledge and speed. There is no place for stars and heroes in Digital Age businesses. In the world of mass collaboration, the leader's role is to make sure that an infrastructure of both physical and social technologies is in place to support the collective learning and the shared understanding of the knowledge workers. In wiki-management enterprises, there are no bosses and there are no subordinates; there are only workers. And it's the collective organization, not the leader, who is the star.

Diminishing the supervisor-subordinate relationship does not mean that organizations are without leaders. It just means that the leaders aren't bosses. They don't give orders or expect blind compliance, and they don't have authority over the vast majority of the people with whom they work. Leaders in wiki-management organizations are catalysts who get things done by building consensus among large numbers of workers. It doesn't matter whether a company is a new child of the Digital Age, such as Google, or a veteran of the Industrial Age, such as IBM, all large organizations in the 21st century will be shaped or reshaped by the great leap in efficiencies made possible by mass collaboration. If established corporations expect to be major players in the new economy, they need to begin now to shift their leadership paradigm and change the profile that they use to select executive leaders. Nothing will stand in the way of an organization's ability to take advantage of the efficiencies of mass collaboration more than authoritative take-charge bosses unwilling to let go of the levers of order and authority.

Corporations can no longer afford to continue to be filling their leadership ranks with traditional bosses skilled in the traditional power dynamics of bureaucratic maneuvering. Wiki-management organizations are not bureaucracies; they are communities of networks of knowledge workers where power has more to do with facilitating speed and innovation than with the exercise of authority.

The move from hierarchical bureaucracies to collaborative communities is already well underway as it is becoming more common for leaders to be responsible for the performance of significant numbers of workers who are located outside their divisions, and in the case of the growing number of business alliances, even outside their companies.

Celebrity leaders and heroic leaders will not do well in business arrangements where accessing collective knowledge and building consensus are the prime leadership tasks. Executive facilitators are much better suited to meet the challenges of leading the communities of Digital Age organizations.

As more and more leaders recognize that they must adapt to the inevitable revolution in social technology, they will discover that, despite the diminishing role of the boss, leadership does matter more than ever. However, it's no longer a matter of someone's got to be in charge or nothing will get done. It's now a matter of someone has to bring us together or nothing will get done. Thus, when we recruit for leaders in Digital Age organizations, the emphasis is more on intellectual honesty than intellectual prowess, more on emotional intelligence than on academic smarts, more on personal humility than on self-promoting confidence, more on a strong will than on a strong ego, and more on building shared understanding than on taking charge.

If you are a board member, a hiring executive, or an executive recruiter, the next time you are involved in the selection of a key leader, do something different. Resist your deep-seated inclination to hire another highly intelligent, authoritative, take-charge boss. Instead, change the profile and search for an intellectually honest consensus builder with that special combination of personal humility and professional will. Take a pass on another celebrity or heroic leader and take a chance on an executive facilitator because the days of taking charge are over.

Chapter 5

TWO TIMELESS ACCOUNTABILITIES

To build people's trust and commitment deep in the ranks and inspire their voluntary cooperation, companies need to build execution into strategy from the start.

- W. Chan Kim & Renee Mauborgne
Blue Ocean Strategy[1]

While the Digital Age has begun to reshape the principles of management and is about to dramatically change the work we do and the way we work, the fundamental expectations for business leaders remain unchanged. Whether the practice of management is organized around order and authority or knowledge and speed, top managers have the same two timeless accountabilities: strategy and execution. What will change, however, is how companies approach and carry out these two core leadership tasks.

Historically, traditional organizations have functionally divided strategy and execution between a chief strategy officer who serves as the central planner and a chief operating officer who serves as the central organizer. Planning and executing have often been considered as distinct activities requiring different core competencies. Planners are seen as the "big sky, out-of-the-box" thinkers who move the business forward while the operators are valued as the "down-to-earth" pragmatists who get things done. Unfortunately, one of the consequences of this functional segregation is that middle managers and workers usually have very little understanding about the connections between these two essential dimensions of the business. As a result, large numbers of both managers and workers are not conversant in strategic thinking and view business execution through the limited lens of performing their assigned tasks.

If you ask the typical manager what strategy is, you are likely to get a canned answer such as "doing the right thing" or "setting the corporate direction" or worse yet, you may get a lot of stumbling and fumbling for words before she comes out with something like "strategy is planning," or "what we do in offsite retreats," or "the CEO's key initiatives." The simple fact is a large number of business managers do not really know what strategy is – which may explain why they spend so little time on this key accountability.

Managers are much more confident when talking about execution. Ask any manager what execution is and she will quickly respond "getting things done" or "meeting our goals." Most managers pride themselves for their successes in accomplishing their tasks and meeting their objectives. They are much more comfortable with the tactical side of business because the associated activities are more immediately understandable, play better to their traditional penchant for problem solving, and provide an immediate sense of accomplishment when completed. This instant gratification is often a two-edged sword insofar as it reinforces the feeling among managers that they know what they are doing as they take pride in thinking that, because of their heroic efforts and personal involvement, things get done.

However, if you check with the workers who report to these managers, you often hear a much different story. They will tell you that their leaders micromanage and impose less than adequate solutions to problems which oftentimes are actually the creations of muddling mismanagement. They are also likely to tell you that their leaders engage in a great deal of crisis management and, most of the time, really don't know what they are doing. Unfortunately, despite both their bravado and their tactical results, the simple truth is that most managers are not proficient at getting the job done and do not understand what it means to excel at execution.

Surveys of some five million people over the last 25 years by FranklinCovey provide alarming evidence of the persistent deficiencies of managers in the performance of both strategy and execution. While the workers give managers high marks for their work ethic, the employees rate their leaders poorly for their capacity to provide clear focus and direction.[2] Thus, Stephen Covey concludes, "people are neither clear about, nor accountable to, key priorities, and whole organizations fail to execute."[3]

Nevertheless, traditional organizations have been able to succeed despite these deficiencies because the relative stability and the slower pace of change in the Industrial Age allowed enough time for their bureaucracies to make the necessary corrections and still keep pace with the market. Companies had time to learn from mistakes, to do rework, and still meet their market goals.

Throughout the last century, there is more than ample evidence that less than effective management has been tolerated as long as managers delivered the bottom line. This is not possible any more. Just look at the automotive industry – perhaps the consummate 20th century industry – and the difficulties that General Motors and Chrysler are experiencing in keeping up with a changing and more demanding automotive market.

The American automotive industry is struggling with both strategy and execution, and the prospects for turning its fortunes around do not look very promising. This is because the pace of change in the market today is much faster than it was in the 20th century and it will continue to accelerate throughout the 21st century. This is true for all industries – there are no exceptions.

The need to organize around knowledge and speed is significantly raising the bar on the performance of the two timeless accountabilities. The disconnects and the delays caused by the functional segregation of these two core tasks may not have been hindrances to business performance in the past, but given the new challenges of an unprecedented pace of change, managers will have to move much smarter and faster than their current bureaucracies allow.

The most important thing to understand about strategy and execution in fast changing times is that they are not separate activities, but rather they are interrelated and interdependent responsibilities. Thus, in the new wiki world, any company that organizes these two core accountabilities into different and distinct departments is making a serious error. In today's markets, organizing effectively means a company's organizational structure must foster and facilitate continual iteration between strategy and execution. Unlike in the Industrial Age, these accountabilities are not sequential events where strategy precedes execution. In the Digital Age, strategy shapes execution and execution, in turn, shapes strategy. This is why Peter Senge's vision of learning organizations is so important.

When new technologies can reshape markets in a matter of months, learning must be built into the day-to-day fabric of organizational life so that companies are effectively integrating new knowledge about strategic necessities into the execution process and new innovations in execution into strategic direction – all in real time. This is what it means to manage at the pace of change. Given their limited competencies in strategic responsiveness and their functional bureaucratic task-oriented approach to execution, command-and-control organizations are simply not structured for effective learning. As a result, hierarchical businesses are ill equipped to manage at the new pace of change. If companies are to successfully transition from command-and-control to wiki-management, they need to become much more competent in their understandings of what strategy and execution are and how differently they work together in the Digital Age corporation.

STRATEGY

Strategy is the understanding and the alignment of the core business infrastructure necessary to fulfill a company's promise to its customers. Strategy begins and ends with customer value. That's because the key to business success is to consistently deliver what's important to customers better than anyone else. Thus, the first job of strategy is to choose your customers and to know what they value most. Perhaps nobody has done this better than Southwest Airlines, despite the difficulties of competing in a uniquely challenged industry.

Much of Southwest's longstanding success can be attributed to its clear focus on its chosen customer, the leisure traveler. With its competitors riveted to the demands of the business road warriors, Southwest saw an opportunity to deliver value to an untapped market segment with a very different set of needs and expectations.

For business travelers, timeliness and comfort are most important. With the many demands on their time, frequent fliers require flight schedules that align with their business meeting arrangements, they want to be able carry-on their luggage, and they need to be able to quickly move on and off the aircraft so that they can spend more time doing business and less time sitting on planes. While in flight, business travelers want a reserved comfortable aisle or window seat, preferably with no one in the middle seat, so they can work more comfortably because, for road warriors, their cushion on the plane is an extension of the office. This is why all the major airlines set it up so that the frequent fliers board and depart first and have the most comfortable seats at the front of the plane. Another important value for business travelers is to receive their timely and comfortable service at a reasonable price so that they keep their corporate finance departments happy back at the office. Thus, the key value set for business travelers can be summed up as timely and comfortable service at a reasonable price.

For leisure travelers, on the other hand, low prices are what's most important, followed by the reliability and the freedom to travel to distant places by plane rather than by car. Leisure travelers don't mind checking luggage as long as they do not have to pay any extra fees. They don't need assigned seats, and they aren't worried about working on airplanes. They're delighted to go to places without having a long drive in a car and without spending more money than it would cost to drive. Leisure travelers want the reliable freedom to travel at an affordable price.

Southwest's strategic challenge was to find a way to align its core business infrastructure with a market segment where affordability was everything. The air carrier met this challenge by building its well-known low-cost business model. Southwest's fleet uses only one type of aircraft, the Boeing 737. This reduces maintenance and training costs and means that its planes are interchangeable for greater operational flexibility. Recognizing that seating preferences were not essential values for leisure travelers, Southwest was able to trim its technology costs by using a system of three seating groups, the now familiar A, B, and C lines. Furthermore, by leveraging its no frills approach, the air carrier dramatically reduced its gate turnaround time to an unprecedented 20 minutes, shattering the industry norm. Getting planes quickly back into the air generated more revenue miles per hour than their competitors, which allowed Southwest to charge lower fares and still remain profitable. Finally, while other carriers have resorted to charging baggage fees to meet their cost challenges, Southwest is able to leverage its low-cost model to meet a very important value of the leisure traveler: no baggage fees.

By building its core business infrastructure around the most important values of its chosen customers, Southwest was not only able to find a way for the cost of air travel to favorably compete with the cost of car travel, but they also found a clarity and a focus to guide the strategy reflected in their well-known company promise, "You are now free to move about the country." And that's exactly what millions of leisure travelers do every year.

Effective strategies are always clear, focused, and real. Southwest Airlines perennially succeeds in one of the world's most challenging industries because its leaders are competent at making sense out of complex and ever changing markets (the reality) by discovering the fundamental drivers of customer value (the focus) and building their infrastructure to deliver what is most important to their chosen customers (the clarity).

Most traditional organizations do not strategize well because they do not have effective management processes to sort through the complexities of the market. Historically, most strategic work has been a trial and error endeavor without any real developed discipline. The typical command-and-control organization has looked to promote the smartest and most effective individuals to executive leadership positions and to rely on their native intelligence for sifting through the business complexities and setting the direction for the company. This desultory approach is often played out in a type of musical chairs where executives are replaced if their strategic directions do not work out until the organization finds a leader who seems to get it right. Unfortunately, the trial and error approach is becoming increasingly perilous as the pace of change continues to accelerate for the simple reason that by the time an organization gets it right, market opportunities may be permanently lost to organizations who do have a more effective discipline for doing strategy.

In the wiki world, strategy needs to be a process that involves all the parts of the organization in creating a shared understanding grounded in evolving market reality and shaped by current operational capacities and future market requirements. When the pace of change is accelerating, effective strategy is interdependent with effective execution – you can't have one without the other.

EXECUTION

Execution is the design and management of business processes to meet or exceed all expectations in the customers' value set. Like strategy, execution begins and ends with customer value. Where strategy is about the focus of the company's promise, execution is about the fulfillment of that promise. For example, FedEx's pledge of "absolutely, positively overnight" would be meaningless without the consistent follow-through to deliver every package the next morning. While strategy gives purpose to execution, it is execution that gives meaning to strategy. Flawless execution lets the customer know that a company really means what it promises.

Consistently delivering what customers value is the surest pathway to success. While this sounds simple, why is it that so many organizations are execution-challenged? Stephen Covey has called execution the great unaddressed issue in most organizations today.[4] Too many companies are plagued by broken promises, quality breakdowns, damage control, and quick fixes. Their attempts at execution are misadventures in crisis management that oftentimes pit frustrated and overworked employees against dissatisfied and angry customers caught in a web of seemingly endless problems. This is not a formula for long-term success!

The key to execution excellence is having a discipline of effective process management where the fundamental business processes are properly and thoughtfully designed to integrate the complete set of activities necessary for the customer to receive promised value each and every time. When companies have well-designed business processes, problem solving becomes an exception activity rather than the primary focus of work.

The prerequisites for effective business processes are clarity – which is the bridge between strategy and execution - and voluntarism. Clarity comes from understanding what is important to customers from their perspective, knowing the sequence and the interrelationships of the activities necessary to deliver customer value, and identifying which activities are the key drivers of success. Clarity is only possible if project plans capture the workers' shared understanding of the sequencing and timing of these activities and if the key drivers of success are measured in a compelling and visibly evident scorecard so that all the workers can see for themselves how well their execution is meeting customers' expectations. Clarity around what we are doing and how what we do contributes to what customers value is a fundamental driver of execution excellence.

Without clarity, there is the continual nagging question of whether or not anybody knows what they are doing around here. Without clarity, work is haphazard, disjointed, and unfocused. Without clarity, no one really knows what the goals are. And without clarity, work is a continual stream of problems and crises, often identified by the customers – a clear sign that nobody really does know what they are doing around here!

Clarity does not come easily or naturally. It's hard work because clarity is not something you dictate – it is something you discover, especially in the wiki world. Beware of bosses who proclaim, "Let me make this perfectly clear" without the benefit of the collective wisdom of the workers. Clarity only comes from learning processes that are able to sift through business chaos by tapping into the creative collective knowledge across the broad perspectives of both the managers and the workers.

Unfortunately, when faced with the inevitable chaos that accompanies accelerating change, many traditional leaders resort to a familiar place of emotional comfort that's worked before when they felt overwhelmed – and that is, "being the boss." When they are in this mode, leaders take charge, become authoritarian, micromanage, stop listening, shut down other points of view, become coercive, and sometimes even abusive. When a business leader is engaged in the worse kind of "being the boss" behavior, the message is clear: "I don't care what you think – I'm in charge here – do what I tell you because if you don't you won't be working here any more." While this kind of coercive pseudo-clarity can work in the short term some of the time, it is not consistently effective. Furthermore, it is becoming less and less effective as markets become more chaotic and as knowledge workers sometimes surprise the bosses by taking up their coercive offer to work somewhere else, taking their knowledge with them.

In the Industrial Age when the corporate bosses were the owners of all the primary assets of capital, facilities, and equipment, they could get away with accomplishing execution through coercion. However, now that the primary assets are capital and knowledge, the bosses no longer control all the economic essentials. While they may still direct the capital, it is the workers and not the corporations who hold the most important knowledge. This new balance of power calls for a different relationship between bosses and workers, one where the leaders and the professionals collaborate as partners to provide excellent products and services to customers.

This brings us to the second prerequisite for effective execution, voluntarism. If workers are truly partners, then workers are volunteers – paid volunteers – yet volunteers all the same. There are no more employees for life. Workers today remain with the same company as long as the business relationship meets their needs. If workers feel their working arrangements no longer suit them, they are not likely to "suck it up" and accept that this is how it is in the "real world." Rather, they are more likely to move on to another company for as long as the next situation meets their needs. With the recent rapid shift in pensions from defined benefit to defined contribution and the increased portability of health insurance, companies have less financial leverage to keep workers in their employ and workers have more choices about where and with whom they will work.

There was a time when the bosses could take the workers for granted and could act as if the workers were assets they owned. Workers have been called "human resources" as if they were available tools along with other fixed assets such as capital resources, facilities, and equipment. Traditional corporate language and structures reflect this attitude of ownership. Bosses are said to be "in charge" of budgets, facilities, equipment – and people, and they are expected to exercise control over all their resources, including the people. The language and the structure of the hierarchical organization continually reinforces the internalization of the mistaken notion, especially on the part of the bosses, that workers have limited voice and are hired to serve as a resource at the discretion of the managers. Thus, no matter how benevolent they may be in their intentions and in their rhetoric, when bosses behave toward workers in ways that limit workers' voices and treat people as discretionary human resources, their behavior clearly communicates that workers are subordinates. This is not the reality in the wiki world.

Today's workers are partners. Because they own the knowledge, they are free agents able to partner with any organization that they choose in the building of outstanding strategic and execution infrastructure. This means that for organizations to truly achieve extraordinary performance, they need workers to willingly and voluntarily work for them. In this new partnership, organizations cannot afford to treat their workers as subordinates. Peter Drucker captured this new reality best when he stated in an interview, "Today the corporation needs them [knowledge workers] more than they need the corporation. That balance has shifted."[5]

Acknowledging that workers are no longer subordinates is a dramatic shift in the way companies view their employees because being a volunteer means the workers have the right to say "No." To be effective in the Digital Age organization, leaders will need to accept and respect this right. In a true partnership, one partner does not get to command or control the others. Partners collaborate, respecting each other's right to object and working issues until a mutual consensus is reached. This means leaders can no longer consider it their prerogative to issue orders and directives or expect workers to do what they are told "because I'm the boss." While more companies are calling their employees "associates" in recognition of changing realities, the true test for whether the company is serious or just paying lip service is whether or not the leaders respect the worker's right to say "No," and whether or not they will honor the voices of all their workers until a mutual consensus is reached.

The command-and-control leader will bristle at this notion, calling it an invitation to corporate chaos. "How will anything get done

around here," she will protest, "if people have the right to say 'No'."
She will further argue that work will come to a standstill if she has to
take the time to be responsible for achieving a consensus among the
workers. For the traditional leader, respecting the worker's right to
object is completely incompatible with her notion of execution excellence. Ingrained in the mindset of command-and-control leaders is the
assumption that the exercise of hierarchical authority is the key to
what makes organizations work well and that the chain of command
must be respected above all if a company has any expectation of execution excellence. This mindset assumes that if employees are allowed
the right to say "No" then they will undercut the chain of command,
creating all kinds of unnecessary problems and inconsistencies which,
in turn, will lead to a complete loss of control and ultimate business
failure. These managers will be quick to point out that they are not
opposed to input from their employees, and that they, in fact, involve
their subordinates by soliciting their ideas and taking them into
account as they make their decisions. However, more often than not,
these managers feel no sense of responsibility to follow-through with
their employees on how their ideas are used or to find out whether or
not the workers agree with the use of their input. At the heart of the
mindset of command-and-control leaders is the belief that execution
excellence will happen if only everybody would just do what she's
told.

In the wiki world, nothing could be farther from the truth. Quite
the contrary, consensus is the key to getting it right the first time.
Honoring the voices of the employees, listening to the "No's" and
taking the time to reach mutual consensus is actually the path to
faster and more effective execution. An organizational learning session that I personally facilitated in the spring of 2001, when I was
with Blue Cross Blue Shield, boldly demonstrated this fact.

LISTENING TO THE "NO'S"

By way of background, the objective of our learning session, using
a process called Work-Thru that is fully described in Chapter 7, was
to design a new health insurance product to replace one of the two
options Blue Cross Blue Shield offered in the Federal Employees
Health Benefits Program (FEHBP). In this program, federal employees
across the nation choose their health insurance from product options
offered by over 250 different national and local offerings. Blue Cross

Blue Shield was the market leader with 49 percent of the market share at that time. Over the preceding 15 years, Blue Cross Blue Shield had steadily increased its market share by 10 percentage points on the strength of a then new PPO (Participating Provider Option) product that, over that time, had grown to become the carrier's flagship product in the FEHBP.

In designing and executing a new product option to replace the unpopular and financially-challenged second product offering, the charge was to create a new option which would be more attractive to customers without diminishing the appeal of the carrier's flagship product. The new product was to be part of a growth strategy to expand into segments of the federal employee market where Blue Cross Blue Shield had historically been weak. A market segmentation analysis had been shared with the Work-Thru participants and it had become clear very quickly that the best product design to attract enrollment into the new option, without jeopardizing the strength of the flagship product, was to build a lower priced EPO (Exclusive Provider Option) offering. This would be a completely different product model from the flagship product as well as from the offering it was replacing, which was also a PPO product. In exchange for its lower price, the proposed EPO product, while providing generous benefits for using doctors and hospitals in the carrier's network, would not provide any out-of-network benefits. This means that if a customer were to use the services of a doctor or a hospital that was not part of the carrier's EPO network, the customer would be responsible for 100 percent of the costs. The flagship PPO product, on the other hand, would continue to have both in-network and out-of-network benefits, with lower cost sharing for customers who use the carrier's network of participating doctors and hospitals.

There were two major challenges to the successful execution of this strategy. First, Blue Cross Blue Shield was not certain that the Office of Personnel Management (OPM), which has responsibility for administering health insurance benefits for federal employees, would agree to an EPO product option. Second, the execution of this new product model would require significant time-challenged modifications to the carrier's claims processing systems that would need to begin well before the annual date that Blue Cross Blue Shield and OPM agree on product options for the next calendar year.

Given these two challenges and knowing that continuing with the current unpopular second product was not an option, I had instructed the Work-Thru participants to meet in small group discussions to identify alternative product designs in the event that the employer would not accept an EPO product. I explained that, by having an alternative, we could begin systems work on both alternatives until product discussions were concluded enabling us to complete the systems installation of whichever product alternative was ultimately accepted by OPM. It sounded like a reasonable business plan in view of the fact that the board had already decided that the current second product was unsustainable and had to be replaced immediately in the next benefits year. Being prepared with alternative options would allow us to be able to handle any outcome from the product negotiations with OPM, while at the same time meeting the board's requirement to install a new second product.

As was my usual practice at the start of small group discussions, I asked the participants if they had any questions before beginning the exercise. One individual from the information systems discipline spoke up and said, "I understand the exercise and what you're asking us to do, but we can't do this. It's the wrong thing to do." He went on to explain that there really was no alternative to the EPO product model for the new second product if we were serious about the new offering promoting a growth strategy. He asserted that what we needed to do was to make a commitment to the EPO model and to do whatever was necessary to make it happen, even if it meant waiting an additional year to get OPM comfortable with this new product design. He further stated that, from the systems perspective, the existing resources could not support working on two alternative product designs concurrently, and thus, we could not reasonably expect to do either one before the start of the next benefit year at the level necessary to deliver the expected excellent service. He reiterated that a commitment needed to be made to the EPO model and that the group should not waste any time on alternative models.

Having encountered objections to small group exercises in facilitating previous organizational learning sessions, I responded to the participant by acknowledging the importance of doing everything possible to make the EPO model happen and affirmed the difficult challenge of beginning systems work on two alternatives at once. Nevertheless, I emphasized the importance of identifying a back-up alternative given the established annual schedule for product negotiations and the board's expectation for a new second product in the next benefit year. I then begged the group's indulgence and once again asked the participants to begin the small group discussions to identify a back-up product design just in case an alternative is needed. Once again, the same participant raised his hand and said, "With all due respect, I have to continue to push back. We will be wasting our time – it's just the wrong thing to do if we want our new product to be a growth opportunity." This time I noticed nods of agreement among the other participants and realized that the speaker was, in fact, a spokesperson for the group. If there was ever a "No" on the part of the workers, this was it!

There was an air of suspense building in the room, as everyone was aware that we were in uncharted waters. While I was quite experienced at facilitating Work-Thrus, I had never before been faced with participants refusing to go into a small group exercise. As I looked around the room, I realized that all eyes were on me to see how I would handle this moment and to find out whether or not Work-Thrus were for real or just another example of empty rhetoric about employee involvement. It was moment-of-truth time.

I was very uncomfortable and felt under enormous pressure at that particular moment. On the one hand, the board wanted a new product now. On the other hand, the Work-Thru participants were insisting that there was only one new product model that fit the strategy, even it meant waiting a year to make it happen. I was also aware that this was an integrity moment for the Work-Thru process that would have ramifications about our commitment to organizational learning and collaboration far beyond this particular session. With all this in mind, I asked the participants a third time if they would indulge me and go into the small group exercise. And for a third time, the same participant respectfully pushed back with even more nodding agreement on the part of the participants – the "No" was loud and clear. It was then that I realized that there was something important happening in the room and that I needed to stop fighting it and let it be.

And so, I turned to the group and asked, "What do others think?" And one by one, several other participants voiced their agreement that a commitment had to be made to the EPO product model and that it would be counterproductive to work on any other alternative. Acknowledging the clear will of the group I smiled and said, "Well, I guess we won't be doing this small group exercise this morning." Instead I opened up a large group discussion, sharing with the group the pressures I felt to both acknowledge the wisdom of the Work-Thru participants and to comply with the will of the board.

Over the next hour, a genuine dialogue developed as we together worked the problem of resolving these seemingly irreconcilable positions. As the discussion evolved and the participants built upon one another's comments and observations, a breakthrough emerged as one member of the group suggested that we escalate the date for reaching agreement with OPM on the form of the new product option. If that could be done, the new product design would be known before beginning critical systems work and the board's directive would be met. The creative energies of the participants then moved to outlining the compelling presentation needed to convince OPM to accept an earlier date for closure on the second product model. At the end of this large group discussion, we were all very comfortable that we had created the tools to secure OPM's agreement to an earlier product closure date and, more importantly, to fully execute the systems requirements for the operational excellence that customers had come to expect from us. In the end, both of these actions were successfully achieved and the new second product exceeded the strategic growth expectations to the delight of the board, the executives and the staff alike.

As a final note on this Work-Thru experience, after the participants had concluded their work in the large group discussion, the participant who had continually pushed back against the small group exercise raised his hand one more time, and I remember thinking "What now!" However, he looked at me and said, "Before we move on, I'd like to thank you for allowing us to push back and for your patience with us. I know that this wasn't comfortable for you. I think we all agree that, over the last hour, we did some really fine work and that we landed in the right place. We wouldn't have gotten here if you hadn't allowed it. Thanks for not shutting us down." At that point, all the participants broke into spontaneous applause. It was clear to me that I was looking at 45 very enthusiastic and committed volunteers who would make this new product work – excellent execution was assured. It was also very clear that organizational learning, despite its uncomfortable moments, works to drive faster and smarter execution. Honoring the voices of the workers, listening to the "No's," and taking the time to reach mutual consensus – all of this accomplished in less than an hour – did indeed drive a faster and more effective execution.

This single hour saved countless months of what would have been wasted energy and resources. Clearly this example demonstrates that it is consensus, and not control, that is the key to getting it right the first time, and that clarity and voluntarism are the prerequisites for effective execution. The clarity of commitment to building the EPO product and the willingness to approach the workers as volunteers and as true partners in the design and management of the business processes supporting the new product did, in fact, result in an execution that clearly exceeded the customers' expectations.

TWO DIFFERENT APPROACHES

A key difference between command-and-control and wiki-management organizations is how they approach the two fundamental accountabilities of strategy and execution. As noted above, strategy and execution are interrelated and interdependent. The level of the performance of both of these accountabilities is what drives a company's results, as reflected in what could be called the basic business formula:

$$STRATEGY + EXECUTION = RESULTS$$

Simply stated, this means the right strategy (doing the right thing) and the right execution (doing things right) produces the right results. That's the job of management in a nutshell. However, before focusing on the differences of the two management mindsets, let's probe a little more deeply into understanding this basic business premise and why this apparently simple formula is becoming increasingly challenging for so many companies as we transition into the Digital Age.

Let's begin with the critical observation that the real work of strategy has more to do with understanding why we do things rather than what we do. That's because the "why" is more important than the "what." Understanding why we do things is only possible if we focus on the right questions. Thus, the key to the right strategy is to ask the right questions. While this sounds simple enough, this is where the challenge lies because the right questions are not always immediately apparent. Meeting this challenge requires knowing what's important to customers, where their values are, and how their values are changing. Once again, strategy begins and ends with customer value. Focusing on the right questions to understand what's important to the customer (the strategy) will lead us to what needs to be done (the results) and how we need to do it (the execution). Thus, another way to look at the basic business formula is:

WHY + HOW = WHAT

The reason that the "why" is more important than the "what" is because the "why" helps determine the "what." Before we can proceed with what we are going to do (the answers), we have to understand the why or the purpose (the questions). Only then will we be able to deliver on the how (the actions). Thus, still one more way to look at the basic business formula is:

QUESTIONS + ACTIONS = ANSWERS

It is the questions that lead organizations to the "right thing" and it is the capacity for action that defines an organization's ability to do "things right." Thus, the "answers" are a product of exploring the "questions" and growing the capacity for "actions." This is why, especially in fast changing times, the power of an organization has less to do with its knack for making the right decisions and more to do with its capacity to make the right discoveries.

Decision-making is concentrated on finding the answers, whereas discovery is focused on discerning the questions. When organizations fasten their strategic efforts on discovery and asking the right questions, the answers emerge and are often self-evident. As a result, the decisions become easier and more reliable as a clear connection between what we are doing and why it is being done becomes obvious to the whole organization. This clarity produces a shared understanding that drives consistent excellence in execution among willing volunteers who believe in what they are doing and know why they are doing it. When organizations focus on discovery as their pathway to decisions, they create a workforce of willing volunteers who find both meaning and purpose in their work.

Unfortunately, for too many organizations, strategic work is difficult and confusing because executives embark on a search for the right answers based on the limited understanding of a small group of decision-makers. The resulting decisions do not have the benefit of the knowledge and the understanding of the workers who are usually more aware of what's most important to customers. The difficulties become exacerbated as workers become disengaged when they conclude that the decisions are wrong as they correctly see the flaws in executive thinking and know that they have no realistic way for their voices to be heard. When this happens, execution becomes an exercise in coercion as workers perform tasks that make no sense to them, knowing that the corporate effort could have been so much better had they had the opportunity to contribute in a meaningful way.

In today's fast changing times, strategy is not the domain of the elite. Strategic work is everyone's work because you cannot separate strategy from execution and because nobody is smarter than everybody. Organizations that do strategy and execution well begin with the questions, have a capacity for discovery that expands the knowledge and know-how of both the executives and the workers, and an adaptability to both extend the limits of their delivery capacity and then to execute well within those limits. The simple business formula of "Strategy + Execution = Results" is so hard for many companies because they do not understand that, in fast changing times decisions are not made, they are discovered.

This is a reality that is lost on command-and-control managers who tend to confuse strategy with action. As a consequence, when doing strategic work, they tend to start with the "what," skip the "why," and move to the "how." Once traditional managers have settled on their course of action, they then plan, organize, and direct how work will be performed and tasks are assigned accordingly to staff down the chain of command. Because they have ignored the "why," whether or not they are doing the right thing is a gamble at best. And whether or not they are doing things right is questionable because of the likely minimal up-front involvement of the workers who know the customer and the business processes best.

Command-and-control managers often confuse action with progress and therefore pride themselves on being action-oriented. But far too often this action-orientation is nothing more than a mask for a continual pattern of crisis management. When leaders start with the answers, skip the questions, and go straight to action, the results are wrought with the problems so typical of a "ready-fire-aim" management approach that so poorly utilizes scarce resources and drains the morale of the staff.

Wiki-management organizations, by contrast, are results-oriented. Wiki-leaders understand that strategy and execution are iterative and interrelated processes that require the integrated involvement of both managers and workers. They understand that it is results, and not activities, which delight customers. Being quick to action diminishes the short-term anxieties of bosses. Being quick to results meets the needs of customers and helps to turn them into long-term purchasers.

When organizations are results-oriented, they understand that you have to slow down to move fast. Thus, results-oriented leaders take the time to start with the questions, align the actions, and discover the answers. They appreciate that "ready-aim-fire" always works better than "ready-fire-aim."

No manager, especially those who practice it, really wants to operate by "ready-fire-aim." It's just that, when the going gets tough, they often do not have any experience in proceeding any other way. However, with the recent development of collective learning processes such as Work-Thrus, leaders now have the reliable means to practice "ready-aim-fire" in the most challenging circumstances. They now have the unprecedented ability to quickly discover the most important questions and get clear about the "why" behind the needed action. Once this clarity of purpose becomes a shared understanding, the organization is poised to identify breakthrough possibilities and then build the infrastructure necessary to deliver real results that continually exceed customers' expectations.

Results-oriented companies understand that leaders need to organize their work processes around knowledge and speed if they want to continually remain competitive in the new business world of accelerating change. And speed does not mean quick to action – it means quick to results. Having the capacity to tap into the organization's full knowledge at any time is what makes a company nimble and drives better and clearer strategy. This, in turn, fosters a clarity, focus, and shared understanding throughout the organization that drives fast and effective execution as workers, who understand fully why they are doing things, become engaged volunteers in the expansion of the organization's delivery capacity. When this happens, things are done right the first time. This is what is meant by quick to results.

In wiki-management organizations, the leaders understand that the key to delivering results is to recognize that they don't have to have all the answers themselves because their primary job has much more to do with making discoveries than with making decisions. They are not concerned with being in charge because they fully appreciate that in today's new economy, we all work for the customers, not the bosses. This explains why wiki-leaders are extraordinary facilitators and excel at building consensus and shared understanding among large numbers of people. It is much more important for them to know that they are fully connected with their workers and their customers, because only then will they be able to leverage the rich reservoir of their collective knowledge to effectively integrate strategy and execution. That is the secret to the achievement of extraordinary performance in carrying out these two timeless accountabilities in the new wiki world. And that is why it is so important to reset the managers from being bosses to being facilitators.

Chapter 6

THE FIRST RESPONSIBILITY: CUSTOMER VALUES

Without customer value, there is no sustainable business.

- Michael Treacy & Fred Wiersema
The Discipline of Market Leaders[1]

For most of the 20th century, the bosses dominated market economies. They set the pace of product development, and through their offerings, they created markets for customers all too eager to purchase whatever latest conveniences came off the assembly line. Mass production capacity equaled market power, and the greater the capacity, the more the bosses had the sense that they were in control. For them, the economic world was like a machine that they could design, assemble, and manipulate. Through long-term planning, these managers could analyze current trends, forecast their futures, and then make them happen. They were the engineers of the market and the captains of their destiny. The relative stability and predictability of industrial markets reinforced the universally perceived power of the bosses, while the customers were taken for granted. The managers did not concern themselves with consumers; rather they worried about the other bosses in their industry and always kept their competition in sight. The managers were in charge and all the workers inside corporations were well aware that they worked for the bosses.

Toward the end of the 20th century, the world changed. Customers are no longer the passive recipients of corporate offerings. They are now educated, knowledgeable, and discriminating consumers who have options and exercise choices. The customers' power of choice has supplanted the bosses' power of capacity, and thus, market definition has shifted from the bosses to the customers. Markets shaped by consumer choice are more volatile and less predictable than those driven by production capacity. This makes long-term planning extremely difficult, if not impossible, and means that it's now more important for companies to keep their eyes on the customers rather than the competition.

Customers make choices based on what they value. If your capacity does not match what's most important to them, they will literally search the globe and find the company that does provide the best match. And that company may not be your perceived competition or even in your industry. Craigslist, for example, does not focus at all on competition. In fact, according to CEO Jim Buckmaster, Craigslist has no interest in competing with anybody.[2] Their whole focus is on creating customer value. "We consider our mission to be one of public service," Buckmaster says. "We're just trying to create something as useful as possible. If people use it, great. If they don't find it useful, that's great too. Yet we keep reading that we're one of the newspaper industry's deadliest competitors."[3]

Keeping your eye on the competition is no longer a useful reference point. In the Digital Age, you must never take your eye off the customer because in the new wiki world, managers and workers alike better understand that everyone inside corporations now works for the customers, not the bosses.

The first responsibility of management is customer values. Corporate work no longer begins with planning around what the bosses think. In the Digital Age, the starting point for business is always what the customer values. And what's important to customers is likely to be very different from what the company values. Also, what customers prefer today might be very different from what they valued yesterday and will certainly be different from what's most important to them tomorrow.

Customer values are never found inside executive suites. In fast changing times, only the most arrogant managers would forgo asking the question and presume they already know the answer to what's most important to customers. Customer values are only discovered outside the organization, and because they evolve and change, managers need to continually inquire and look outside to be instep with market reality. Effective decision-making requires organizations to have processes for actively listening to their customers and understanding what they value most.

Michael Hammer makes the point, "When companies know only about themselves and not about their customers, they make all kinds of decisions with inadequate information."[4] This was a lesson that IBM learned the hard way. When Lou Gerstner was appointed CEO in 1993, IBM was in serious trouble and in a downward spiral that could have spelled its demise in a market that it had actually created.

It took someone from the outside to get IBM to understand that it had lost touch with the market, had become too arrogant and insular, and as a result, had stopped listening to its customers. Instead of fragmenting Big Blue into smaller companies as had been planned, Gerstner successfully kept IBM together by refocusing the company to look outside its walls, to come to terms with new market realities, and to reconnect with its customers.

KNOWING YOUR CUSTOMERS

When you step outside your company, the first thing you have to do is to walk in your customer's shoes. You need to learn to see your organization and your products from their perspective. It is especially important for senior executives to get out of their offices and to go out into the marketplace to meet their customers face-to-face. In the heyday of the Industrial Age, senior executives could go their entire careers without ever meeting an end user of their products. Their only contact with customers was usually through well-organized data in neatly prepared analytical reports. While customer data is important, it is not enough. If you really want to know whom you're working for, you need to talk to customers, hear their voices, look them in the eye, and know how it feels for them to do business with you. Even if you spend only a couple of hours each month listening to service center calls, you need to take the time to directly connect with your customers' experience. As you listen to them, find out why they buy your products and don't be surprised if they use them for different reasons than you had in mind. This kind of knowledge, which you can only get by engaging with your customers, is emotional intelligence, and you're not likely to find it in data charts and reports. Only when you walk in their shoes will you truly know the strength of your emotional bond with your customer and the power of your brand.

Toyota is a company that understands the importance of starting initiatives by walking in the customer's shoes. In 2003, the automaker undertook a major redesign of its Sienna minivan, which is primarily marketed in North America. In addition to the traditionally available market data, Yuri Yokoya, the chief engineer for the project, went to his director and requested time to take a trip to North America so he could drive through every U.S. state and Canadian province as well as all parts of Mexico.[5] Unlike many traditional companies that might have viewed such a trip as a wasteful and unnecessary travel expense, Toyota appreciated the importance of looking outside to understand what customers value and encouraged Yokoya to engage in his firsthand consumer research.

By taking the time to see their product through the customer's eyes, the Toyota engineers were able to discover several important values that would not be readily apparent in the usual market data reports. For example, they learned that Canadian highways have a higher crown than Japanese, American, or Mexican roads, and therefore, they needed to control the "drift" of the minivan.[6] They also found out the importance of side-wind stability by driving through gusty winds on a Mississippi River bridge and by seeing how easy it was for trucks to blow a minivan aside in the crosswinds of Ontario.[7] And perhaps, most importantly, by driving the longer trips between the more spread-out U.S. cities, Yokoya saw firsthand the value of cup holders to American drivers who are more likely to eat and drink while driving.[8] By going outside into the market and experiencing driving from the customer's perspective, Toyota was able to better align its minivan with customer values and was rewarded for its foresight when the redesigned 2004 Toyota Sienna was voted best minivan of 2004 by *Car and Driver* magazine.

UNDERSTANDING NONCUSTOMERS

In addition to seeing the world through your customer's eyes, you also need to get to know your noncustomers and find out why they don't buy your products. Peter Drucker continually emphasized the importance of understanding your noncustomers because he felt that they were the prime catalysts for change. He often observed that, "very few institutions know anything about the noncustomers – very few of them even know that they exist, let alone who they are. And even fewer know why they are not customers. Yet it is with the noncustomers that changes always start."[9]

Understanding your noncustomers is critical to managing at the pace of change. The sooner you have information about market changes, the more time you have to act. Your noncustomers are often the best sources for the information you need, provided you are prepared to hear it. Unfortunately, the recording industry is an example of a group of companies who were not prepared to listen to their noncustomers, and as a result, may be on the verge of being overtaken by a fundamental restructuring of their industry.

From the mid-1980's through the late 1990's, the recording industry had enjoyed a financial bonanza as a whole generation of baby
boomers replaced their vinyl album collections with compact discs.
The CD was an innovation engineered by the record companies that
maximized the most important value to baby boomer customers,
quality of sound. The CD was also the ultimate manifestation of the
longstanding business model of the industry, the record album. Just
when it appeared that the CD was the golden goose that would keep
on giving, along came the Internet and a whole new generation of
post-boomers with very different values about how they liked their
music. Until this time, for all practical purposes, there were no noncustomers in the recording industry. Whether they were vinyl records
or CD's, until the late 1990's everybody bought albums.

Beginning in 2001, the world of recorded music experienced the
equivalent of a seismic shock when, for the first time, noncustomers
began to populate the recording industry's market. Brian Hiatt and
Evan Serpick, in a comprehensive article on *RollingStone.com*, chron-
icle the industry's precipitous decline.[10] After the CD bonanza of the
1980's and the 1990's, sales of albums decreased by over 25 percent
from 785.1 million in 2000 to 588.2 million in 2006. Meanwhile,
legitimate digital singles sales, which were nonexistent in 2000,
reached 582 million in 2006. However, this number does not take
into account the countless billions of illegal downloads that continue
to increase each year. This means that, even after the recording industry's successful legal action that shut down Napster, the first file-sharing enterprise, the vast majority of digital music continues to be
downloaded illegally. Despite the industry's much publicized copy-
right-infringement lawsuits against over 20,000 file sharers, tens of
millions of noncustomers continue to illegally download digital music
each year.

The incredible amount of change in the recording industry may be
a harbinger of a massive transformation that will quickly reshape
every major industry. It started in recorded music because this is one
of the first, if not the first, economic market in which a young person
participates. The teenagers of this first decade of the 21st century are
the first generation to come of age in the Digital Age and embrace the
new network mindset. As they move through their 20's, 30's and 40's,
they are likely to dramatically change each industry they touch as they
propagate the market with the new values of the network mindset.
What is happening in the recording industry today is that the non-

customers are shifting the market from mass production to mass collaboration, demonstrating Drucker's astute observation that changes always start with the noncustomers.

Today's post-boomer generations do not value the industry's perennial mass production album format; they prefer the mass collaboration digital download, and they will likely carry this preference throughout their adult lives. This means that unless the recording industry radically adjusts its view of the market, willingly abandons its historically successful mass production business model, and wholeheartedly embraces a new innovative mass collaboration model, it will find itself on the outside looking in at new market players who will have found a way to turn these noncustomers into customers. Right now the recording industry is fighting the trend toward mass collaboration and doing everything within its power to try to preserve its mass production world. However, the recording industry is pursuing a doomed strategy. It will not turn noncustomers into customers by suing them. The ranks of the tens of millions will only continue to grow as new generations are born into the Digital Age, and laws will evolve to match the values of the new network mindset. Remember in the Agrarian Age, charging interest for loaned funds – known as usury – was considered both immoral and illegal, but that changed once the Industrial Age mindset became established.

Hiatt and Serpick point out that the recording industry missed a big opportunity to steer their own fate into the new world of digital music by failing to make peace with Napster.[11] At the time the industry sued the file-sharing service, Napster was the overwhelming preference of the digital market. Had the industry embraced this new mass collaboration business model and worked out licensing fees with Napster, it would have well-positioned itself for converting all these noncustomers into customers and would have reestablished a market in which everyone was once again a customer. Instead by shutting down Napster, all the industry accomplished was the dispersion of these 30 or 40 million noncustomers among a larger number of file-sharing services.

Mass collaboration is the new market reality and it is not going away. If the recording industry is to rebound, it will only do so by embracing and not fighting the noncustomers' values and by accepting that theirs is one of the first of many industries that will transform from a mass production to a mass collaboration platform.

VALUE SETS AND VALUE PROPOSITIONS

Continually understanding both your customers and noncustomers is the key to staying in touch with your current market reality and the foundation for building innovative strategies for the future. The most powerful information that you can have about either customers or noncustomers is a clear understanding of their value sets.

A value set is a particular combination of needs and expectations that is meaningful to a group of customers. Different customer groups in the same market may have different value sets. For example, as we discussed in Chapter 5, frequent fliers and leisure travelers have two very different value sets. Frequent fliers want timely options and comfort whereas, for leisure travelers, the freedom to travel at an affordable price is what's most important. It is very difficult for one airline product to align with both of these customer segments. Different value sets usually call for different products and different supporting infrastructure. Michael Treacy and Fred Wiersema, in *The Discipline of Market Leaders*, make the point that "no company can succeed today by trying to be all things to all people."[12] For this reason, organizations need to understand the current and the changing values of both customers and noncustomers so that they can choose their customers and align their corporate value propositions with the value sets of their chosen patrons.

Treacy and Wiersema define a value proposition as "the implicit promise a company makes to customers to deliver a particular combination of values."[13] Accordingly, management's first responsibility is about making sure that the company's promise delivers what's most important to the customers. For the leisure traveler, low-cost freedom to travel that beats the car is what it's all about, and that's the promise that Southwest Airlines delivers.

Many traditional executives often ignore the critical tasks of choosing customers and aligning value propositions. When they are out of touch with their customers and are unaware of the array of value sets, executives know only their view of the market and tend to see consumers as a homogenous group with the same values as the company. As a result, product differentiation becomes nothing more than alternative versions of a corporate value proposition, which may have once worked with the customers, but is no longer relevant in today's more dynamic and customized markets. These executives learn the hard way that, especially in the Digital Age, customers are not homogenous and that they no longer adjust their value sets to match the corporation's value proposition. As the executives in the recording industry are painfully learning, success in today's markets means that corporations have to adjust their value propositions to match the customers' value set.

Knowing and keeping up with customer values is the starting point for effective management in the new wiki world. Because all customers do not have the same values, businesses need to have a deep understanding of the market segmentation within their industry and be thoroughly familiar with the value sets of each customer segment so they can intelligently choose who will be their customers. They need to know which segments are growing, which are declining, and how customer values are shifting. Companies also need to become aware of untapped market opportunities by identifying market segments where none of the current competition is meeting the particular customer value set, especially if that segment is expanding.

Understanding market segments and value sets gives an organization a distinct competitive advantage because this knowledge is a roadmap for efficiency in the selection of customers and in the design of business processes that form deep connections with a company's chosen patrons. Executives who are competent at understanding customer values accept and embrace that they will not be everything to everyone. They understand that every business has customers and noncustomers. What separates the skillful leaders is that, by working outside-in, they have the reality-based knowledge to proactively choose who they want as customers and who they will leave as noncustomers.

In today's markets, sustainable business success is increasingly dependent on an organization's ability to cultivate an emotional bond with its customers. This is why it's so difficult, if not impossible, to be all things to all people. Forming a genuine emotional bond means focusing your execution on the delivery of a particular combination of values, which by necessity means abandoning other attributes that are not compatible with what's important to your chosen customers. This also means you will probably not be appealing to your noncustomers. As long as this is your choice, it is not a problem. In fact, William C. Taylor and Polly LaBarre, in *Mavericks at Work*, make the point that "one test of how committed a company is to its most important customers is how fearless it is about ignoring (even offending) customers who aren't central to its mission."[14]

However, while managers are right to focus their efforts on the values and needs of their chosen customers, they nevertheless need to continually stay in touch with both customers and noncustomers to keep a sense of the pulse of the market and to guide their future customer affiliations should markets shift. Technology breakthroughs, significant value shifts, or even repositioning in corporate strategic direction could mean today's noncustomers are tomorrow's customers. Competency in customer values means that managers are constantly focused outside the company, continually choosing their customers, and adapting and evolving their processes to deliver an aligned value proposition.

ADDING VALUE

Business leaders who are skillful in the first responsibility of management acknowledge the new market reality that everyone in their company works for the customers and not the bosses. Accordingly, they understand that efficiency and profitability have much more to do with the focused adding of value than with arbitrary cost cutting. This is why Apple has Genius Bars in its retail stores. What might appear to be an unnecessary cost that cuts into profits is actually a revenue generator. Apple's customers like hands-on face-to-face technical support and Genius Bars fulfill that important need. Apple understands that it is not just selling computers and electronic devices, but rather a complete customer experience that includes follow-up support. The fact that the Genius Bars are conveniently located at no additional cost delights Apple's customers, enhances their experience, and solidifies an emotional bond and a brand loyalty that contributes to increased sales. Indeed, the purpose of a business and the pathway to profitability is to deliver customer value, and you never lose sight of this when you work for the customer.

The connection that Starbucks has cultivated with its customers is another example of how building value propositions that delight customers is the foundation for realistic, innovative, and profitable strategies. In the 1990's, Starbucks discovered an untapped market opportunity by identifying a market segment with an unmet value set. Who would have ever thought that people would pay a premium for a commodity that is generally available for free at most offices? Twenty years ago, most of us would have thought you'd have to be crazy to think that you could build a successful business by expecting people to pay four dollars for a cup of coffee on their way to work. Yet that is exactly what 25 million people do every week.[15]

The Starbucks success story demonstrates how the skillful exercise of the first management responsibility sometimes reveals a customer segment with an unmet value set that calls for the creation of a new innovative business model. And often these customers are willing to pay a premium for a product that adds an important value to their lives.

When Howard Schultz bought Starbucks in 1987, it was just another coffee shop in Seattle with 17 stores and 100 employees.[16] By understanding its market, choosing its customers and its noncustomers, and investing in a value proposition to deliver the unmet value set of its chosen customers, Starbucks has created a whole new industry with over 10,000 stores of its own along with several look-alike competitors. Starbucks discovered that sometimes a cup of coffee is more than a cup of coffee – at least for a sizable customer segment of 25 million middle class workers. In a fast paced world of ever increasing change, sometimes customers need more than just a cup of coffee. They also want a place between home and work where they can slow down, relax, take a breath, check e-mails, or just chat with someone who knows their names. Starbucks customers are buying more than coffee; they're buying an experience – and they're willing to pay a premium for it.

Starbucks is very clear about who are their customers, but equally important, they are also definite about who are their noncustomers. If you want a cheap cup of coffee or a quick soft drink and nothing more, Starbucks is not the place for you. In fact, Starbucks doesn't even sell soft drinks. Starbucks chosen customers are coffee lovers who share a special language when placing their orders and who want a sense of community with their lattes. And so Starbucks stores are more like living rooms than retail shops where you feel invited to take a little time to sit down and enjoy the music as you chat with friends or just quietly relax. Starbucks doesn't just sell coffee; it sells grandes mixed in with a touch of identity, a sense of community, and a feeling of connectedness. By turning the sale of a commodity into the delivery of a value proposition that meets a complete set of needs around a community experience, Starbucks has cultivated a genuine emotional bond with its customers that is at the core of its meteoric success.

Starbucks is a company that embraces the new market reality that, to succeed in business today, management practices and organizational cultures need to be structured around serving, delighting, and adding value to customers. That is why everyone at Starbucks fully appreciates that they work for the customers, not the bosses. When a new recruit joins Starbucks, he receives a pocket-sized pamphlet, known as the *Green Apron Book*, which summarizes the five core "ways of being" that are the foundation for personalizing relationships with customers: be welcoming, be genuine, be knowledgeable, be considerate, and be involved.[17] Guided by this framework of the principles and examples contained in the pamphlet, Starbucks partners (the term Starbucks uses for its employees) are empowered to use their own judgment to respond to the unique needs of their customers without needing to obtain a supervisor's approval. Should you need to return to the counter and order again because you inadvertently spilled your coffee on the way to your car, the barista has the authority to make sure that you don't have to pay for "the one that got away."[18]

The latitude that Starbucks gives partners to meet the needs of its customers demonstrates the priority that the company places on adding value over cutting costs and is a testament to the atypical relationship that exists between the workers and management.

When the management at Starbucks refers to its workers as partners, this is not empty rhetoric, but rather reflects a fundamental financial and operational reality. Stock options are available to everyone working 20 hours a week or more.[19] Thus, the server behind the counter fixing your morning latte is likely a shareholder with a stake in the profitability of Starbucks. But more importantly, the managers understand that the workers are their direct link with the customers and that effectively working for the customers is more likely to happen in a culture based on employee partnership rather than on management control. Starbucks managers realize that the partners are the ones who know the customers best and that they will be the first to recognize when customer needs are not being met or if customer values are shifting.

When you work for the customers, your business processes need to be designed to amplify their voices, and in a retail business, the best way to hear the customers is to design your organizational culture around listening and responding to the voices of those workers who are closest to the customers. If there are better ways to meet or exceed customer needs or new ideas for product improvements that will delight customers, Starbucks managers don't want to be the last to know, as frequently happens in hierarchical organizations. By genuinely listening to the voices of their partners, Starbucks not only has immediate access to the knowledge of their workers for product improvements, but they also involve the customers in product design. What better way for Starbucks to cultivate an emotional bond with its customers than to make them drink designers? This is how Starbucks began offering soy milk in its beverages. Originally, Starbucks didn't carry soy milk, but the voices of the customers were heard through the voices of the partners and today almost 10 percent of drinks sold at Starbucks include soy milk.[20]

Starbucks is a company designed around adding value for customers. The managers at Starbucks understand well the reality that if you want your employees focused on the customers, you need to treat your workers as partners and not subordinates. If an important part of your value proposition is cultivating relationships with your customers, you will only succeed if you honor your relationships with your workers. This is why Starbucks is a partnership where everyone, whether in an office or behind a counter, has the opportunity to share in the profits, knows that his voice will be heard, and is clear that he and his partners are all working for the customer.

CONFRONTING REALITY

Becoming experts in customer values means that managers have to be competent at confronting and clarifying reality. The essential work of this responsibility – understanding customers and noncustomers, keeping current with their value sets, choosing customers, and formulating value propositions to match the value sets of those chosen customers – is challenging enough in ordinary times. It becomes daunting in fast changing times. Unfortunately, given the acceleration in the pace of change brought about by the Digital Age, meeting this challenge will perilously stretch the current capabilities of most companies. The simple fact is most organizations are not competent at processing reality in real-time. A recent study by Mercer Human Resource Consulting found that only 39 percent of employees believe that senior management does a good job of confronting issues before they erupt into major problems.[21] And that percentage is likely to decrease as the pace of change continues to accelerate.

Effectively confronting reality means that managers have to let go of illusions that have defined their identities and have yielded them significant psychological payoffs in the past. They will necessarily need to distribute their coveted power and they will need to manage through collaboration rather than control. They will need to adapt to new realities and have the courage to let their worlds be turned upside down.

The successful enterprises of the 21st century will be led by a new breed of leaders who will have the courage to abandon wishful thinking, the filtering of information, the silencing of dissent, and the dissemination of corporate views reinforced by fear and coercion. These Digital Age managers will facilitate processes that amplify the voices of the workers and the customers through an array of multi-media conversational opportunities integrated with collective learning methods and techniques for quickly accessing the collective knowledge of both the managers and the workers to reach a speedy broad-based consensus. These collective learning processes, designed to promote knowledge and speed, will be essential for managing at the pace of change because businesses will no longer be able to survive by riding out a successful business model for 40 years, the average life of a corporation.

In the Digital Age, the new reality is that businesses will need to reposition, perhaps reinvent themselves, every seven to ten years. Ram Charan, based on his observations in consulting with many of America's leading corporations, anticipates that "over the course of a forty-year career, most twenty-first-century leaders will have to reposition businesses four or more times."[22] Leaders and organizations that lack the courage or the processes to confront reality and to quickly reposition themselves will be severely disadvantaged in the face of this unprecedented level of change.

Keeping pace with market reality requires organizations to put in place learning processes that can quickly access the collective knowledge of both the customers and the workers. Market segmentation studies, focus groups, and customer satisfaction surveys are some of the ways to listen to customers and to learn about what is important to them. But they are not enough. To manage at the pace of change, organizations need faster access to consumer intelligence than these vehicles provide.

Knowledge is power, and that has never been truer than in today's Digital Age markets. However, in these fast changing times, the knowledge that is most important to organizations is more likely to reside with the customers and those workers who are closest to the customers than with the senior executives. Turning this knowledge into power means a fundamental transformation in organizational conversations. Keep in mind that the basic task of managing large numbers of people is no longer about making the machines more efficient by prescribing worker behavior and having protocols for compliance. The current challenge of managing large numbers is now about making the networks more efficient, and this can only happen if managers accept that they can longer control the corporate conversation.

The necessary transformation in conversations will call for building open communication processes designed to quickly transport knowledge located outside and on the fringes of the organization into the core of corporate decision-making. This is what Starbucks was able to do by listening to the voices of its partners and learning that soy milk was important to its customers. Companies that are competent at collective learning have different and better conversations than traditional hierarchical organizations. They have processes that break down the distance between organizational levels so that critical information, innovative ideas, and collective knowledge cannot be blocked by bureaucratic maneuvering or a single voice in the chain of command. If organizations are to be nimble in their response to what customers value, then the conversations need to change so that the pursuit of the truth about market reality takes precedence over the politics of corporate dogma. If managers are to effectively lead learning processes to provide quick access to the collective knowledge within their organizations, they will have to accept that they can no longer script the corporate conversation. This explains why the essential work of resetting the managers is to transform executives from bosses to facilitators.

There is an incredible amount of knowledge and wisdom about the market distributed throughout organizations and most of it remains untapped. If an organization is serious about working outside-in, it has to be able to tap into this resource. When you have to get it right the first time to keep pace with fast changing markets, you need access to the best available knowledge. And having that access means that leaders must be highly skilled listeners and facilitators. How many times have we seen tone-deaf senior executive bosses march down a single-minded path completely confident that their pet strategy was a market winner only to have it fail the test of market reality? Do you remember New Coke?

In the early 1980's, Coca Cola's flagship product was in danger of losing its century-old position as America's most popular soft drink.

Coke's chief rival, Pepsi, had been steadily gaining in market share on the strength of a very effective advertising campaign touting blind taste-tests that showed that even Coca Cola drinkers preferred the taste of Pepsi. Unfortunately for Coca Cola, their own independent taste-tests validated Pepsi's claim. With a sense of urgency, Coke embarked on a comprehensive market research project using surveys and focus groups in combination with taste-tests to interview almost 200,000 consumers. By the fall of 1984, Coca Cola executives were confident that they had a winning strategy to preserve the preeminence of their flagship product. The technical staff had mixed a formula of Coke that was handily beating Pepsi in blind taste-tests. However, the results from the focus groups and the survey data were not entirely consistent in projecting the amount of customer satisfaction that might convey with a reformulation of the world's oldest soft drink. While both the focus groups and the surveys indicated there would be customer dissatisfaction, the survey results projected that the dissatisfaction would be limited while the focus groups suggested the displeasure would be widespread.[23] Trusting the results of the taste-tests, Coca Cola executives put more weight on the survey results than the focus groups in interpreting the differences in their market research, and on April 23, 1985 unveiled the reformulated version of their flagship product, New Coke.

New Coke turned out to be one of corporate America's biggest business debacles. In the end, the focus groups were right. The negative reaction among Coke's customers was so widespread, that just 78 days after the lavish launch of New Coke, on July 10, 1985, old Coke was brought back and reintroduced as Coca Cola Classic. Coke's executives had been so myopically focused on taste that they failed to fully understand that when it came to their soft drinks, their customers valued more than just the flavor of Coke. While taste is important, many customers valued Coca Cola as a source of social connection and a personal reflection of their identity. Coca Cola was a meaningful American icon that was an important part of their lives. Coca Cola executives were completely unprepared for the massive emotional backlash coming from both their customers and their bottlers. As one executive put it, "We did not know what we were selling. We are not selling a soft drink. We are selling a little tiny piece of people's lives."[24]

At first, Coke's executives denied the market reality as the protests mounted. They were convinced that their taste-tests were correct, and that the backlash would die down once their customers came to appreciate the improved taste. However, the customer dissatisfaction continued to build to the point where the bottlers, who were much closer to the customers, prevailed upon Coca Cola's senior executives and forced them to come to terms with the reality that, for Coca Cola lovers, old Coke was the real thing.

As mentioned above, while surveys and focus groups are important tools for understanding what customers value, they are not necessarily enough for a complete grasp of market reality. Sometimes there are forces at work that are difficult to measure. Coca Cola's reliance on the supposed sovereignty of blind taste-tests was misplaced and, in the end, only blinded the executives from their customers' true values, some of which were not easily accessible by traditional quantitative research.

If the Coca Cola executives had broadened the conversations and had the skills to access the collective wisdom of their own bottlers as well as other voices within the company closer to the customers, perhaps the fiasco of New Coke could have been avoided. In all likelihood, these voices would have put the executives in touch with their customers' values and would have identified far more effective alternatives for addressing Coke's declining market share. Fortunately for Coca Cola, both the customers and the bottlers found a way to make their voices heard before it was too late, and the executives learned the hard way the most important lesson of the new market reality. The market doesn't care what the executives think; today we work for the customers, not the bosses.

Part Three

RESETTING
THE MEETINGS

Chapter 7

FROM STRATIFIED VOICES TO OPEN CONVERSATIONS

When our imperfect judgments are aggregated in the right way, our collective intelligence is often excellent.

- James Surowiecki
The Wisdom of Crowds[1]

Changing the focus of work from bosses, tasks, and activities to customers, processes and results requires a significant transformation of the social structures and the day-to-day practices of organizations. Developing a collective learning core competency that enables businesses to effectively manage at the ever-increasing pace of change means shifting the driver of consistency within organizations from control to shared understanding, which in turn, means changing the quality of conversations inside companies.

The primary vehicle of managerial work is conversation. Whether they are in one-on-one discussions or in larger group gatherings, people in organizations spend much of their time moving from conversation to conversation in different types of meetings. Effective conversations are critical to the development of shared understanding. Yet, in the hierarchical organization, there is probably no more dysfunctional activity than the typical meeting. When organizations are focused on control, conversations quickly become monologues or debates where people talk past or over each other focused only on what they think, with little real interest in hearing what others have to say. By its design, the structure and practices of the typical meeting in command-and-control companies drive and enable limited thinking.

The traditional meeting follows the committee format where the leader sits at the head of the table, where individuals follow the cues of their superiors in bringing forth ideas, and where often what needs to be discussed isn't talked about as candid reality takes a back seat to political correctness. Indeed, when an organization's focus is about control, conversations are not vehicles for listening or a true interchange of ideas, but rather are oftentimes nothing more than broadcast mechanisms to promote everyone "getting on board with the program."

Committee-style meetings are essentially controlled events where voices are stratified by position or function and all the voices are not equal. The opinions of the senior executives and the functional experts count more. Thus, they speak more often and more forcefully in forums where defending one's position and preserving the accepted ways have more value than exploring the novel notion or facilitating an inclusive dialogue. In a business world where the future is changing almost daily, most corporate meetings are nothing more than formal rituals to preserve yesterday's order where bosses set the agenda, decide who's in the "need to know," and carefully script the conversations in closed gatherings where they make certain that everyone is clear about what is speakable and what is unspeakable. And they make most unspeakable the very fact that some issues are unspeakable.

The ritualistic norms of the committee-style meeting are so well established that most participants are unaware that they engage in conversational practices that dismiss the opinions of others and shut down any opportunity to explore new directions. Even managers who consider themselves more enlightened participative leaders fall prey to the well-established norms if the only gathering format is the committee-style meeting. While these leaders may encourage everyone to speak her mind and make sure that everyone is heard, if the meeting itself is not a vehicle for integrating thinking and creating collective knowledge, then all you have is a polite respect for different opinions where nothing really changes because the same people continue to control the same levers of power and authority when everyone leaves the room.

While making it safe for everyone to express her opinion is an important first step in opening up corporate conversations, it's not enough and may actually do more harm than good by fostering cynicism if expectations that things will be done differently are unmet when we leave the meeting room. There is no time for the destructive dynamics of cynicism when 21st century markets are rapidly shifting business platforms from mass production to mass collaboration.

As shared understanding replaces control as the fundamental driver of business consistency, the conversations, and thus the meetings, have to be radically transformed such that listening is valued, ideas are depoliticized, differing views build on rather than clash with each other, and creative collective thinking displaces myopic groupthink. In short, for shared understanding to become the primary driver in the organization and for collective learning to become a core competency, meetings must become highly functional management tools.

Two examples of innovative meeting formats that support collective learning and shared understanding are General Electric's legendary Work-Out sessions and the Work-Thru technology that we used when I was with Blue Cross Blue Shield. Because resetting the meetings is so important to implementing the wiki-management discipline, the remainder of this chapter is dedicated to outlining the principles and the practices of these meeting alternatives, including a step-by-step description of the Work-Thru process for leaders who are ready to use this powerful tool to gain quick access to their collective knowledge.

GENERAL ELECTRIC'S WORK-OUT

One of the first business leaders to appreciate the importance of transforming meetings as a powerful competitive advantage was Jack Welch during his time as General Electric's CEO. Welch understood that GE's bureaucratic culture was an impediment to its ability to manage at the increasing pace of change that began emerging as a permanent business phenomenon in the late 1980's. If GE was to continue winning in the marketplace, then moving faster from breakthrough idea to quality action would need to become a way of life across the company. Welch knew all too well, however, that bureaucracy hates speed because speed decreases control.[2] Welch felt that GE needed a business tool that would guarantee the free flow of ideas, a candid and realistic assessment of those ideas by the people closest to the actual work, quick decisions on whether or not to proceed with an idea, and a commitment to action to implement agreed-upon conclusions. That tool is the "Work-Out."

Work-Out is a different type of corporate meeting modeled after the traditional New England town meeting.[3] The format is specifically designed to take unnecessary work out of the processes of the organization, hence the name Work-Out. These meetings are two to three day sessions with 40 to 100 employees who gather to share views on how to break through the bureaucracy that gets in the way of doing their jobs. Because Welch was concerned that the business leaders would inhibit the openness necessary for the meetings to work, GE uses outside professional facilitators to serve as the Work-Out leaders. Business leaders are invited to participate at the beginning and at the end of the Work-Out sessions, but the majority of the meeting involves just the group members and the facilitators.

A typical Work-Out session starts with a presentation by a business leader on a particular challenge or issue, after which the boss leaves the session. The facilitator then leads the Work-Out members through a series of small group discussions to identify problems and solutions and to prepare the participants for selling their ideas to the business leader when she returns at the end of the session. A powerful dynamic that enables Work-Out sessions to cut through the bureaucracy is the expectation that, when the boss does return to receive the proposals from the Work-Out members, on-the-spot yes or no decisions are to be given on no less than 75 percent of the ideas. For those proposals that cannot be decided immediately, a definite agreed-upon date is set for the final decision.[4] This expectation assures that no good idea is going to get lost in a never ending committee process.

Work-Outs have changed the quality of conversations at GE. The use of meeting facilitators, small group discussions, and on-the-spot decisions promotes openness, increased listening, and fosters speedy action to improve both the work performance of the company as well as employee morale. These sessions assure that the voices of the people closest to the work – who also know it best – are clearly heard. Work-Outs drive a culture where leaders lead rather than control and where specific actionable items with clear deadlines are more quickly identified and executed.

It is important to note that, while Work-Outs have expanded the voices in addressing business issues, these sessions have not turn GE into a democracy. The executives are still accountable for the decision-making. However, by not controlling the conversation of the employees, the bosses have a better meeting tool for quickly collecting and integrating the best thinking of all their employees and for improving both the quality and the speed of executive decision-making – all at no extra cost. As one GE middle-aged appliance worker put it: "For 25 years you've paid for my hands when you could have had my brain – for nothing."[5] The GE Work-Out experience demonstrates that when meetings become highly functional management tools where listening is valued, ideas depoliticized, and speedy creative collective thinking is a business asset, a company is very well positioned to successfully manage innovation at the speed of fast changing times.

WORK-THRUS

In the mid-1990's, during my time with the Blue Cross Blue Shield Federal Employee Program (FEP), we recognized that, given FEP's unique business configuration and the then new pace of change erupting across all industries, we needed to improve the effectiveness of our meetings and the quality of our corporate conversations if we were to remain the market leader in this faster business environment. FEP is a business alliance of the 39 independent Blue Cross and Blue Shield organizations to provide private health insurance to over 4.5 million federal employees and family members nationwide, with annual premium revenues of over $19 billion. FEP is the largest privately underwritten health insurance account in the United States. Among the various health insurance choices available to federal employees in 2009, six out of every ten federal employees purchased Blue Cross Blue Shield FEP coverage.

The unique management challenge for FEP is bringing together these 39 separate and sometimes competing organizations into a collaborative infrastructure to deliver a seamless uniform health insurance product. With so many independent moving parts in the business configuration, meeting this challenge sometimes felt like "herding cats." When the pace of change was slower, we had the time needed to work the usual politics of forming a consensus among so many autonomous partners. But with the emerging new pace of change and the well-publicized cost challenges in the health care industry, we knew we needed a more effective meeting mechanism to move us beyond the usual politics and to help us achieve faster and smarter consensus. Thus, we invented the Work-Thru.

Similar to GE's Work-Out, Work-Thrus are meetings designed to address complex business issues by drawing upon an organization's best collective thinking and moving to a clear consensus on action in a very short period of time. Unlike Work-Outs, the defining idea behind Work-Thrus is to effectively use the business leaders as the facilitators so that the resulting shared understanding from the Work-Thru experience becomes the primary driver of the work in the follow-through execution of a project. Work-Thrus were born from the observation that some of the best meetings inside an organization are offsite sessions that are run by outside facilitators. However, so often the energy and follow-through are lost once everyone returns to the office and the facilitators move on. Well, we thought, what if the business executives were the facilitators, and thus, would have a continuing role in the execution after the facilitated sessions? While this would present a challenging skills and role transition for the typical executive, what better way to shift the social structures and practices in support of effective shared understanding than to train executives to be skilled and competent facilitators?

We recognized that, if we were going to work smarter and faster, we needed a meeting discipline that fostered better conversations, more effective listening, greater participation by all, better processing of ideas, real consensus, clear accountability, and focused action – all in a short period of time. The concept is simple: The secret to extraordinary performance is better conversations inside organizations.

Unfortunately, this simple secret is not practiced inside most companies. In many instances, meetings are nothing more than "hijack" experiences in which two or three people dominate the discussion in a battle of wills and a clash of ideas where the remaining participants become mere spectators. In the absence of a true consensus, apparent agreements and compromises or, worse yet, dictated mandates are undercut as participants who have not been heard or who do not agree find acceptable bureaucratic ways to passively exert their influence. This is because the traditional meeting tends to be a competition of ideas where the focus is on the sport of being right and where the ineffective acting out of passions divides the room into winners and losers – and the losers do not go complacently but rather find ways to thwart the hollow victories once everyone leaves the room. Even in those instances where the gatherings are not contentious, traditional meetings tend to yield less than the best decisions possible because the meeting structure is inadequate to process individual thinking into collective knowledge, and thus, produces inadequate information.

As business becomes more global, as the pace of change continues to accelerate, and as business processes and customers are increasingly dispersed, the exercise of control becomes more challenging and the need for expedient collaboration becomes a business imperative for success in the global marketplace. In this context, meetings that do not create – or worse yet, actually impede – expedient collaboration will become corporate liabilities.

Work-Thrus work because the structure of the meeting and the rules and norms around conversations are very different from the typical committee-style meeting. Work-Thrus are large group gatherings that are designed for working projects, initiatives or issues that involve creating or adjusting complex business processes. They are usually facilitated by a company's own executives, although outside facilitators can be used, especially when an organization is becoming acquainted with the process. Work-Thru sessions are held offsite and usually last for two or three days, depending upon the complexity of the business issue being worked. These sessions are most effective with between 25 and 50 participants, who together represent the full diversity of the business process under discussion. Accordingly, the participants in a Work-Thru are a blend of levels from executives to specialists, a blend of functions from marketing, finance, systems, operations, etc., and a blend of geography from urban to rural or from region to region depending upon the geographical circumstances of the business process. This diversity is critical to the success of the Work-Thru because shared understanding is only accomplished when the participants working the business issue reflect all dimensions of the business process.

The participants are seated at round tables, each accommodating 8 – 10 people. Work-Thrus alternate between three different interactive activities, each with its own purpose and rules for conversation: presentations, small group exercises, and large group discussions. The structure of the conversations and the movement between the different interactive activities ensures that the meeting supports listening and dialogue, the full expression of ideas, the constructive identification of apparent misalignments, the development of creative alternatives and breakthrough ideas, and most importantly, real consensus.

PRESENTATIONS

The first interactive activity of a Work-Thru is always a presentation. These presentations can take different forms. Sometimes project leaders have strong opinions or passionate concerns around the way the company should proceed in addressing a particular initiative, especially if they are responsible for delivering the results. At other times, the topic for discussion may be so new or so perplexing that an orientation or an overview by a staff expert on the nature of the subject is necessary to lay the foundation for the meeting's work. In any event, presentations help seed the work of the meeting.

Presentations are always delivered without interruption. This is the first cardinal rule of a Work-Thru. The underlying dialogue principle at work during presentations is listening. Everyone is asked to listen to the thoughts and the ideas of the presenter. Whether the participants agree or disagree or whether they see the subject differently is not relevant during the presentations. What is important is that the presenters are heard and understood. For individuals who are participating in a Work-Thru for the first time, this is very hard! In our typical corporate cultures, interruptions are generally tolerated and there are usually a few people in every meeting who feel free – and are sometimes even encouraged – to raise questions or to express their opinions, observations, or concerns whenever they want. However, it is often the interruptions and the undisciplined expression of thoughts and ideas during presentations or initial discussions that causes so many meetings to turn dysfunctional.

Before each presenter begins, the facilitator reminds both the speaker and the participants that the presentation will be delivered without interruption and asks the participants to hold all questions until the presentation is complete. Even if a presenter expresses a preference for the participants asking questions throughout the presentation, the facilitator will diplomatically but firmly make sure that all questions are held until the end.

When the presentation is complete, the facilitator invites the participants to ask "clarifying questions only." This is the second cardinal rule of the Work-Thru. Clarifying questions are those that help the participants clearly understand the presenter's point of view to make sure that everyone in the room has correctly heard what the speaker intended. The facilitator advises the group that presentations are neither the time nor the place for the expression of the participants' opinions, observations, and concerns – that will come later during the small group exercises. For the moment, the focus is on making sure that all participants understand the presenter's thoughts and ideas. Again, for individuals participating in their first Work-Thru, restricting questions after presentations to clarifying questions is very hard! But, it is also very necessary.

Beginning the Work-Thru with uninterrupted presentations and "clarifying questions only" radically changes the group dynamics of the meeting because it structures listening into the start of the meeting – and all effective dialogue begins with listening. The simple reason that most corporate meetings are dysfunctional is that most people don't begin meetings by listening to each other. They are usually focused on looking for openings to express their own opinions or to work their agenda or, worse yet, are mentally absent as two or three individuals dominate and "hijack" the meeting. The two cardinal rules of "no interruptions" during presentations and "clarifying questions only" when the speakers are finished means the participants have no choice except to listen and to understand the thoughts and the ideas of the presenter. It puts in place the simple provision that before we agree or disagree or express another opinion, let's be sure that we've heard what's being said first. These two cardinal rules are a simple discipline to structure into the Work-Thru one of Stephen Covey's habits of effectiveness: "Seek first to understand, then to be understood."[6]

It is very important that the facilitator makes sure that all participants adhere to these two cardinal rules. Every once in a while, especially where there are individuals participating in a Work-Thru for the first time, someone may attempt to interrupt a presentation with a question or, during the clarifying question period, may start to express an opinion. When this happens, the facilitator needs to immediately interject and diplomatically remind the questioner to hold all questions until after the presentation is complete or to hold any opinions, observations, or concerns until the small group discussions.

While the insistence on the rules of "no interruptions" and "clarifying questions only" may appear to be authoritarian and controlling, the result is actually quite the opposite. As a matter of fact, strict adherence to the "clarifying questions only" rule, in particular, sometimes leads to one of the most powerful moments in a Work-Thru.

When the facilitator intervenes to make sure a participant holds her opinion or concern until the small group exercises, it sends a clear signal to the group that the Work-Thru session is going to be a different experience from the typical meeting. People who tend to dominate or "hijack" meetings are used to speaking their minds quite freely, whether on topic or not. For the individual attempting to express her point of view during the "clarifying questions only" period, it is often the first time that anyone has ever inhibited that person's usual practice of freely interjecting whatever is on her mind at the time. As the facilitator diplomatically reminds the person to hold observations, opinions, and concerns until the small group exercises and then asks if the individual has a clarifying question, you can feel the energy rise within the room as all the participants realize that this meeting is not going to be "hijacked" and that the possibility for an effective and productive conversation is very real. It is often in this moment that all the participants become truly engaged in the Work-Thru.

SMALL GROUP EXERCISES

When the initial presentations are complete and the clarifying questions are answered, the Work-Thru shifts to the second type of interactive activity, the first small group exercise. Having heard what is important about the process, project, or issue from some of the key stakeholders, it is now time to find out what is important to everyone else in the room. More often than not, the focus for the first exercise is for each group to list the 3 – 5 most important observations, opinions, or concerns about the particular Work-Thru topic. However, before beginning this first small group exercise, there is one very important logistical adjustment the facilitator needs to make.

Before the opening of the Work-Thru, as the participants arrived in the room, they should have been invited to sit at any table. Invariably, individuals sit with those they already know. Because one of the goals of a Work-Thru is to depoliticize ideas, it is important for the facilitator to "remix" the groups so that individuals are more likely to be in discussions with people that they normally might not work with, and are thus, less likely to be inhibited in expressing their ideas. If a person is initially sitting at a table with her boss, she may be less likely to differ with one of her supervisor's observations than with a comment from someone with whom she infrequently works. To "remix" the groups, if there are four tables in the room, the facilitator asks each participant to count off by four's, with all the number 1's moving to Table 1, all the number 2's moving to Table 2, etc.

Once the groups are "remixed," they are ready to begin the exercise. The facilitator instructs each group to first agree on a scribe and a presenter before beginning the discussion. The role of the scribe is to capture the ideas of the group on a flip chart during the discussions, while the presenter's job is to report the results of the small group's conversation at the end of the exercise. In describing the work to be done in the small group exercise, the facilitator focuses the groups on a specific outcome. As indicated above, the assignment for the first discussion is to list the 3 – 5 most important observations, opinions, or concerns about the Work-Thru topic.

This focus is important for two reasons. First, it establishes a clear and common deliverable for all the groups. Second, it reinforces the discipline of separating the more important from the less important, a practice that is so critical for effectively managing at the pace of change. While many observations and concerns may be shared in the small group exercise, the listing of only the 3 – 5 most important items helps to begin the process of forming a consensus around identifying the small number of actions that are the key to process improvement or project success.

With this in mind, the facilitator advises the groups that, in the event that their list exceeds five items, they will need to go back and identify the top 3 – 5 most important items for their presenter to share with all the participants at the end of the small group exercise. This is the third cardinal rule of Work-Thrus: Small group exercises are always focused on clear and specific deliverables for reporting out to all the participants. The facilitator writes the deliverable expectations as either a statement or a question on a flip chart that is clearly visible and available to all the small groups during the exercise.

The use of small group exercises for the initial vetting of ideas is the key dynamic that drives the effectiveness of Work-Thrus. When 25 – 50 individuals gather for the purpose of reaching agreement on how to address a complex issue in a short time frame, it is almost always impossible to do so immediately in the context of the large group. Unless the issue is first discussed in smaller groups, a few dominant individuals will inevitably "hijack" the meeting.

Unfortunately, the most dominant people in a large group are not necessarily the most intelligent, the most thoughtful, or the most effective people in the room. They do tend to be the more extroverted people and are very comfortable with endless debates, talking over each other, and with any form of verbal interaction, whether it gets the group somewhere or not. It is often said of these individuals that they love to hear themselves talk! These dominant souls, in their passion for advocacy and in their ease in large groups, always seem to take over the meeting. Once the "hijack" becomes apparent, the introverts in the room tend to shut down. Introverts are usually not comfortable speaking up in large groups, and become even more reticent in "hijacked" meetings, especially when it's clear that no one really is listening to each other. This is unfortunate, because more often than not, it is the thoughtful introverts who have the best ideas or, perhaps, a different way of looking at an issue that might build on another's idea and create a breakthrough observation.

Small group exercises are more effective venues for the initial vetting of complex issues because they increase the chances that both the extroverts and the introverts will participate in the discussion. In addition, small group exercises diminish the influence of the hopelessly dominant individual in that, even if she does manage to "hijack" one of the small groups, the other groups will probably create effective output that will productively move the meeting along.

At the conclusion of the small group exercises, each of the presenters reports the results of her table's discussion. The rules for presentations are applied once again. That is, each presenter gives her entire report without interruption and, at the conclusion of the report, there is a time for clarifying questions only. At this point, the focus of the large group is to understand the thinking coming from the presenter's table and not on whether people in the room agree or disagree with the reporting table's ideas, opinions, or concerns. Until all the presenters report the results from the small group discussions, the facilitator employs great care to make sure that the large group does not become an open forum for the general expression of opinions that is so common in the typical business meeting.

Also up to this point, there has been no attempt at problem solving because formulating solutions without a shared understanding of the key issues and concerns around the problem is counterproductive. The first hours of a Work-Thru are about taking the time to listen and to understand the different perspectives in the room around an issue before attempting problem-solving or agreeing on needed actions. All too often in the typical corporate meeting, the problem solving begins before the issue is sufficiently understood and actions are taken without truly knowing whether they will work or not. Too much of corporate behavior is trial and error driven by a bias for action and fueled by a misplaced sense of urgency in the face of poorly defined complexity. In a world in which the degree of business complexity and the speed of change is ever increasing, a bias for action is no virtue as, more often than not, premature problem-solving and indiscriminate execution result in unnecessary work or major rework that, in the end, actually slows the company down and hampers its ability to respond in market time.

Work-Thrus have a strong bias for results and are based on the premise that companies need to slow down to move fast. Taking the time in those first hours of a Work-Thru to effectively process the thinking of everyone in the room before attempting problem-solving assures an early shared understanding among the participants around what exactly is the problem to be solved and fosters a sense that people know what they are doing. With this understanding comes a clear focus about what are the right actions that will lead to the best solution of the problem. In fast changing times, there is increasing pressure to "get it right the first time" and that means moving slow in the beginning in order to move fast at the end. The discipline of the cardinal rules of Work-Thrus – no interruptions of presentations, clarifying questions only, and clear focused deliverables for small group exercises – are how Work-Thrus slow down to move fast. By taking the time to listen to everyone's ideas and to focus on what is most important, we are now ready for the third type of interaction where most often consensus on right actions is reached, the large group discussion.

LARGE GROUP DISCUSSIONS

Presentations are the time for clarifying questions, and small group exercises are the place for observations, opinions, and concerns. Large group discussions are the time and the place for the conclusions and agreements that become the foundation for the shared understanding that creates an unbeatable execution advantage.

Work-Thrus are designed for knowledge and speed, and this is most evident in the large group discussions. Normally, a meeting of 40 to 50 individuals is more likely than not to be a dysfunctional experience with little hope of getting anything done quickly. Because of the difficult challenges of the typical large group discussion, important matters are often delegated to smaller committees where issues are either subject to a prolonged death or, if successfully handled, take weeks or months of precious time to reach closure. Because large group discussions in Work-Thrus are built upon the work and the shared experience of the presentations and the small group exercises, the whole group is far more likely to reach a speedy consensus on its conclusions and agreements.

One of the most dramatic examples of how Work-Thrus cultivate effective large group discussions involved the design of a new insurance claims processing model to coordinate benefits between the central processor of the existing Blue Cross Blue Shield FEP health insurance product and the central processor for a new proposed dental insurance product. Two very different processing models had emerged, one proposed by the health product processor and the other proposed by the dental product processor, each passionately advocated by its proponent. Because of speed to market requirements, a definite selection of one of these models was critical to moving the project forward. As the Work-Thru meeting approached, many of the participants were skeptical about whether or not a timely consensus on a model could be reached and were dreading expected tense and difficult conversations in the upcoming Work-Thru session.

Recognizing the importance of this selection and the passionate advocacy of both central processors, the Work-Thru facilitator invited each of the processors to open the meeting with a presentation of its proposed model. Each presentation was delivered without interruption and a period of "clarifying questions only" followed. Afterwards, the facilitator remixed the four tables in the room using the "count-off" method and asked each table to select one of the two models and to list the top three to four reasons for their selection. Following 45 minutes in the small group discussions, each table reported its results with all four tables selecting the health product processor's model for reasons that were obviously consistent across the four groups.

When all the table reports were complete, the facilitator opened the large group discussion by observing that it appeared from the table reports that there was a clear consensus for using the health processor's model. Everyone in the room nodded in apparent agreement. To be absolutely sure that true consensus and agreement had been reached, the facilitator asked "Is there anyone in the room who cannot live with this selection?" The facilitator cautioned the group that no one should agree for the sake of going along. Neither should anyone hang on to their preference just for the sake of not giving up on their personal druthers. Rather if there is any individual – even just one person – who truly believes the selected method will fail and thus, she cannot live with the selection, then that individual needs to come forward and the group needs to stay with the discussion. Many times that one person sees something that the rest of the group does not, and that insight might very well move the group in a different direction. The facilitator pointed out that consensus is not about "majority rules" but rather about identifying the optimal workable solution that everyone can live with.

In response to this final question, all 40 participants – including those who advocated the model not selected – agreed that they could live with and support the chosen model. With true consensus and agreement achieved, the project could move forward in meeting its speed to market requirements. Because of the effectiveness of the presentations, the clarifying questions, and the small group discussions, this large group discussion achieved a speedy consensus on a highly charged issue – a rare occurrence in the traditional meeting format.

Not all large group discussions lead to resolution as quickly as the one described above. More typically, large group discussions are opportunities to refine the initial work done in the small group exercises. Large group discussions may take different forms depending on the results reported from the small groups. The conversation described above is an example of a Clear Consensus discussion where it is obvious that all the small groups have arrived at the same conclusion. Other types of large group discussions include: Focus List discussions, Creative Alternative discussions, Key Questions discussions, and Timeline discussions.

FOCUS LIST DISCUSSIONS

This form of discussion is most appropriate when the facilitator observes a wide variety of observations and concerns among the reports from the small groups. The facilitator might open the large group discussion by acknowledging the diversity of ideas and opinions in the small group reports and then inviting observations from the Work-Thru participants. As the conversation progresses, if it becomes clear that a consensus is not emerging around what are the most important observations, the facilitator should request the small group presenters to take their flip charts and tape them on one wall of the room, with the pages lined up one next to another. The facilitator then invites all the participants to stand around the wall.

When all the participants are gathered, the facilitator then asks the group to look over all the flip charts and identify items that may be identical or similar across the different small group reports. As items are identified, the facilitator checks with the individuals from the two small groups to see if they agree that the two items are indeed the same. If the two groups agree, the facilitator checks with the large group as to which item should remain and which one should be deleted. Once agreement is reached, the facilitator draws a box around the retained item and draws a line through the deleted item. It is very important that the facilitator does not make the decision as to which items to retain or delete unilaterally or she risks losing credibility with the participants at a very critical time in the Work-Thru. The conclusions and agreements must be those of the participants for this process to result in the desired shared understanding.

Oftentimes, the conversations around which items to retain or delete lead to greater understanding of the original observations from the small groups and increases everyone's knowledge of the complexities related to the project or initiative under discussion. As a result, sometimes it becomes obvious which items will be retained or deleted. Other times, it becomes clear from the discussion that the two items are actually not similar at all but rather reflect very different aspects of the issue at hand and, therefore, both items should be retained after editing the language on the flip charts to further clarify each of the items. In all instances, the final word on whether to retain, delete, or edit an item is the prerogative of the group participants and not of the facilitator. The facilitator may make suggestions to the group and may even challenge the group's thinking, but in the end, the decisions on the composition of the list of items are to be made solely by the participants. This can be very challenging and uncomfortable for a new executive facilitator who is used to managing by control, especially if she has a history of editing the views of her work team when they differ from her own. In a Work-Thru, the facilitator does not get to exercise this type of control in the development of the ideas. Conclusions and agreements about the group's ideas rest with the group – period! This is the fourth and final cardinal rule of Work-Thrus.

This does not mean that the ultimate decisions around work necessarily rest with the group. These decisions as well as the commitment of resources can remain the prerogative of the organization's executive leadership. However, in Work-Thrus, the conclusions about the ideas to be presented for the executives' consideration rest with the Work-Thru group. If executives have the advantage of work processes that make available to them the fastest, most comprehensive, and uncensored thinking of the individuals in their organization, then they have a powerful competitive advantage in quickly identifying breakthrough solutions to complex issues.

In addition, the shared understanding that results from this iterative process between the staff and the executives positions the company for fast and effective execution once decisions are made and resources are committed. This means that executives don't have to lose time educating the staff or getting the employees "on board" with their decisions because the workers and the managers have already mutually educated each other before the final conclusions were reached.

When all the items on the flip charts have been condensed into a mutually exclusive list, the facilitator passes out small strips of "stick-on dots" with anywhere from three to five dots per strip. When each person has one strip, the facilitator requests the individuals to place their dots adjacent to the items that are most important to them. Each person is free to vote her dots anyway that she wants. Thus, for example, if each strip contained four dots, an individual could place four dots on four different items, or all four dots on one item, or two dots on one item and two dots on two different items, etc. This flexibility in applying dots assures two things. First, all dots are placed only on the most important items. If a particular individual considered only three items on the list to be most important, then the fourth dot is applied to one of the three items already selected rather than being placed on a fourth item of lesser importance. Second, the ability to apply more than one dot to a particular item provides the opportunity for minority points of view to remain a part of the continuing dialogue.

Once all the dots have been applied to the items on the condensed list, the facilitator tallies the votes and observes where the natural "break point" is in the voting results. For example, if 40 people voted four dots each on a list of 10 items and the voting results were 30, 29, 27, 26, 15, 14, 8, 5, 4, and 2, then the natural "break point" would be after the fourth item, meaning that the top four items would be the candidates for the Focus List of the most important issues to address in the remainder of the Work-Thru. In this example, the facilitator writes the top four items in the order of their votes on a separate flip chart page with the number of votes received noted next to each item.

There is one last step before concluding that we have our Focus List. At this point, the facilitator reviews the list with the large group and asks if the list feels right or if there is an item that anyone feels strongly should be added to the list. The production of a Focus List is not a "numbers game." Voting is merely a tool to help identify a "sense of the group" about the most important work that needs to be done first. This final check-in before concluding that we have identified our Focus List is to assure that we have consensus and agreement on the most important issues before we proceed. Usually, the Work-Thru participants affirm that the list feels right, but every once in a while, the group adds an item from below the "break point" that, after further discussion, everyone agrees needs to be on the list. The Focus List discussion is complete once everyone agrees with the final list.

Focus Lists are very valuable tools in making Work-Thrus both speedy and effective because they position the group to quickly and successfully move through complex issues. Complexity, by definition, means that there are many aspects, details, or moving parts to a process, project, or initiative – some known and understood and others not. Establishing a clear focus early in a complex project on the most important issues to be worked lays a powerful foundation for effectively developing a shared understanding of the key fundamental relationships among the activities necessary to successfully complete the project. Working through the most important issues first assures that, as the work becomes more detailed, the details are far more likely to come together as the work proceeds.

It is often said that the "devil is in the details." This is generally true because, all too often, organizations driven by a bias for action dive into the details prematurely and inevitably the details do not come together as much last minute work and rework is done to fix what the devil has done. The power of Focus Lists is that they take the devil out of the details. When organizations are driven by a bias for results, they take the time at the beginning of a project to cull from the complexity the most important issues and work on these first. When the most important issues are worked well and worked first, then the detail work is much more likely to come together at the end without any sign of the devil!

In Work-Thrus, Focus Lists are tools to identify the most important issues and these issues become the work for the next round of small group exercises. These issues are usually handled in concurrent small group discussions. Thus, if the Focus List consists of four issues, then four different discussions could be held at four different tables with each of the Work-Thru participants self-selecting which table discussion they wish to join. In the event that more than 10 – 12 people select one issue, the facilitator could consider dividing this group into two groups with both groups working on the same topic. When many individuals choose a particular topic, it is a sign that the issue is very important. By dividing into two groups, we assure that all the voices will be heard in the small group exercises as well as providing the Work-Thru with two different points of view on a very important issue.

CREATIVE ALTERNATIVE DISCUSSIONS

Creativity cannot be planned; it can only be facilitated. This is why large traditional organizations have so much difficulty with creativity. The centralized planning that is pervasive in command-and-control organizations is designed to eliminate surprises. Unfortunately, the only surprises that centralized planning seems to eliminate are the "good surprises." Far too often, the dysfunctional silo structures of command-and-control organizations inadvertently lead to "bad surprises" in the later stages of complex projects.

Good surprises are the breakthroughs and alternative ways of thinking that result in cost or time reductions, operational efficiencies, product innovations, or new business opportunities. More often than not good surprises are discovered by entrepreneurs who are not saddled with the controlling infrastructures of traditional organizations. Bad surprises are the unintended consequences of centralized planning in bureaucratic structures when things do not come together at the end as planned because different parts of the bureaucracy had different understandings – or worse yet – different agendas.

Surprises in organizations are like cholesterol in the human body. Just as an abundance of bad cholesterol and a low amount of good cholesterol can lead to cardiac arrest, an abundance of bad surprises and the absence of good surprises can lead to significant business failure. Likewise, as the body needs good cholesterol for sustained health, organizations need good surprises for sustained business success. This is even more important in fast changing times because good surprises can greatly improve established organizations' capacity to keep up with entrepreneurs, compete with new players, or leverage the power of an existing brand into new markets. In the 21st century, companies that desire long term sustainable growth must have the capacity to facilitate good surprises and to be able to quickly convert and execute those good surprises into business results. Given the pace of change in business today, this is not an option but rather a required competency.

The Creative Alternative discussion in Work-Thrus is one of the ways an organization can exercise this competency. Once again, creativity cannot be planned; it can only be facilitated. Thus, Creative Alternative discussions are not planned into a Work-Thru but rather emerge from the discussions of the participants after the reports from the small group exercises. For example, the participants may have been asked to propose solutions for a complex business issue after being divided into four small groups. The report from one of the small groups may result in a breakthrough approach that immediately connects with all the participants in the room resulting in an enthusiastic consensus on the part of everyone. While this is rare, this good surprise does sometimes happen in Work-Thrus.

More often, however, the reports from the small groups will represent four entirely different solutions, none of which can garner an immediate consensus among the large group. Sometimes a participant or the facilitator will suggest combining elements from the observations of the different small groups as a possible solution. If this combination of elements starts to work with the group, it may serve as a catalyst for new ideas to emerge as the participants build onto the evolving alternative solution. Before you know it, a consensus is achieved among all the participants – a consensus that everyone realizes could not be accomplished by any one person but only by accessing the collective knowledge of the group working effectively together.

The functionality of large group discussions in Work-Thrus is in stark contrast to the dysfunctional dynamics so often seen in the typical large group corporate meeting. When large group discussions follow presentations and small group exercises using the cardinal rules of Work-Thrus, the context of the large group conversations is dramatically changed. Rather than the debates of competing ideas so characteristic of traditional meetings, using the Work-Thru format with its cardinal rules creates a context in which the participants become committed to working a collective solution, and so the conversation becomes focused on how to integrate different ideas rather than on which idea is right or wrong.

As so often happens once true breakthrough consensus is reached, the actual solution to a complex issue turns out to be relatively simple once the right elements are put together. This development does two things. First, it creates a powerful shared understanding among the cross-functional group that created the breakthrough, and second, the simple elegance of the solution translates very effectively to both decision makers and workers outside the group, leading to quick adoption of the solution and an even broader shared understanding to drive consistency throughout the organization. The simplicity and the clarity of the results produced from Creative Alternative discussions go a long way to producing good surprises early on in a project and to minimizing or eliminating bad surprises in the final hours of the work effort.

KEY QUESTIONS DISCUSSIONS

Sometimes following the reports from the small groups, it becomes apparent to everyone in the Work-Thru that the issue being discussed is more complex and far more difficult then anyone had realized and that the group is nowhere near knowing how to begin to design a solution. In fact, the disparity and the apparent lack of cohesion of the small group reports may leave the participants with an overwhelming sense of confusion and chaos as they wonder whether or not they are wasting their time in the meeting. This is an important and pivotal moment in a Work-Thru and must be carefully and skillfully handled by the facilitator. For it is this moment that presents a very real opportunity to move the group forward to a deeper understanding of the problem at hand through a discovery of the important but as yet unknown factors that will drive a successful solution.

When this moment occurs, it often works for the facilitator to acknowledge the obvious by asking "Does everyone in the room feel completely confused by where we are right now?" As she looks around the room and sees all the affirming nods, she should encourage and reassure the group by saying "Good – you're exactly where you need to be if we are going to truly get to a breakthrough to solve this problem." This simple statement can ground the group in the midst of their felt confusion by letting them know that chaos is something to be worked through – and not avoided – if they are to achieve real success.

When you think about it, every project has two phases: order and chaos. Our only choice as managers is the sequence. In the typical command-and-control organization, when faced with complexity and confusion, chaos is rarely embraced. The tendency is to choose order by coming up with an immediate plan, organizing resources, designating an accountable leader, and setting up a periodic reporting structure. In other words, when confronted with the anxiety of the unknown, the usual reaction of traditional managers is to embrace the basic activities of the command-and-control management model: planning, organizing, directing, coordinating, and controlling. But all too often, this premature embrace of order is actually counterproductive, leading eventually to chaos in the later stages of projects and resulting in significant cost overruns and delays, if not outright failure. When order is embraced prematurely, managers deny themselves the opportunity to discover what is most important at the start of complex and difficult projects: to find out "what they don't know that they don't know." These are the important factors that are outside our awareness at the beginning of initiatives that inevitably come back to bite us, sometimes fatally, at the end of projects.

When Work-Thru participants experience confusion and chaos in confronting an important and complex issue, this is a sure sign that the group is at a place where "they don't know what they don't know." If the participants are to breakthrough this confusion, they need to embrace the chaos and discover the key questions that need to be addressed so that they may become aware of everything they need to know at the start of the project, and then with the answers to these questions, they will be able to produce a realistic plan and organize resources in a way that has real possibilities of working on budget and on time.

The Key Questions discussion is about identifying what are the important prerequisite issues, factors, or understandings that need to be handled before we can effectively develop and execute a plan of action. The facilitator takes a more active role in the Key Questions discussion, guiding the group through a process of discovery. As a first step, the facilitator might summarize the observations from the previous small group exercises, capturing the main points on a flip chart. When there is agreement on the main points, the facilitator might ask the group what are the major barriers to problem-solving or what work needs to be done to break the impasse. Often the group will identify input or work that needs to be done "offline" and brought back to the next Work-Thru meeting. In any event, the focus of the work at this point is to come up with a complete and concise list of questions that needs to be addressed to move the group forward. Most times the key questions can be formulated in the large group discussion format. Other times, the facilitator may recognize that the large group forum is not working and will shift the participants into small group exercises with the assignment to identify the three to four key questions that need to be answered to move the project forward.

When the discussion is working in the large group format, one of two things happens. Sometimes, after the formulation of the key questions, the group recognizes that they already have the right people in the room and all the information they need to move on. When this happens, there is an incredible sense of accomplishment as the participants realize that they have made a real contribution to solving an important and complex business issue. At other times, the group may realize that they have come up with the right key questions, but either the right people to address the questions are not in the room or more information needs to be brought into the group and, thus, the key questions will need to be worked "offline" and brought back at the next Work-Thru meeting. In that case, the facilitator will record the actions necessary to move the questions forward on an "Actions/Next Steps" flip chart.

Key Questions discussions are a powerful vehicle for embracing chaos at the beginning of projects to identify early on critical success factors that are unknown at the time yet are essential to a well-ordered, on budget, on time, and flawlessly executed solution to an important business issue. Once again, every project has two phases: order and chaos. Our only choice is the sequence. Work-Thrus, especially in the Key Questions discussions, embrace chaos first in a way that works to realize true order at the project's end.

TIMELINE DISCUSSIONS

This form of large group discussion is very useful when the focus of the Work-Thru is a complex project involving multiple parts of the organization, especially if those parts are physically or geographically dispersed. The Timeline discussion usually follows a break during which the facilitator has taped blank flip chart pages, each one next to each other, across a large wall space in the room. Each flip chart page represents a month, with the facilitator writing the name of the corresponding month at the top of each page in chronological order, i.e., March, April, May, etc.

When the participants return from the break, the facilitator invites everyone to gather around the wall containing the flip chart pages. She then asks the participants to identify key dates for important activities that need to be done to successfully deliver the project. The facilitator instructs the group that the activities do not have to be identified in chronological order, rather as individuals think of tasks, they can be recorded on the calendar pages.

For example, the focus of the Work-Thru might be a nine-month project to install a new customer service center that needs to be operational by the end of October. The first participant may identify the obvious activity of having the customer service operational on October 31. The facilitator would then record at the bottom of the

October flip chart "31 – Customer Service Center Operational." The next participant might identify the necessary recruitment activities for customer service representatives (CSR's) with job postings starting on June 1 and all staff hired and reporting for work on September 30. The facilitator would go to the top of the June flip chart page and record "1 – Job Postings for CSR Staff" and at the bottom of the September flip chart page "30 – All CSR's Hired/Start Work."

As the participants continue to identify activities, inevitably significant misalignments are surfaced. For example, participants from the business area may be focused on a completion date of September 30 for the CSR manual so that it is ready for the CSR training, which is to be done throughout the month of October. The participants responsible for training might point out that a September 30 completion date for the training manual will not work because time will be needed to train the trainers if the October CSR training is to be effective. As a result, the completion date for the training manual might be modified to August 31 to provide sufficient time for the training of the trainers. The identification and recording of activities and the appropriate adjustments to the original recordings of activities continues until all key activities are captured on the flip charts and everyone in the room is comfortable with the timeline.

The Timeline discussion is powerful because it accomplishes three things. First, the complete end-to-end process of activities that are critical to success are properly sequenced in time, thus facilitating the effective execution of on-time quality deliverables. Second, by focusing on the project as an integrated process rather than as a distribution of discrete tasks, misalignments of tasks are identified before the work begins. How many times in command-and-control organizations do we see tasks for key initiatives distributed among functional departments without those departments understanding the full process underlying those tasks and without knowing how their jobs interrelate with other departments' activities? When this happens, the project runs into difficulties in the later phases as different departments are actually working to different timelines because of their differing senses of priorities and their differing understandings of the timing of activities in the project. The Timeline discussion eliminates these 11th hour difficulties by "front-ending" the misalignments and fully resolving them at the start of the project. This saves the company both time and money.

The third and most powerful contribution of the Timeline discussion is the creation of a shared understanding among all the Work-

Thru participants. Each participant has a clear picture of the whole process and fully understands the interrelationships among the activities and how her tasks fit into the overall project. By participating in the construction of the holistic timeline, witnessing the conversations as critical potential misalignments are identified and resolved, and visually seeing the entire project mapped on the calendar flip chart pages, everyone in the Work-Thru goes back to their different departments or different locations working toward the same timeline. It is far more powerful for people in organizations to be working to timelines where they truly understand how their part fits into the whole project than to be working to due dates assigned by the boss.

When individuals work to shared timelines that they have helped create, they understand why they cannot be late and the full ramifications that missed deadlines have on the project, whereas if individuals are working merely to due dates, in the face of competing priorities, it is very easy to think so what if this task is missed by a few days. Yet those few days could mean the difference between the ultimate success and failure of the project.

WRAP UPS

As the Work-Thru progresses, moving back and forth between presentations, small group exercises, and large group discussions, the facilitator throughout the day records on flip charts the important observations, conclusions, agreements, and action steps from the group's work. These would include the 3 – 5 items identified from a Focus List discussion or the work plan from a Timeline discussion or a list of "Next Steps" of actions to be done following the Work-Thru.

Each day of a Work-Thru concludes with a Wrap Up session that lasts between 15 and 30 minutes where the facilitator reviews the key observations, conclusions and agreements with the participants. The facilitator will also review the list of Next Steps identified by the group and make sure everyone is clear about exactly what needs to be done, who specifically will do each action, and when each action will be completed.

After reviewing the day's work the facilitator will check with the group about their sense of comfort with the work done that day or, if it is the last day of a multi-day Work-Thru, their sense of the progress made over the whole session. Generally, the participants' sense of accomplishment at the end of a Work-Thru day is very high.

Throughout the course of the facilitated meeting, they have wrestled with the complexity and the confusion of difficult and important issues, they have experienced and worked through the overwhelming chaos that inevitably happens when you confront the realities of change and complexity, and they have discovered breakthrough insights and compelling observations in identifying the focused action needed to meet the challenges of fast changing times.

The most common observation in the written evaluations at the end of a Work-Thru is that the group members are amazed – perhaps stunned is a better word – at how much they accomplished in such a short time. They realize that in the Work-Thru they have accomplished in two or three days what otherwise would take weeks or even months in traditional meeting formats. This is the power and the competitive advantage of Work-Thrus: When an organization has an effective meeting process that expands and diversifies the voices in more disciplined conversations, it can streamline its most important work from many months to a few days with the added bonus of producing better results in less time.

BUILT FOR KNOWLEDGE AND SPEED

Changing the way we work together in meetings is the cornerstone for moving companies from being structured for order and authority to being built for knowledge and speed. In the Digital Age, conversation is the catalyst that drives the corporation. The quality of conversations determines the quality of work. Better dialogue drives better knowledge and the broad early involvement of many and diverse voices delivers faster reliable results. Linda Ellinor and Glenna Gerard accurately capture the essence of organizational work when they say "Conversation, whether dialogic or not, *is* how most everything gets done in organizations."[7]

If corporations need to be built for knowledge and speed, they cannot afford to let the workings of bureaucratic control stratify the voices in the corporate conversation. The only way that companies will be able to make quick sense from the apparent complexity and chaos that always accompanies change is by engaging in open conversations where managers and workers pool their knowledge to create shared understanding. Work-Outs and Work-Thrus are two examples of the new competency of collective learning that can easily be adopted by any organization that wants to improve conversations within its meetings to promote knowledge and speed. Both of these examples expand and diversify the number of voices in the corporate conversation, depoliticize ideas, and eliminate the inappropriate exercise of control over what people think and what they have to say. GE's Work-Outs accomplish this by removing the bosses from the room and putting the workers in the hands of skilled facilitators. Work-Thrus succeed by expanding executive skills and transforming bosses into facilitators.

The common lesson from both of these examples is that learning – especially quick learning – doesn't happen naturally in organizations. It must be facilitated and it must follow a discipline designed to promote dialogue rather than debate. The discipline of Work-Thrus is contained in its four cardinal rules:

1. Presentations are always delivered without interruption.

2. After presentations, clarifying questions only.

3. Small group exercises are always focused on clear and specific deliverables.

4. Conclusions and agreements about the group's ideas rest with the group – period.

The executive facilitator following the cardinal rules creates a safe environment that promotes real listening, that keeps the group focused on what it defines as the most important things, and that assures that the group reaches its own consensus on important ideas.

Collective learning processes, such as Work-Outs and Work-Thrus, show that facilitated learning is essential for executives who are serious about managing at the pace of change. The breakthrough concept behind Work-Thrus is the development of the role of the executive facilitator. The idea that executives serve as facilitators who do not express their own opinions and who do not exert influence toward specific outcomes flies in the face of the assumptions of command-and-control management. In traditional meetings, where idea generation tends to be intertwined with decision-making, executives are expected to have strong opinions, to exert influence over outcomes, and to take charge. In Work-Thrus, idea generation is separated from decision-making. In fact, Work-Thru participants generally are not responsible for decision-making. In Blue Cross Blue Shield FEP, the senior executives and the board continued to be responsible for corporate decisions, which was something that was made clear at the start of a Work-Thru session.

Collective learning processes enable a company to focus on generating the best ideas possible in a short period of time by providing quick access to the full collective knowledge of both the managers and the workers. The discoveries and the breakthrough thinking that emerge from well facilitated learning processes provide optimal input for executive decision-making. When better ideas from the collective wisdom of knowledge workers drive better decisions by executives, the result is the foundation for a powerful shared understanding throughout the organization as workers clearly see their input reflected in management decisions.

The arrival of the Digital Age, along with its emerging network mindset, is bringing about a complete transformation of the practice of management as new assumptions about work, new relationships between executives and workers, and new management responsibilities change the work we do and the way we work. The primary responsibilities of managers are no longer planning, organizing, directing, coordinating, and controlling. Those command-and-control activities structured around order and authority worked in the relatively stabile context of mass production. In the Digital Age, the context is now mass collaboration and the market requirement for companies is knowledge and speed. The new work of wiki-management organizations and the new responsibilities of managers today are: customer values, collective learning, shared understanding, focused measurement, and collaborative community. Work-Thrus are designed to support these new responsibilities.

Chapter 8

THE SECOND RESPONSIBILITY: COLLECTIVE LEARNING

Team learning is vital because teams, not individuals, are the fundamental learning unit in modern organizations.

- Peter M. Senge
The Fifth Discipline[1]

One of the deepest beliefs of command-and-control management is the assumption that the smartest organization is the one with the smartest individuals. This belief is as old as scientific management itself. According to this way of thinking, just as there is a right way to perform every activity, there are right individuals who are essential for defining what are the right things and for making sure that things are done right. Thus, traditional organizations have long held that the key to the successful achievement of the corporation's two basic account-abilities of strategy and execution is to hire the smartest individual managers and the brightest functional experts.

Command-and-control management assumes that intelligence fundamentally resides in a select number of star performers who are able to leverage their expertise across large groups of people through proper direction and effective control. Thus, the recruiting efforts and the promotional practices of most companies are focused on compet-ing for and retaining the most talented people. While established management thinking holds that most individual workers are replace-able, this is not so for those star performers whose decision-making and problem-solving prowess are heroically revered. Traditional hier-archical organizations firmly believe in the myth of the individual hero. They are convinced that a single highly intelligent individual can make the difference between success and failure, whether that person is a key senior executive, a functional expert, or even a highly paid consultant.

The firm grip of this myth is reflected in *The War For Talent*, a book published in 2001 by three consultants with the prominent firm McKinsey & Company. The authors contend that, based on their research and experience with some of America's most successful companies, corporate competitive advantage comes from having better talent at all levels.[2] The best companies, according to the authors, have a "talent mindset" that is riveted on a relentless courting of "A players," putting a premium on degrees from the top-tier business schools, investing heavily in the individual development of these star performers, and making sure that they are handsomely compensated. *The War For Talent* is a manifesto for the belief that the smartest organization is the one with the smartest individuals.

Unfortunately, one of the model organizations in the McKinsey & Company study was Enron, whose precipitous demise followed just a few months after the publication of the book. Enron was a fervent proponent of star performers and believed in the myth of the individual hero. However, Malcolm Gladwell in a 2002 New Yorker article suggests that perhaps smart people are overrated and Enron's belief that organizational intelligence is a function of individual talent was actually an enabler of its failure.[3] Gladwell makes the point that "companies work by different rules. They don't just create; they execute and compete and coordinate the efforts of many different people, and the organizations that are most successful at that task are the ones where the system is the star."[4]

The assumption that individual experts are the key to extraordinary performance has long been a driving force behind the "war for talent," especially with the emergence of MBA programs in the later part of the 20th century. In the myopic pursuit of the very best expertise, corporations have continually placed a disproportionate value on academic intelligence. Yet scholastic excellence is only one of many competencies necessary for effective management performance, and it is not necessarily at the top of the list. This is not said to negate the value of scholastic intelligence. Indeed, academic credentials are a value in recruiting – they're just not the only value or even the most important value in selecting who will join the company.

As we transition into the Digital Age with its accelerating pace of change, it will become obvious to more companies that no single individual or even an elite cadre of star performers can adequately process the ever-evolving knowledge of fast-changing markets into operational excellence in real-time. The original ideas and concepts behind

Enron's business model may have been very sound – even brilliant. After all, Enron was designated by *Fortune* magazine as the "most innovative company in America" for six consecutive years. However, the Enron experience is a testament to the fact that, when it comes to sustained business success, the ideas and the concepts of star performers are not enough. Successful companies, especially in the wiki world, need sound processes and systems for bringing together and for integrating the best ideas and efforts of all the people in the organization, whether they're "A players" or "B players."

Academic excellence does not necessarily correlate with leadership effectiveness. Star performers are not necessarily equipped for the task of organizing large numbers of people in dynamic fast-changing markets. While the talented graduates of MBA programs have demonstrated that they are quite capable of working individually, nothing in their scholastic experience has prepared them for today's new challenge of quickly accessing the collective intelligence of large numbers of people. There's probably little doubt that Enron did recruit some of the brightest talent in America, but in the absence of processes to integrate the collective knowledge from this rich talent pool, the individual star performers remained selfishly focused. And in the end it was the misplaced and self-centered focus of very talented people that led to the downfall of "the most innovative company in America." Innovation in the Digital Age has more to do with creating collective intelligence than is does with chasing experts, because as Enron has made perfectly clear, today the smartest organization is not necessarily the one with the smartest individuals.

COLLECTIVE KNOWLEDGE

While most mainstream organizations have yet to learn the value of collective knowledge, the companies in one peripheral industry have known for years that the sagacity of the masses usually outperforms the judgment of the experts. If you're in the business of sports betting, there is no illusion about the talents of star performers when you have state-of-the-art systems to access the collective knowledge of all the bettors. If you want to stay consistently profitable in the gaming business, you learn quickly that the system is the star.

MGM MIRAGE owns and operates 16 hotel and gaming properties in Nevada, Mississippi and Michigan. The company also has a 50 percent interest in four other properties in Nevada, New Jersey,

Illinois, and Macau. A major portion of its revenue stream comes from its sports betting operations in its Nevada hotels. While MGM MIRAGE hires talented and experienced experts to manage its sports gambling business, it also maintains highly sophisticated computer systems to track the wagers of its bettors. MGM MIRAGE doesn't make its money by picking winners and losers, but rather by correctly setting the point spread such that half of the gamblers will win and half will lose. Because the company pays out less when wagers win than it collects when they lose, the sports betting operations will always make money when the number of winners equals the number of losers. While the staff experts do set the initial point spreads, MGM MIRAGE's computer systems track all the incoming bets and adjust any spread if more than half the wagers are on one side of the betting line. Thus, the final value of the point spread is determined by the collective wisdom of the crowd rather than by the savvy judgments of the experts.

MGM MIRAGE is consistently profitable in its sports betting operations because rather than relying on the expertise of a few star performers, it has the capacity to quickly access the collective knowledge of its customers. MGM MIRAGE understands a business secret for success that most organizations have yet to learn: Nobody is smarter than everybody.

James Surowiecki, in his insightful book *The Wisdom of Crowds*, provides numerous examples of where, under the right conditions, groups are highly intelligent and consistently outperform even the smartest individuals in them.[5] In his study of collective intelligence, Surowiecki found that if four conditions are satisfied, groups can provide incredibly sound and accurate judgments.[6]

The first condition is diversity of opinion. Having different perspectives – even eccentric notions – broadens the available information, provides the capacity for evolving ideas, makes it easier for individuals to be candid, and protects against the negative dynamics of shortsighted groupthink.

The second condition is independent thinking, which means that each individual is free to express his own opinions without editing and without any pressure to conform to the beliefs of others in the group. Surowiecki makes the point that, "paradoxically, the best way for a group to be smart is for each person in it to think and act as independently as possible."[7]

The third condition is local knowledge. In order to truly access collective knowledge, the group must be able to draw upon specialized and localized intelligence because the closer a person is to the problem or the customer, the more likely he is to have a meaningful contribution. This is why social networks such as the Internet, which include large numbers of people and where no one is in charge, are so valuable; they allow important information to quickly and freely flow from the fringe to the core.

The fourth and final condition is aggregation mechanisms. Without the capacity to collate and integrate the diverse and independent thinking of large numbers of people, there is only chaos and cacophony. Surowiecki emphasizes that "a decentralized system can only produce genuinely intelligent results if there is a means of aggregating the information of everyone in the system."[8] Aggregation mechanisms are processes or systems for learning the integrated content of collective knowledge.

There is an important distinction regarding this fourth condition: aggregation should not be confused with centralization. Centralization always emphasizes order and authority. In command structures, the desired outcomes are predetermined through a strategic planning process that inevitably leads to a dependence on the knowledge of experts and a reinforcement of their organizational authority in the pursuit of those preordained outcomes. Aggregation, on the other hand, emphasizes knowledge and speed. Accordingly, the primary task of aggregating mechanisms is learning. By quickly collecting the decentralized observations of its many stakeholders and discerning the inherent patterns and trends, organizations are able to use the collective knowledge of their customers and workers to guide and align their activities in the pursuit of market-driven outcomes.

The sports betting business would be risky business if it relied on a centralized business model, depended solely on the judgments of its pundits to set the point spreads, and set up organizational structures to reinforce their authority. Because the gaming industry fully understands that the crowd is smarter than the experts, sports betting operations employ aggregation mechanisms that collect and collate the independent betting patterns of their many customers and use this real-time collective knowledge to successfully guide the establishment of their point spreads. Unfortunately, unlike the companies in the gaming industry, most organizations have been extremely reluctant to abandon traditional planning practices to embrace the learning processes necessary to access collective knowledge. Consequently, as Gary Hamel correctly observes in his book *The Future of Management*, "there is more wisdom embedded in the average sports bet than there is in the typical corporate investment decision."[9]

PLANNING AND LEARNING

Whether starting a new initiative, dealing with an unexpected crisis, or solving an emerging business problem, the first step of the traditional manager is usually to draw up a plan of action. Planning provides comfort in the face of complexity because, by defining and sequencing a set of action steps, the manager has the sense that a reliable path to a certain outcome has been put in place. Planning assumes that the world is stable and predictable.

This assumption reinforces the notion that long-term business planning is both desirable and possible. It has been common practice among Industrial Age corporations to spend significant time and money on three-year, five-year, or even ten-year business plans. While these long-term strategies have not always turned out precisely as expected, given the relative stability of the pace of change for most of the 20th century, these business blueprints nevertheless did serve as reasonable guideposts for decision-making in the deployment and allocation of corporate resources. For most of the span of the Industrial Age, planning worked because the future was reasonably foreseeable. Planning can serve as the foundation of strategy when the future is clear or at least clear enough. In stable circumstances, planning and analysis generally do cultivate sound business decisions.

However, what happens when markets are not so stable and predictable and the pace of change continually accelerates? What happens when a steady stream of new technologies continually reshapes the business landscape? What happens when your business environment is no longer local or domestic and you find yourself competing in global and multi-cultural markets? What happens when the rules of the game change and you need to transform your organization from an Industrial Age establishment to a Digital Age innovator? In the new wiki world where innovation, flexibility, and adaptability are necessities for business survival and where knowledge has replaced the machines as a critical economic asset, mechanistic planning technologies that assume a known and stable business environment can no longer serve as the foundation for strategic work.

In the fast-changing times of the Digital Age, planning is no longer a strategic activity; it is now only a tactical exercise. Today's continually changing and uncertain markets make it impossible to predict the future much beyond the immediate horizon. Consequently, traditional long-term planning is likely to be counterproductive by locking organizations into what may become obsolete strategies or by blinding them from discerning the opportunities in newly emerging technologies or markets. This, unfortunately, is where the recording industry appears to find itself today as it persists in trying to preserve its mass production business model in a mass collaboration world.

In times of accelerating change, strategy is less about the strategic plan and more about the strategic options. This means that businesses need to be able to rapidly synthesize a plethora of information, realistically anticipate the different directions that markets could take, and develop options for each of these probable paths. If companies are going to need to reposition their businesses every seven to ten years, there's a lot to learn and they have to learn it fast. In the wiki world, strategy is a continual iterative dance with changing market realities and there are no slow dances on this dance floor!

In the past, the starting point for strategic work was based on what organizations knew from sophisticated analyses or forecasts prepared by talented experts. They could count on this expertise to successfully navigate markets with certainty and confidence. All that has changed. Today, the starting point for strategic work is the unknown, and the most important strategic task for business leaders today is to quickly uncover "what they don't know that they don't know." This is vital because if you know what you don't know, you can fill the gap by hiring staff or engaging a consultant. However, when you don't know what you don't know, you are not even aware that you have a gap, and that can spell trouble when markets are changing fast.

Thus, for the recording industry, it appears that the fundamental restructuring of their world was completely off their radar screen. Because they didn't know what they didn't know, they missed a golden opportunity to form a partnership with Napster that could have firmly repositioned their business in the mass collaboration world. Instead the recording trade's strategic response was based on its existing industry paradigm in an attempt to preserve what will surely become an obsolete business model. When you don't know what you don't know, you not only run the risk of missing new opportunities, but you also may be sowing the seeds for new competitors to bring about your creative destruction.

If you want to be competent at continually uncovering the unknown, strategic processes needs to be based on learning not planning. Traditional corporate planning is not designed for delving into the inscrutable or producing discoveries. It's designed for assimilating everything we know so we can come up with the best decisions. However, in the fast paced wiki world, the focus of strategic work is no longer about making decisions – it's about making discoveries. It's about discovering what you don't know that you don't know.

COLLECTIVE LEARNING

When you believe that the smartest organization is the one with the smartest people, the organizational learning paradigm is focused on individual development. That's why traditional companies sponsor tuition reimbursement programs, encourage professional certifications, pay for weeklong business seminars and conferences, and establish in-house "corporate university" programs. In the traditional paradigm, learning has been about training individuals and increasing their functional expertise.

While individual development will continue to remain important, it's not enough to succeed in a new global economy where digitization and robotics are recasting operational platforms, where the Internet and other collaborative technologies are driving the reinvention of old business models, and where whole new industries can come and go in less than a decade. Managing at the pace of change is only possible if companies have a mature core competency in collective learning. This means not only hiring and training smart individuals but also possessing the technology to quickly access the collective knowledge of workers and customers. While you want both, should you have to choose between smart individuals or collective knowledge, bet on collective knowledge because, in the wiki world, the smartest organization is the one that has quick access to its collective knowledge.

If you are going to be a smart company in the new economy, you will have to develop and embrace new and unfamiliar business processes to get the access to your collective intelligence. These learning processes will require investments in systems technology to collect and collate the many observations at the periphery, glean the inherent collective wisdom, and make the information readily available to everyone in the company. Being a smart company will also call for the incorporation of innovative social technology that will belie the traditional notions of order and control. This is because both the social and the systems technologies supporting collective learning must meet Surowiecki's four conditions of diversity of opinion, independent thinking, local knowledge, and aggregation mechanisms if they are to generate useful collective knowledge.

ELECTRONIC LEARNING PLATFORMS

Technological advances, especially since the arrival of the Internet, are expanding the possibilities for systems architects to create unprecedented learning platforms that dramatically deepen organizational capacity for both knowledge and speed. The systems technology at MGM MIRAGE is just one example from an array of computer applications that provide comprehensive up-to-date access to the collective knowledge of the crowd in literally fractions of a second. Amazon and eBay are two other examples of companies that have built their systems architecture as learning platforms to not only access the collective knowledge of their customers, but to also make that knowledge available to everyone online. Amazon uses its online data to construct its own best-seller lists and to aggregate and publish ratings of books by its customers. eBay keeps vendors in its online market honest by collecting, collating, and publishing buyers' ratings of the sellers. This real-time access to the available collective knowledge of all the buyers makes purchasing on the Web a better customer experience.

No single expert or even group of experts can come anywhere close to matching the completeness of knowledge or the incredible speed of well-designed electronic learning platforms. Before the Internet, we were substantially limited in our ability to quickly access the collective wisdom of the larger community. Although it has always been true that nobody is smarter than everybody, because we had lacked the technology to organize the intelligence of large numbers of people, access to collective knowledge was simply not practical. Thus, in the days before the Web, seeking out the expertise of the brightest among us was the most expeditious course for navigating business success. However, the current state-of-the-art technology is making it perilous for organizations to endeavor to meet today's market challenges by relying on the judgments of a handful of experts. We are already beginning to see, even among Internet companies, that customers will swiftly abandon established products and gravitate to companies that provide superior alternatives built on collective intelligence.

At the beginning of 1998, Yahoo's web directory was on the verge of breaking away from a small field of upstarts who were fiercely competing to establish themselves as the web surfer's first choice for searching the Internet. Using a horde of expert editors, Yahoo had organized the myriad of web pages into an impressive practical catalogue. If you wanted to find information on the Web, most people were finding their way to Yahoo because their cataloging experts were better than their competitors. However, cataloging takes time, and by 1998 the popularity of the Internet had begun to explode. The prodigious effort to keep up with the ever-growing number of web pages was becoming a challenge for even the best of editorial experts.

It is at this time that two innovative entrepreneurs who had met at Stanford University as students, Sergey Brin and Lawrence Page, came up with the idea for a more effective and efficient way to catalog web pages that would not require the use of experts. They created a systems learning platform, which they called PageRank, that would rely on the collective knowledge of all the Internet users to catalog and rank web pages. Thus, Google was born.

PageRank is an algorithm that lets users decide which web pages are most relevant to a search based on the number of links and visits to a particular site. By tracking user search patterns and trends, Google's decentralized learning platform did a better job of quickly finding the right pages than Yahoo's centralized expert editors. It wasn't very long before Google's learning platform easily supplanted Yahoo as the search engine of choice.

Although Yahoo is an Internet company, its business model reflected the machine mindset, and thus, the work of cataloging web pages was seen as a planning and organizing task to bring order to complexity based on the authoritative knowledge of experts. Brin and Page, however, operating from the network mindset, saw the work effort as a learning and collaborating task to discern the collective knowledge of all the Web surfers, using the speed of systems technology. While Yahoo's business model, like those of most traditional companies, was organized for order and authority, Google's electronic learning platform was designed for knowledge and speed. The dramatic preference shift from Yahoo to Google clearly manifests that nobody is smarter than everybody and that today's Digital Age customers value the products of companies focused on knowledge and speed over those from organizations structured around order and authority.

The systems architectures at Amazon, eBay, and Google are examples of how the Internet is dramatically revolutionizing the business landscape. In addition to Web-enabled technologies that transform simple transaction information into collective knowledge, the Internet has opened up a whole new world of possibilities for creating electronic learning platforms that allow organizations to reach out to incredibly large numbers of people and to effectively engage all willing participants in collaborative dialogue. Why limit your strategic learning to the knowledge of a handful of executives within your organizational walls when some of the most intelligent people in the world are eager and willing to work with you – sometimes even for free! When the market demands knowledge and speed, the more voices you can get into the same room at the same time, the better the knowledge and the faster you can transform that knowledge into execution – provided that you have workable collective learning processes. Web-based learning platforms are furnishing an unprecedented capacity for organizations to reach outside their walls and expand the available knowledge in their strategic conversations.

For example, IBM is using the Internet to bring fresh ideas into its walls by inviting more than 100,000 customers, outside consultants, and employee family members to join in the strategic conversation. In July 2006, Big Blue hosted an online "Innovation Jam" where the participants were encouraged to offer their ideas and to brainstorm on important strategic issues that would shape the company's future. IBM had populated the website with an array of background information on transportation, healthcare, the environment, finance, and commerce to seed the electronic learning platform. The Innovation Jam gave IBM access to valuable collective knowledge by providing a vehicle for the company to aggregate the diverse, independent, and localized reflections of key stakeholders. By employing this learning process as a foundation for discerning strategy, IBM gave itself real-time access to a range of ideas and knowledge far beyond the limits of its organizational walls, in stark contrast to the typical inbred planning processes of traditional management practices.

THE GOLDCORP CHALLENGE

Another company that has discovered the power of using the Internet to reach beyond its walls and expand the strategic conversation is the Canadian gold-mining firm, Goldcorp Inc. In the late 1990's, Rob McEwen, Goldcorp's CEO was wondering if he had made a big mistake five years earlier when he acquired a fifty-year old gold mine that yielded lots of rocks but not many nuggets. In fact, facing increasing production costs, mounting debts, and almost no productivity, Goldcorp had been forced to cease mining operations.[10] Although it seemed as if the best days of the Red Lake, Ontario mine were long behind, McEwen was convinced that there had to be substantial undiscovered deposits of ore somewhere beneath the 55,000-acre site. All Goldcorp had to do was find them. And so, McEwen invested $10 million in exploration and sent his geologists prospecting on a last-ditch expedition.

Although the geologists were skeptical, they nevertheless gave the exploration their best efforts and were pleasantly surprised a few weeks later to bring back some astounding news: Test drilling in nine of the exploratory holes suggested vast deposits of new gold with an average concentration of ore as much as 30 times richer than Goldcorp was currently producing.[11] However, this remarkable discovery did not solve the productivity problem. While the geologists found strong indications of fresh gold, there was still the question of finding the exact location of the ore, and that would require deep drilling, which is much more costly than test drilling.

After a year of further exploration, running up more costs, and not locating the elusive ore, a frustrated McEwen decided he needed to step away and take a break from the office. He enrolled in a weeklong program about trends in information technology that MIT was sponsoring for presidents and CEO's. Part of the program was an orientation on Linux and open-source software. McEwen was fascinated by the story of how Linus Torvalds used the Internet to build a world-class computer operating system written by volunteer programmers distributed all over the globe. By the end of the lecture, McEwen was convinced that he had found the solution to the problem of locating the elusive gold. If Goldcorp's geologists couldn't locate Red Lake's new gold, perhaps the company could open the exploration process and invite drilling strategies from geologists around the globe.

As soon as McEwen arrived back at his Toronto office, he outlined his plan to Goldcorp's geologists and executives. The company would sponsor a contest with a total of $575,000 in prize money to be divided among 3 finalists and 25 semifinalists submitting the best drilling plans to help the company achieve its goal of locating 6 million ounces of gold. Goldcorp would take the unprecedented step of posting every bit of information about its 55,000-acre site on its website. This included 50 years worth of maps, charts, and reports, as well as detailed geological data. Goldcorp would use the power of the Internet as a learning platform to reach out to the worldwide community of geologists and engineers to locate the elusive gold.

The immediate reaction of Goldcorp's geologists and executives to McEwen's plan was shock. They were aghast to think that the company would make public all of its proprietary data, and they were concerned about how Goldcorp's geologists would be viewed by members of the scientific community when they learned that the company was sponsoring a contest to prospect its gold. The Goldcorp staff shared the traditional mindset of Industrial Age corporations that believe the smartest company is the one with the smartest individuals and keeps its knowledge to itself as a competitive advantage. They felt that the contest would fly in the face of conventional wisdom and would publicly embarrass Goldcorp's geologists before their professional peers. Goldcorp's staff it seemed was more concerned about looking smart than being smart.

McEwen was not to be rebuffed. In the wake of his MIT experience, he understood that conventional wisdom is no substitute for collective wisdom. Goldcorp needed to abandon its 19th century thinking and catapult into 21st century technology if it was to have any hope of turning itself around. Thus, the "Goldcorp Challenge" was launched in March 2000. The enthusiastic response from the international community of scientists and geologists was immediate. The Challenge Website received over 475,000 hits, and more than 1,400 online prospectors from 51 countries registered as Challenge participants. Within weeks, submissions from all over the world were appearing on Goldcorp's virtual doorstep, and by the contest deadline, the company received detailed drilling plans from over 140 registered participants.

The Challenge identified 110 geological targets, more than half of which had not been previously nominated by Goldcorp's geologists. Over 80 percent of the designated targets were found to be rich in new gold with a yield of over 8 million ounces, far exceeding Goldcorp's initial goal of 6 million ounces. Astoundingly, at the March 2001 Goldcorp Challenge awards presentation, McEwen was able to proudly announce that Goldcorp was once again profitable and debt free!

When McEwen first came up with the idea for the Goldcorp Challenge, all he was hoping for was a way to locate the new gold on his Red Lake site. What he did not anticipate was the astonishing and unexpected learnings from the contributions of the participants that would revamp the company's mining business model. In presenting the awards to the contest winners, McEwen acknowledged, "These individuals and teams represent the leading edge of mining in the 21st century. We congratulate them on their initiatives, skills, and understanding of how new economy tools are transforming the mining industry."

The Goldcorp Challenge taught McEwen an important lesson about knowledge as an economic asset: Knowledge is an abundant not a scarce resource. Before the contest, Goldcorp was mired in an Industrial Age mindset that believes organizations need to compete for scarce resources and should hold their most important knowledge as proprietary to maintain their competitive advantage. McEwen learned that, because knowledge is an abundant resource, the only way that it grows is by giving it away. He was amazed at the number of innovative ideas that Goldcorp received back by making its once-proprietary data available on the Internet. By sharing its trade secrets with the world's scientific community, Goldcorp was able to tap into a rich diversity of technical expertise beyond the borders of its organization, and in the process, significantly expanded the wealth of its corporate knowledge in addition to paring two to three years from its expected exploration time. "We have done something nobody has ever done in the mining industry and in the process fundamentally changed the way Goldcorp thinks about mining," says McEwen. "We have created a new exploration frontier for Red Lake and have given the international mining community a model to work with that we have proven to be successful."

Collective learning competency is essential for wiki-management leaders. If corporations are serious about managing at today's pace of change and organizing around knowledge and speed, embracing the new power of electronic learning platforms is one way that organizations can quickly access the potent resource of collective knowledge. Today Goldcorp continues to profit from its collective learning venture. A one hundred dollar investment in the company in 1993 was worth about $3,000 in 2006.[12] But the most enduring benefit for the Canadian company is that a plodding Industrial Age mining firm, more interested in looking smart than being smart, transformed itself into an innovative Digital Age juggernaut. The Goldcorp Challenge is a testament to today's reality that the smartest company is the one that has quick access to collective knowledge.

CHANGING CORPORATE CONVERSATIONS

The recent developments in systems technology, especially within the past decade, have created an extraordinary capacity for facilitating collective learning. Through the power of electronic learning platforms, organizations now have timely and unprecedented access to a global reservoir of information. However, while a growing number of businesses are making exponential progress in developing systems technology to access the invaluable collective intelligence of customers and professional peers beyond their walls, an abundant reservoir of collective wisdom in the very backyard of organizations remains largely undiscovered because companies are lacking in the social technology needed to tap into this rich resource. What is amazing is that this untapped reservoir requires no financial investment because it's already fully paid for. What it does require is a radical shift in the social technology of the company and in the personal preferences of the managers. This rich abundant resource is the collective knowledge of an organization's own workers.

Accessing this collective knowledge is only possible if managers have the courage to radically change their corporate conversations. With the recent transition into the Digital Age, conversation has taken on much greater importance in the execution of work as it replaces the assembly line as the fundamental catalyst that propels the corporation. In an age where the challenge of organizing large numbers of people has shifted from leveraging the machines to leveraging the networks, tightly controlled top-down conversational norms will not get the job done. The persuasive tactics and savvy negotiations so common in the advocacy debates of traditional committee-style meetings are incompatible with the active listening and deep inquiry necessary for competent collective learning.

Mass collaboration is all about open conversations in many different electronic and interpersonal forums. The advances in technology brought about by the proliferation of the Internet means it is impossible to control the conversations anymore. That's why, for example, it is increasingly difficult for governments to spin or conceal events within their borders when anyone can view live video on YouTube. The days of scripted conversations are over.

Unfortunately, the first evidence of the futility of controlling conversations is being lost on traditional organizations as they struggle to attract the talented younger workers they so very much covet. Even when they entice recent graduates to join the company, they can't seem to retain the younger talent much beyond a year or two. For the brief time that younger workers are with traditional organizations, it's a mutually difficult experience. The most common complaints heard from the corporate bosses is that today's younger workers don't know how to learn, they don't speak up and participate in meetings, and they spend all their time fingering their PDA's.

Traditional managers are insistent that the current generation of younger workers, much like the many cohorts before them, needs to learn the corporate ways of order and authority. They expect this first vanguard of instant messengers to adapt to the conversational norms and practices of Industrial Age committee-style meetings and view their unwillingness to conform as a serious learning disability. Nothing could be farther from the truth. What is really happening is that we are witnessing a clash of mindsets with very different views about learning.

Today's younger workers are the first generation raised with the new network mindset and also the first generation reared in parallel education systems. In addition to their participation in the regular formal education system, they have been schooled on the ways of mass collaboration on the Internet. While applications such as Twitter and Facebook may appear trivial to older generations, these interactive innovations are imparting transferable collaboration skills that will mature into economic value as the millennials become mainstream in the new wiki-management organizations. After all, with their almost innate aptitude in computer technology, they already are the first generation of children to teach their parents about something of economic value.

On the Internet, everyone's voice is equal, anyone can make a contribution, and you can learn from all kinds of people. In cyberspace, if you have an idea or workable knowledge, then your voice counts. This new generation of workers finger their PDA's, are silent in committee-style meetings, and quickly leave traditional organizations because they know a better way of working and learning together and they won't settle for less. Fortunately for them, they don't have to acquiesce because there are real options for them as more companies are transitioning to the new work of the Digital Age, discovering the power of collective knowledge, and truly opening up the conversations.

The inability of traditional organizations to attract and retain younger workers is becoming so troublesome that some companies are considering programs to hire back retired workers on a part-time basis. However, these programs will only postpone the issue because the retirees will inevitably move on or pass away and the ranks of network-minded knowledge workers will only continue to grow.

If organizations want to sustain themselves in the new wiki world, they will need to open up the conversations, and do everything in their power to discover what they don't know that they don't know. In the age of knowledge and speed, executives can't afford the cultivation of "blind spots" or the impediments to change that come with the corporate conversational norms and practices of a century-old management model.

As more organizations discover the astonishing power of systems technology to open up the world of collective knowledge, expectations will be raised for what happens when managers and workers gather in the same room. The ever-widening gap between the advances in 21st century systems technology and the stagnation of century-old social technology will force everyone inside organizations to wonder why, when they are able to quickly collaborate in cyberspace with all kinds of people from all over the globe, is it so hard to get anything done whenever they get together in the same room.

The answer goes back to Surowiecki's four conditions of diversity of opinion, independent thinking, local knowledge, and aggregation mechanisms. Electronic learning platforms work because they are containers in which organizations are able to effectively integrate the specialized and localized points of view of a large variety of people who are free to express their opinions and whose voices are equally heard. These four conditions are generally not present when individuals gather in the typical corporate meeting. Electronic learning platforms work because they minimize the pitting of one point of view versus another and maximize the building of ideas on top of each other. In an electronic learning platform, there is no notion of who is right or who is wrong; there is only the search for the best in everyone's ideas. This systems technology achieves a level of dialogue that is not present in the social technology of the typical corporate meeting. If corporate gatherings in physical space are to equal the access to collective knowledge that is now possible in cyberspace, then the social technology around how we conduct meetings needs to promote dialogue.

Dialogue happens when diverse points of view are brought together in a forum where there is an effective process for integrating the ideas and opinions of all the participants into a collective consensus. However, dialogue is not as easy as it sounds. In fact, dialogue in face-to-face conversations is very difficult and challenging. The degree of listening and the capacity for the suspension of initial judgments that are necessary for dialogue rarely happen naturally in small group conversations and almost never in large group meetings. For this reason, changing the corporate conversations will require that meetings be facilitated. Given the long history of committee-style meetings where the natural tendencies are to advocate strongly held positions, to interrupt and talk over each other, to dismiss each other's ideas, and to debate rather than build on each other's thinking, a new social technology that employs facilitator leaders will be needed if large group gatherings in the same physical space are to be containers that meet the four conditions necessary for quickly accessing collective knowledge.

GE's Work-Out meetings, which we discussed in Chapter 7, are so effective because they meet these conditions. The large number of participants, usually between 40 – 100 workers, assures that the discussions benefit from the full diversity of different points of view as well as the specialized and localized intelligence of contributors who are both close to the customers and the actual work. The use of professional facilitators encourages a safe environment for independent thinking and the free expression of ideas in addition to the benefit of practitioners skilled in leading group dynamic exercises that help to aggregate the collective wisdom of the group.

The Work-Thru process, which we also described in Chapter 7, is another example of how face-to-face conversations can be effective pathways to collective knowledge. You will recall that the defining idea behind Work-Thrus is training executive leaders to be competent facilitators to assure an effective connection between organizational learning and business execution. Transitioning the role of the leader from boss to facilitator can be very challenging when an executive is used to getting things done by pulling the levers of order and authority. When executives serve as Work-Thru facilitators, their primary job is to listen and to learn by guiding the participants to their own sense of their collective knowledge, following the four cardinal rules of Work-Thrus. This means the executive facilitators have to fight the urge to impose order when, inevitably, chaos and confusion present themselves in the early stages of the session. Instead, they need to create the conditions where the participants can work through ambiguity and complexity by practicing the discipline of clarifying questions, by making it safe for all individuals to express their ideas, and by guiding a process of dialogue where people can build on each other's thoughts and ideas and discover their collective knowledge.

Perhaps the most difficult transition for the executive facilitator is the commitment to not express his own opinions during Work-Thrus. This is critical because, should the leader express his own thinking, many of the participants are likely to alter their views or keep their thoughts to themselves, and, as a result, access to collective knowledge will be greatly diminished, if not lost altogether. The role of the executive facilitator is not to exert his influence over the group's thinking, but rather to lead the group to discover its own collective wisdom. It is when managers learn to sometimes set aside their own ideas and opinions that they are able to make the transition from boss to facilitator and become skilled in the social technology of collective learning.

Work-Thrus are powerful vehicles for quickly accessing collective knowledge because they also satisfy Surowiecki's four conditions. When preparing for a Work-Thru, the most important activity for the executive facilitator is determining who will be the 25 – 50 participants in the session. The Work-Thru participants need to be a microcosm of the relevant business process with representatives from every function and level. This assures that the group is both diverse and localized with a variety of points of view from a wealth of specialized perspectives. The executive facilitator safeguards the independence of everyone's thoughts and opinions by orchestrating a free and productive flow of ideas. Through the focused deliverables of the small group exercises and the skillful facilitation of the large group discussions, the executive leader guides the participants on a learning journey as the group aggregates its own thinking and discovers its collective knowledge.

Traditional managers often scoff at the thought of checking in with large groups of workers and say they simply don't have all the time it would take to build consensus, especially when they are feeling the stress of accelerating change. However, the truth is not that they don't have the time; it's that they don't have the skills. When managers take a little time and are competent in accessing the collective wisdom of their workers, they are able to facilitate highly productive meetings that change the corporate conversations and accomplish great things in short periods of time.

The new management responsibility for collective learning radically changes the nature of the challenge of managing large numbers of people. The challenge is no longer about planning and controlling complex sets of corporate activities as if business were nothing more than one big machine. In the wiki world, the new challenge of managing large numbers of people is about getting the most out of knowledge networks and having the business processes to quickly learn and aggregate the collective wisdom contained in the decentralized observations of both customers and workers, and then using this learning to build a shared understanding to guide strategy and execution.

As we progress deeper into the Digital Age, more managers will come to understand that they can no longer survive by assuming the role of engineers and controllers manipulating the levers of order and authority. Managing at the new pace of change means that managers are now pathfinders and facilitators leading their organizations in partnership with their workers on collective quests for knowledge and speed in service of their customers. Managers skilled in both the social and the systems technologies of collective learning understand well that the smartest company is the one with quick access to collective knowledge and they also fully appreciate that, now more than ever, nobody is smarter than everybody.

Chapter 9

THE THIRD RESPONSIBILITY:
SHARED UNDERSTANDING

Shared Understanding is not the same as "same under-standing." It's about agreeing on disagreements.

- Eugene Eric Kim[1]

Execution is the bottom line of business, and consistency is the prime attribute of execution. If a company does not consistently deliver quality products on time, it won't be in business for very long. The same holds true for executives. If a business leader wants to keep her job, she needs to deliver consistent results. Customers don't want unpleasant surprises when they purchase goods and services; they expect a company to consistently deliver on its brand promise. And when a business continually meets or exceeds consumer expectations, its brand becomes the customers' bond, and that bond delivers the bottom line.

Maintaining consistency is one of the biggest challenges of any business. In the small businesses of the Agrarian Age, farmers and craftsmen could personally observe all aspects of work as it was performed. Because they knew everyone in their small enterprises, they were well aware of whether quality and production were on target. If something was awry, they could correct it immediately because all the work was within their sight. In the small business, observation is the driver of consistency.

As work transitioned from the farm to the factory with the advent of the Industrial Age, managing the challenge of consistency became much more difficult. The ascent of the corporation and the need to organize the work of large numbers of people meant that it was impossible for corporate owners to personally observe all the work. Because they still needed to know if quality was on target and production was on schedule, the early corporations developed sophisticated control structures that employed an array of bosses organized into hierarchical reporting arrangements with top-down communication protocols to direct the work and bottom-up reporting requirements to provide the owners with the information they needed to assure themselves that the mass production processes were working as planned. In the Industrial Age corporation, control became the driver of consistency.

Over the years, the effectiveness of these control structures reinforced the notion that authoritative take-charge leaders are essential for achieving consistent results. According to this widely held belief, bosses make the corporate world go around, and without them organizations would quickly fall into disarray and chaos. Deep down, whether they like their bosses or not, most people in large organizations believe that somebody's got to be in charge and everybody has to report to somebody or nothing will get done. Somebody's got to have the "big picture" and coordinate the scores of activities that need to come together if there is to be any hope for delivering consistent results. Most of us simply cannot conceive of an organization without bosses.

In the command-and-control organization, effective communication between the bosses and the workers is seen as the key ingredient for successfully bringing all the work together. When things work well in large organizations, most individuals will cite good communication as the reason why. They will tell you that everyone understands what they're doing and why they're doing it. Unfortunately, good communication seems to be more the exception than the rule inside most large businesses and is becoming more problematic as the pace of change continues to accelerate. The common sentiment heard among workers inside many traditional organizations today is frustration with the almost complete lack of communication. And nothing frustrates knowledge workers more than not understanding what they're doing or, more importantly, why they're doing it.

In a survey of over five million people over 22 years, Franklin-Covey has found that most workers rate managers low on their ability to provide focus and clear direction.[2] This means that, in the typical company, most people couldn't tell you what the corporate goals are and, therefore, lack the clarity to easily connect their day-to-day work with the corporate mission. When the frustrations and the lack of clarity begin to adversely affect business results and can no longer be ignored, the usual management response to the chorus of complaints is always the same: more meetings, more memos, and more reports. In other words, when the voices of complaints from the workers about poor communications reach a crescendo, the bosses' response is to amplify their own voices through the reengineering of one-way communication channels. Managers assume that, if they are more vocal, then the complaints from the workers will go away. However, far more often than not, this assumption turns out to be false, and despite the bosses' efforts to be more informative, the complaints of poor communications persist. The lesson from this common recurrent experience seems lost on traditional managers: Increasing one-way top-down communications rarely solves communication problems. Transforming the fundamental systems of interaction among managers and workers and changing the nature of corporate conversations is usually what's needed. Effective communication is almost never a one-way process, especially in the Digital Age.

KNOWLEDGE WORKERS

The continuing shift from manual workers to knowledge workers means that workers can no longer be fully productive by merely being told what to do. In the early days of the Industrial Age, when work was about leveraging the machines, this was possible. There was a right way to run the machines of the assembly line and there was a right sequence of activities, and, if manual workers performed their tasks as instructed by the bosses, both the workers and the assembly line were indeed incredibly productive. However, now that work is primarily about leveraging networks, we are discovering that knowledge workers are most productive when they manage themselves. They don't need to be told what to do. Rather what they do require is to understand how their contributions fit into the larger corporate mission and how they add value to meeting or exceeding customer expectations. Relying on a hierarchy of authoritative take-charge bosses to relay information up and down a chain of command does not necessarily drive consistency when traditional control structures can't keep pace with the speed of change and when the workers are often smarter than the bosses.

Knowledge workers are very different from the industrial workers and the farmers who came before them. The workers of both the Agrarian and the Industrial Ages primarily toiled with their hands, applying skills and becoming experts in a relatively fixed and simple body of knowledge learned on the job. Once trained, their acquired knowledge and skills remained essentially constant throughout their work lives. Knowledge workers, on the other hand, engage in a substantial amount of formal education before they even begin a day of work. Their knowledge is evolving and complex and much of what they learn in their initial education is obsolete in less than five years. Consequently, knowledge workers are constantly involved in formal and informal venues of continuing education.

Unlike industrial workers and farmers whose trade and expertise is generic and standard, the know-how of knowledge workers is highly specialized. As a result, the typical knowledge worker knows more about the fabric of her tasks than her boss. While workers were often taken for granted in the Industrial Age corporation because skills were easily transferable, Digital Age managers need to cultivate partnerships with their workers and treat them as highly valued volunteers if they want to retain their specialized knowledge. Control is not the best driver of consistency when the workers are smarter than the bosses and the pace of change is accelerating.

Knowledge workers do not need bosses to tell them how to do their work either. They don't need to be tightly managed because they are very capable of "connecting the dots" between their activities and those of their co-workers once they understand the framework of what needs to be done. When they have this understanding, they are more likely to be fully engaged in their work because their efforts are more directed by what they are working toward rather than whom they are working for. There are not many knowledge workers who get psyched up on their way to work in anticipation of finding out what the boss has planned for them today.

Full engagement happens when workers are allowed to manage their own work and to independently connect with the purpose of their contribution. Unfortunately, in extensive polling with approximately three million workers over the last 25 years, the Gallup Organization has found that only 29 percent of American workers are engaged in their work.[3] The remaining 71 percent are either not engaged, or worse yet, actively disengaged. In fast changing times, no organization can expect to keep pace with only 3 out of 10 workers engaged. This means that as companies come to terms with the new demands of the Digital Age, one of the greatest challenges facing managers today is how to increase the full engagement of knowledge workers.

While managers may be tempted to drive greater worker engagement through improved management communication, we already know that increasing top-down communications doesn't make a difference. The only way to increase the engagement of knowledge workers is for managers to embrace the new reality that, in the wiki world, everyone has a need-to-know and everyone needs to be part of the corporate conversation. Corporate knowledge can no longer be restricted to the elite few and doled out in carefully scripted communiqués. All of the company's knowledge needs to be available to all the managers and workers in multimedia formats. Most importantly, the collective knowledge gleaned from advances in both systems and social technologies needs to be immediately available to everyone via business processes that expand and transform collective knowledge into a broader shared understanding across the corporation. In the Digital Age, shared understanding is the new driver of consistency.

Shared understanding is the vehicle that allows knowledge workers to connect the dots between their work and the larger picture. It is also the missing ingredient that will catapult knowledge worker engagement and will provide organizations with full access to the new means of collaboration.

Shared understanding is essential to managing in the Digital Age because it is this business discipline that assures that an organization remains continually connected to the means of collaboration as workers move from company to company. If organizations persist in maintaining their preoccupation with control, they may one day find themselves disconnected from critical knowledge assets when they finally realize that knowledge workers don't want to work with them. It is then that they will discover that managing the challenge of consistency is impossible when you're disconnected from the means of collaboration. If corporations want to survive in the wiki world, they will have no choice but to embrace shared understanding as the new driver of consistency. This means that managers will need to open up the corporate conversations and engage their workers as partners, not subordinates. Most importantly it means that managers have to give up being bosses.

KNOWLEDGE MANAGEMENT

In the Industrial Age, shared understanding wasn't necessary. There was no need to partner with workers to fully understand the work. Managers already knew everything that they needed to know. After all, they owned the machines and they designed the assembly line. Workers were subordinates, and the only thing that industrial laborers needed to understand was what their bosses wanted them to do and then to do what they were told. When the means of production was the primary vehicle for creating economic value, organizational management was about directives and controls, and asset management was about maintaining sufficient capital and keeping the machines running and up-to-date. Now that the workers own the new means of collaboration, management's job is to maintain access to individual and collective knowledge and to build shared understanding. Thus, while maintaining sufficient capital is still an important goal, the new requirement for asset management in the wiki-management organization is knowledge management.

While knowledge management has become a topic du jour and organizations are embarking on new corporate initiatives to keep up with current management trends, few companies truly grasp just what knowledge management is all about. Most of these new initiatives are data storage exercises to record and catalog current and historical factual information. In the thinking of the machine mindset, knowledge management is a massive library effort that leverages the power of an electronic assembly line to make facts and figures instantly available in any format a user could possibly want. While generating instant information certainly provides valuable analytical input, these corporate initiatives are merely information retrieval applications. The essential work of knowledge management is about leveraging networks and building shared understanding, and has as much to do with social technology as it does with systems technology.

Knowledge is uniquely different from other types of economic assets, and thus, the normal asset management rules do not apply. When managing plant, property, or equipment, the goal of asset management is to preserve and grow scarce resources through ownership, investment, and acquisition. The proprietary accumulation of wealth through legal ownership has been the long-standing charge of asset managers. Knowledge, however, is an abundant resource, and the only way it grows is by giving it away. Holding knowledge as proprietary only diminishes its value over time. Knowledge is most valuable when it is commingled with other knowledge. Although it may seem counterintuitive, when knowledge is shared, especially in networks, everyone's intelligence is increased and all the contributors get far more back than they give away. This is the surprising lesson, as we saw in Chapter 8, that Goldcorp discovered when it posted all of its previously proprietary information on the Internet. By commingling its knowledge with the intelligence of the global community of geologists, Goldcorp was able to locate the hidden treasure of its gold reserves and restore itself to profitability. When it comes to knowledge, the Goldcorp experience clearly demonstrates that, unlike capital or tangible property, owning the asset doesn't necessarily produce wealth. This explains why knowledge workers will always need to partner with corporations or other knowledge workers. In a networked world, knowledge produces wealth when it is shared and aggregated with other knowledge.

Ralph Welborn and Vince Kasten observe that knowledge is nonconsumable, which means, "the more you use it, the more there is to use."[4] Thus, while facilities and equipment tend to depreciate with use, knowledge always appreciates when it is shared. Wilborn and Kasten also point out that knowledge is also nonrevocable, that is, "once someone has it, it cannot be taken away."[5] This means that knowledge cannot be exclusively and legally owned. While you can dispossess somebody of property, you cannot dispossess knowledge. Keep in mind that knowledge should not be confused with intellectual property rights, which apply to particular works, inventions, or brands through the ownership of copyrights, patents, or trademarks. A copyright, for example, preserves the legal rights of an author to exclusively distribute her particular analysis of an industry market segmentation study, and to sell those rights if she so chooses. However, this does not prevent a reader from using the knowledge contained in that analysis to deliver products that better meet the customer value sets identified in that analysis. The written report is proprietary and protected by copyright, but the knowledge discovered in the analysis is nonrevocable.

Because knowledge is abundant, nonconsumable, and nonrevocable, the fundamental work of knowledge management is about building processes to continually access the rich reservoir of workers' knowledge and to quickly share this knowledge throughout the organization. This will not be accomplished through top-down communication activities or massive data storage projects, but rather will require the interactive processes of a new social technology where workers are able to contribute their knowledge and influence the consensus around the work to be done.

The basic tasks of knowledge management are collective learning and shared understanding. Collective learning provides the capacity to quickly access collective knowledge and shared understanding is the vehicle for using collective knowledge to build consensus around the framework of the work to be done. When these tasks of knowledge management are performed well, workers have the necessary frame of reference to connect the dots between their work and the corporate mission, and it is this frame of reference that is so essential for driving consistency in the Digital Age.

SHARED UNDERSTANDING

One of the most common platitudes in corporate America proudly proclaimed in countless executive speeches and annual reports is the affirmation that "our people are our greatest asset." While the sentiment is often well intentioned, there are two troubling enigmas with this predilection. First, the statement is usually more lip service than fact because most organizations, as workers are usually aware, are lacking in the basic business infrastructure or corporate culture to back up the belief. The second anomaly is more subtle and perhaps more revealing of managers' true feelings. Referring to the workers as "our greatest asset" is the same as saying that people are "our most prized possessions" – and therein lies the problem. No matter how benevolent the intention, the statement is off the mark for the simple reason that the corporations do not own the people.

Workers, especially knowledge workers, are not assets, and they don't want to be treated as human resources available for disposal at the discretion of the bosses. Workers want to be treated as partners in service of a common business purpose. They want to contribute their knowledge, and they want their voices to be heard. They also need to understand how their work fits into the larger business picture, and they hanker to know the satisfaction of achieving results that make a difference in customers' lives. People are not assets – the knowledge of the people is the asset. And it is the workers, not the corporations, who own this critical asset.

Managers are much more comfortable viewing workers as assets because they are used to controlling assets. If workers are partners, then they are essentially volunteers, and you can't command or control volunteers. Managers prefer to be in charge and like it better when the workers are dependent on the bosses. However, given the recent ascent of knowledge as the new means for creating economic value, managers will need to lessen their reliance upon managerial control practices, adopt the new social technology of shared understanding, and embrace their workers as true partners.

The first rule of shared understanding is that the understanding is shared and not mandated. In wiki-management organizations, the leaders don't inform the workers what they need to understand in a memo. They engage the workers in forums of cross-functional teams where the participants are invited to speak candidly, where all voices are equally heard, where anyone is free to agree or disagree without political repercussions, where the managers and the workers are jointly accountable to each other, and where consensus is achieved through state-of-the-art social technology that promotes dialogue and the rapid integration of the best of everyone's thinking. Only when this consensus is reached will the organization be ready to document the shared understanding in a memo. When it comes to conveying shared understanding, memos are the last step – not the first step – in the communication process.

After meetings, memos are the next most dysfunctional activity inside traditional organizations. Memos are the epitome of the one-way communication channel and are reflective of the paucity of the social technology in the command-and-control organization. The typical memo is either a command document that expects no response and only compliance or is an advocacy argument prepared for the record (whatever that is!) that often results in a series of back-and-forth written jousts that are far more likely to promote entrenched positions than shared understanding. The typical corporate grumbling and wrangling that flows from the inevitable misunderstandings inherent in these penned pronouncements often leads only to confusion and procrastination as far too much time and effort are redirected from value-adding activities to internal political distractions. When the market demands that organizations are built for knowledge and speed, reliance on memos as the primary communication tool is usually counterproductive. Tapping into the rich asset of collective knowledge and expanding this resource into a broad-based shared understanding to drive consistent execution will challenge executives to abandon the traditional memo and venture into the new social technology of the Digital Age. Shared understanding isn't something executives mandate; it's something they facilitate.

TOWN HALL CONFERENCE CALLS

When I was with the Blue Cross Blue Shield Federal Employee Program (FEP) and we first began using Work-Thrus to access the collective knowledge of the staff throughout the various independent Blue

Cross and Blue Shield Plans, we were concerned about whether or not
the insightful learnings and the innovative ideas discovered by the 40
– 50 Work-Thru participants would translate well to the thousands of
workers scattered throughout all 50 states. Work-Thrus would be of
no value if we only advanced the understanding of 50 people. If we
were to successfully manage at the new pace of change, we needed a
vehicle to quickly and cohesively cross pollinate the collective knowledge of the Work-Thru participants with the working knowledge of
the thousands of people responsible for the day-to-day work into a
shared understanding that would drive consistent business execution.
Given the extraordinary level of innovation that can emerge from
Work-Thrus, we were certain that communication by memorandum
fiat would only produce mass misunderstanding. We needed to facilitate a broad-based shared understanding, and we needed to do it fast.

As we searched for a solution, we noted that the dynamic that
drove both the penetrating insights and the incredible speed of Work-
Thrus was the power of having everybody in the same room at the
same time in facilitated conversations. Effective conversation, where
the members of a cross-functional team reach agreements on disagreements, is the catalyst that makes Work-Thrus work. Well, we
began to think, what if we could bring together all the interested
workers all over the nation into the same conversation? What if we
could, in effect, gather everybody into the same room at the same time
into a facilitated dialogue? Thus, we created the second innovation in
our social technology: the "Town Hall Conference Call." These calls
were generally two hours in length and were open to anyone in the
Blue Cross and Blue Shield organizations who worked with FEP. Our
hope was that simulating the same dynamic of open conversation
with everybody "in the same room at the same time" would work as
well in a conference call as it did in a Work-Thru room. Nevertheless,
we were concerned that, should the dynamics not translate to a conference call, we might generate nothing more than the worst form of
mass confusion that any of us had ever seen. But given that we already
knew that the alternative of communicating by memo was guaranteed
to produce confusion, we decided that going ahead with Town Hall
Conference Calls was worth the risk.

As with Work-Thrus, an executive facilitator, whose exclusive role
is to guide the conversation process, moderates Town Hall Conference Calls. The executive facilitator opens the conference call by
introducing the topic for discussion and providing an overview of

how the call will work. For those conference calls convened to share the results of a Work-Thru, the call begins with a presentation by one of the Work-Thru participants, who summarizes the key issues and conclusions of the Work-Thru session. In Town Hall Conference Calls, presentations are also delivered without interruption to effectively seed the discussion. Following the presentation, the executive facilitator invites questions or comments from any of the participants on the call. The remainder of the conference call is a dialogue between the callers and many of the original Work-Thru participants where questions are answered, suggestions that build on the outcomes of the Work-Thru are clarified, unaddressed concerns are identified and handled, and the initial consensus constructed in the Work-Thru room is extended into a shared understanding among the conference call participants.

Given our past experience with the ineffectiveness of memos as conduits for innovative ideas and our concern that the calls could backfire and produce mass confusion, we were pleasantly surprised at how amazingly effective the Town Hall Conference Calls promoted a practical shared understanding. Time and again, the conference calls proved themselves to be very effective communication vehicles. This is not to say that everyone on the calls readily accepted every Work-Thru idea. While most times this was true, there were occasions when the callers would disagree or offer suggestions, and we would wind up modifying the Work-Thru conclusions based on a consensus of everyone on the call. This was easily possible because, in sharing the results from a Work-Thru, we were not advocating a position; we were sharing ideas. If someone could build on the initial thinking of the Work-Thru and offer a modification or a better idea, their contributions were welcome. On those calls where the participants readily accepted the Work-Thru results, we quickly achieved a workable shared understanding that drove consistent execution far better and far faster than traditional command memos. And in the instances where the callers modified the Work-Thru results and helped to create an even better shared understanding, we were grateful for having identified issues or anomalies that could have impeded execution before the actual work had begun.

When managers take the time at the beginning of projects or initiatives to slow down and involve everyone affected in building a broad-based shared understanding, the result is a powerful tool that drives speedy and consistent execution. The time invested in finding common ground and treating workers as partners always pays itself back many times. Managers who experience firsthand the power of shared understanding learn a valuable lesson about managing in fast changing times: You have to slow down to move fast. When workers know that their voices count and when managers have the social technology to quickly access collective knowledge and build a widespread shared understanding, then organizations are ready and able to successfully manage at the new pace of change.

As we continued to be surprised by the effectiveness of the Town Hall Conference Calls, we soon realized that it was actually the way we processed ideas in Work-Thrus that enabled the speedy path to shared understanding across the workers. In the days when we used to develop new initiatives through central planning and via top-down communications, we generally had to spend a great deal of time defending our approach and getting everyone on board. The time consuming process of negotiations and compromises subsequent to sending the memo often felt like "herding cats." This changed dramatically after we began to use Work-Thrus and Town Hall Conference Calls because we replaced central planning with collective learning to steer both strategy and execution. By assembling a diversity of perspectives in the facilitated conversations of the Work-Thrus, all the various interests and points of view were effectively integrated into the developing consensus because everything in Work-Thrus is worked out with everybody in the same room at the same time. As a result, when the nuances of the issues and the collective thinking of the Work-Thru participants were put in context during the presentations in Town Hall Conference Calls, each of the callers was able to see how her particular interests were integrated into the Work-Thru consensus. Thus, the typical response of the conference call participants was usually to acknowledge and accept the good sense of the Work-Thru consensus.

As we became more proficient in facilitating Town Hall Conference Calls, we found other opportunities to use this new and powerful tool. Perhaps the most significant application involved the installation of a new claims processing system throughout 2002. In the health insurance industry, the claims processing system is the operational core of the business. With continual developments in the world of systems technology, health insurers need to overhaul and replace their claims systems every 10 – 15 years. FEP's previous systems replacement in 1985 had not gone smoothly, had been fraught with several major problems, and it took almost a full year to solve all the issues before the system was fully functional. Installing a new system in FEP is a particular challenge because the business is actually an alliance of all the independent Blue Cross and Blue Shield Plans, which means replacing the system is not one installation but rather 40 separate installations at each of the 39 Plans and the national Operations Center.

As we approached this challenge, we not only wanted to avoid the difficulties we had encountered in the 1985 installation, but we also had to stay on budget because of the requirements under our contract with the federal government. We knew this was an enormous task because our outside systems consultants had advised us that the failure rate for new computer systems across all industries was about 50 percent and that cost overruns were more the norm than the exception. Because we had to ensure that the system didn't fail and we had to stay on budget, we began to use the Town Hall Conference Calls as our primary communications channel during the installation of the new system.

The two-hour conference calls were held every week and were forums for updates, problem solving, and sharing of best practices. The facilitated conversations were open and candid. When you have to get it right the first time and on budget, there's no scripting of the conversations. Because we found a way to bring both the systems staff and the business staff together on the same call, the cross fertilization of learnings was immediate and comprehensive. This continuous interchange between systems and business staffs is unusual for the typical corporate initiative, which may explain the high failure rate of systems projects. Because systems requirements – like everything else in fast changing times – keeps evolving, continuous connection between the systems designers and the end users is essential if systems initiatives are to succeed. When you meet in two-hour conference calls in open conversations every week, a community of systems and business partners starts to form and the participants begin to find each other offline when issues arise. The shared understanding that evolved over the course of these conference calls drove a level of consistent execution that clearly exceeded our expectations. When we threw the switch on the new system on January 1, 2003, not only did the system work as designed, but it came in under budget as well.

While the Work-Thrus were the primary tool we used to access collective knowledge, it was the Town Hall Conference Calls that served as the primary vehicle for building shared understanding among the managers and workers in all the independent organizations that made up the FEP business alliance. These two innovative applications of Digital Age social technology formed the cornerstone of our transition from command-and-control to wiki-management. We set aside central planning and embraced collective learning; we replaced control with shared understanding as the driver of consistency; and we changed the corporate conversations to access the rich reservoir of the collective wisdom of all our managers and our workers. We learned the power of getting everybody – or at least a critical mass of everybody – in the same room at the same time. We also learned that managing at the new pace of change meant that we had to slow down to move fast. And finally, we learned that organizing for knowledge and speed was far more effective than organizing around order and authority.

Over the five-year period from 2001 to 2006, FEP increased its market share from 49 percent to 59 percent and improved operational performance by 33 percent while consistently keeping premium increases two to three percentage points below the national average. In meeting the challenge of organizing large numbers of people in fast changing times, shared understanding is indeed a far more effective driver of consistency than control.

SELF-ORGANIZED WORK

Management is the discipline of efficiently getting the right things done by organizing the work of large numbers of people. The masters of this discipline have an uncanny ability for orchestrating a seamless order from a cacophony of complexity. For most of the 20th century, the complexity challenge was defined as an organization's ability to handle a multitude of detail. The early successes of the first industrial executives in meeting this challenge solidified the assumption in the developing machine mindset that the only way to effectively manage the complexity of organizing the work of large numbers of people is through hierarchical organization. Thus, managers, emboldened by the thinking and the practices of scientific management, came to believe that the most effective way to handle business complexity was through a division of labor where the planning and organizing of work was accomplished by a small group of top executives, the coordination of the details of the necessary activities was delegated to a hierarchy of bosses, and the performance of the related tasks was carried out by functional workers who followed the instructions of their supervisors.

In the early years of the Industrial Age, the beliefs and assumptions of command-and-control management may have made sense because the original assembly line workers were not highly educated and were limited in their capacity to coordinate the then new complexities of the assembly line. Central planning and hierarchical authority probably were necessary in the first days of mass production. And even if there were alternative ways to organize the work of large numbers of people, hierarchical organizations were getting the job done and everyone's quality of life was dramatically improving. Who could argue with the incredible pace of progress? For a while it did work when the bosses organized the activities and the workers performed their tasks exactly as instructed.

However, by the late 20th century, it was obvious that much had changed since the early days of the first corporations. Better-educated knowledge and service workers had gradually replaced industrial workers. Over the years, a steady succession of business, operational and technological innovations had reshaped the business landscape. Yet, despite all this change and innovation, most executives still insisted on employing a century-old management model that's grounded in the belief that execution excellence is about workers doing what they're told.

If you want to bring an organization to its knees in today's business world, one of the quickest and most effective ways to accomplish this feat is to have the workers do exactly what they are told and only what they're told. If workers were to precisely follow the policies and procedures manuals, productivity in most organizations would grind to a halt. In fact, there are times where this tactic is used as a job action by unions to get management's attention. There are many times when the world doesn't fit with the policy manual nor conform to the boss's instructions. In these instances, workers need to apply common sense judgment to get work done.

Given today's pace of change, operational and technological innovations happen faster than the policy and procedure manual revisions. This is because the transition into the Digital Age has changed the complexity challenge. Managing complexity in fast changing times is no longer limited to keeping the details straight; it's also about keeping up with the dynamics of market developments that could redefine the details. That's why in the recording industry, the steps in the mass production of compact discs won't define tomorrow's details; they will be prescribed by the requirements of a new mass collaboration business model.

Fortunately, most companies are not yet feeling the full consequences of this shift in the complexity challenge because, despite the illusions of the bosses that they are in charge, many of today's knowledge and service workers are able to negotiate some of this complexity by finessing their bosses, by not doing everything they're told, and by finding ways to self-organize the work themselves out of the sight of their bosses. The simple fact is that a significant amount of the most important work in many organizations is self-organized today. But because the managers are not part of the collaboration process, companies are not benefiting from the full potential of self-organization as a business practice to successfully navigate the white water of accelerating change.

Self-organization is only possible when there is a shared understanding. In those instances where workers clandestinely self-organize out of the bosses' sight, they take the time to develop a consensus among themselves to get the job done in a politically acceptable way. However, because they are working "under the radar," their innovative shared understanding is usually limited to the small group that created the consensus. When workers have to go around the bosses, quietly access their own collective knowledge, and keep their shared understanding among themselves to avoid possible adverse political consequences, this is a clear sign that an organization is not doing a good job of knowledge management. While this clandestine self-organization may be saving some companies from themselves in these early years of the Digital Age, the limited collective knowledge and shared understanding crafted by small enclaves of workers "under the radar" will only work for so long. It's just a matter of time before the Digital Age and mass collaboration will redefine business in the 21st century, just as the Industrial Age and mass production shaped the enterprise of the 20th century.

With knowledge as the new means for creating economic value, the success of corporations in the new world of mass collaboration will depend upon the quality of their knowledge management. This changes the fundamental challenge of organizing large numbers of people. Because the two dimensions of knowledge management are collective learning and shared understanding and because the critical knowledge asset is owned by the workers, the fundamental relationship between companies and workers needs to evolve. As we rapidly move deeper into the wiki world, it won't be long before most businesses will suddenly discover that they have to abandon the politics of control and embrace the politics of partnership if they want to remain connected to the new means of collaboration. They will also quickly learn that bosses are not all that important when workers have both the technology and the capacity to self-organize their work. As further developments in technology create more options for knowledge workers to employ their knowledge, companies will need to accept the new business reality that, in the Digital Age, workers are partners and not subordinates.

As we discussed above, knowledge workers don't need bosses to tell them what to do or how to do it. They are very capable of self-organizing their work. What knowledge workers do need from organizational leaders is their facilitation of the creation of collective knowledge and the building of corporate-wide shared understanding. When leaders focus on knowledge management rather than micromanagement, they fully connect with the new means of collaboration, fully engage their knowledge workers, and avail themselves of the full benefits of shared understanding and self-organization to meet today's market imperatives for knowledge and speed. As more companies begin to experience the power of shared understanding as the new driver of consistency and witness the incredible efficiencies of self-organization, they will come to appreciate that, in the world of mass collaboration, leaders are not bosses but facilitators and that self-organizing teams operating from a shared understanding – not authoritative take-charge managers – are essential for achieving results. They will also learn to appreciate what seems so inconceivable to the practitioners of traditional management: It is possible to have organizations without bosses.

AN ORGANIZATION WITHOUT BOSSES

At W.L. Gore and Associates, there are no bosses and there never have been since the company was founded in 1958. For over 50 years, the makers of Gore-Tex and countless other innovative products have used shared understanding and self-organization to build a very successful learning organization with $2.5 billion in annual revenues and approximately 9,000 associates in 30 countries around the world.

With its consistent appearance on *Fortune* magazine's annual list of the "Best Companies to Work For" and its enviable track record of 50 consecutive years of profitability, Gore is living proof that corporations can organize large numbers of people into a sustainable business without bosses.

While Gore does have a CEO and a small number of designated leaders for its four divisions and its companywide support functions such as human resources and information technology, these leaders don't assign work to anyone.[6] Nobody at Gore – not even the CEO – tells anyone what to do or how to do it. There are no vice presidents or supervisors; there are only associates. Some of the associates may serve as leaders from time to time, but another leader never assigns this role. If you want to lead a project at Gore, you have to recruit followers. In true self-organizing form, the followers determine the leaders, and the leaders remain in their roles as long as they continue to maintain the respect and support of their peers.

For the most part, leadership at Gore is not a permanently assigned position, but rather a temporary role that is continually earned for as long as a particular project may last. And even when it comes to selecting who will fill those few designated leadership positions, the associates usually have a voice in the choice. Before Terri Kelly, the current CEO, was selected to replace the retiring Chuck Carroll, the board of directors polled a wide cross-section of Gore associates and asked them whom they'd be willing to follow. "We weren't given a list of names – we were free to choose anyone in the company," Kelly recalls. "To my surprise, it was me."[7]

When Bill Gore started his company in 1958, he had just concluded a 17-year stint with DuPont. He was familiar with the workings of traditional companies, and he knew that he wanted his new business venture to be different, especially in how people communicated with each other. Gore often said that, in hierarchical organizations, "communication really happens in the car pool," meaning that the car pool was the only place where people felt free to talk to each other without worrying about the chain of command.[8] In his new company, Gore did not want any impediments to conversations because he understood that the free interchange of ideas was the soil of innovation. Gore was clearly ahead of his time in recognizing that conversation would become the catalyst that would drive the corporation. And so, Gore built what he called a lattice organization where there would be no traditional organization charts, no chain of command, and no predetermined channels of communication. All work would be self-organized by teams and projects would be accepted rather than assigned. In Gore's lattice organization, workers are partners and volunteers who are accountable to their teams, rather than to a boss. Everyone is free to talk to anyone else in the organization, and there is no scripting of the conversations when Gore associates gather for meetings. Compensation is determined using a peer review process, similar to that used in law firms. Thus, the associates are rewarded based on their contributions to team success and they have an incentive to commit to more rather than less work.[9]

Bill Gore's organizational approach was extraordinarily innovative for the 1950's and a precursor of the wiki-management discipline of the coming Digital Age. There is no central planning at Gore and Associates. No single person or elite group determines strategy, sets the direction or drives execution. Strategy is determined by the collective wisdom of the associates and, because there are no bosses, no one individual can kill a good idea or keep a worthless project alive. All voices count at Gore and whether or not a project goes forward is determined by how many associates are willing to work on the proposition. Once a project goes forward, the self-organized team determines its own direction and its own requirements based on its own shared understanding.

Gore's consistent success over half a century is clear proof that the decentralized collective wisdom of workers is an alternative to the centralized planning of a managerial elite. However, as the focus of business continues to shift from mass production to mass collaboration, we are likely to find that companies such as Gore are better capable of managing at the new pace of change and responding to the market's increasing demands for knowledge and speed. While on the surface it may appear that Gore's approach to strategy and execution is haphazard and inefficient, their outstanding performance in developing innovative products across a variety of industries is testament to the reality that nobody is smarter or faster than everybody.

It is perhaps ironic that an engineer who was trained in the core scientific discipline of the machine mindset designed one of the first organizations built according to the ways of thinking of the network mindset. Bill Gore's lattice organization is probably the first American corporation built on the principles of wiki-management. Gore fashioned his organization on the platform of an innovative social technology designed to take full advantage of the collective wisdom of his many knowledge workers.

While he knew from his previous experiences at DuPont that bosses could drive results, Gore was convinced that the workers would achieve better results if his organization had the processes to hear and to aggregate all their perspectives. Without any bosses, there would be no one who could silence a voice or abuse the power of her position to coerce her point of view. By tying compensation to performance and then having a collective peer review process to determine each individual's pay, Gore assured that the associates would be working for and listening to each other as well as having an incentive to collaborate to produce the best results for the company. Gore understood that peer pressure is a far more effective motivator than pleasing the boss as long as you have the right social infrastructure.

Early on, Bill Gore learned that there were two prerequisites that were critical to using the collective wisdom of his workers to drive strategy and execution. The first is that all the different contributors needed to be together in the same place. This means that product design, sales, marketing, and production staffs work together in cross-functional teams so that everyone continually understands how their contributions shape and reshape the underlying business processes of the company's value proposition. Gore recognized the value of having everyone in the same room at the same time and the importance of having workers focused on collective processes rather than individual tasks.

Second, Bill Gore noticed that things got awkward when the number of workers reached about 150 – 200 people. There seems to be a tipping point in the human scale where the effectiveness of peer pressure and the physical ability to self-organize begins to break down.[10] When there are more than 200 people in the same location, the individuals don't feel as personally connected to each other and it becomes difficult even to know everyone's name. We can understand why, in the early factories of the Industrial Age, the owners resorted to hierarchical management to organize the work of large numbers of people. When the efforts of a sizable group of workers have to be brought together and they are so many that they can't possibly all know each other, the corporate pioneers of mass production felt that authoritative bosses were necessary to get the job done. Bill Gore, however, did not want to resort to the employment of bosses when he noticed the tipping point. Instead he put in place a simple practice to preserve his self-organizing management innovation that continues to this day. When a plant approaches 200 people, the group divides, and Gore opens another plant. The new plant may be a stone's throw from the original location, but nevertheless, each plant is completely autonomous to assure the human scale necessary for self-organization to work.

Bill Gore was very proud of the egalitarian principles and practices of his lattice organization. Gore wanted all associates to know that he considered them partners on a shared journey toward innovative excellence. Even though Gore and Associates is a privately held company, after their first year at Gore, new associates receive 12 percent of their salary in company stock, which the partners can cash out if they leave after they are fully vested.[11] The stock's appreciation depends on the company's ability to continue growing and its value is periodically determined by independent consultants.[12] At Gore and Associates, every worker is truly treated as a partner with a stake in the profits of the company.

Perhaps Bill Gore's greatest accomplishment is that his vision of a lattice organization without bosses lives on long after his death in 1986. Gore and Associates demonstrates that companies built around shared understanding and self-organization are not subject to the usual disruptions when successful leaders move on. Wiki-management organizations are not dependent upon star performers or heroic leaders because they have the capacity to quickly access collective knowledge. Succession planning and consistent execution are not issues when companies are guided by the collective wisdom and the shared understanding of the workers and when organizations truly appreciate that workers are partners, not subordinates.

Part Four

RESETTING
THE MEASURES

Chapter 10

FROM CONTROL TO TRANSPARENCY

Greater openness is the path to greater order.

- Margaret J. Wheatley
Leadership and the New Science[1]

A hundred years from now, when the economists, sociologists, and historians recap the course of progress throughout the 21st century, two of the major influences that they are likely to cite are the rise of the Internet and the advances in our knowledge of the complexity sciences. These learned scholars will probably reference how the Web revolutionized global commerce at the start of the century by creating unprecedented capacities for businesses to quickly access collective knowledge, facilitate expeditious organizational learning, and build effective shared understanding among large numbers of geographically dispersed workers. They will likely enumerate the many ways that mass collaboration reshaped every social institution as the world was progressively transformed into both a virtual and a physical global village.

The surveyors of our progress will also note that, while the decline of the machine mindset and the corresponding ascendance of the network mindset began with the spread of the Internet, it was the breakthrough scientific advances in the developing complexity sciences – especially in the emerging fields of biotechnology and network science – that escalated the dramatic shift in the prevailing social mindset during the first decades of the 21st century. Hopefully by then, our understanding will have evolved to the point where we will have a clear definition of the complexity sciences. However, while there is no commonly accepted definition today, there are clear differences that distinguish this new field of knowledge from the traditional reductionistic sciences.

The machine mindset of the Industrial Age traces its roots to the insights and discoveries of the 17th century scientist, Isaac Newton. In the world of Newton's classical physics, the whole is equal to the sum of the parts. Thus, the whole is best understood by studying the individual components and by identifying the linear relationships that determine the behavior of an entity. Classical physics is the prototypical framework of the reductionistic sciences. Even though its natural laws may be complicated, because the tenets of physics are both reliable and precise, we learn to see the world as a fairly predictable place. When the universe operates like clockwork, the mission of science is to discover nature's secrets by applying the scientific method to solve the intricacies of the precision formulae that govern the cosmos. It is this mission that defines the work of both the theoretical physicist and the practical engineer.

The significant expansion of our knowledge of physical laws throughout the 19th century is the foundation for the practical offshoot of physics, the modern discipline of engineering. Over the last century, this knowledge has shaped the way we see the world as the invention of a multitude of machines gave us an incredible capacity to master our everyday lives. The automobile and the airplane, in particular, reinforced the notion that, with the right machines, we could effectively control our environment. Because so many of us still see the world as essentially a machine, control continues to remain a prime social value.

However, in the universe of the complexity sciences, the whole is not equal to the sum of the parts. It is different from and is often greater than the aggregation of its components. The only way that the whole can be understood is by discovering the patterns of mutual causality that shape an entity's behavior. Unlike the workings of classical physics, a particular set of factors forming a pattern through mutual causality does not always produce the same result. This is because biology is the prototypical framework of the complexity sciences where phenomena are probabilistic and adaptable, and they follow the simple rules of the fractal laws of self-organization. Thus, these phenomena can never be fully understood by breaking them into their parts; their workings are inherently interdependent and can only be studied holistically. In the framework of the complexity sciences, the mission of science is to understand the secrets of self-organized growth and to identify the conditions and the simple rules that guide the evolution of complex adaptive systems. The great scientific developments of the 21st century will likely be practical applications of this new field of knowledge that will revolutionize the energy and the healthcare industries, dramatically improve the quality of our lives, and firmly establish the network mindset as the new prevailing worldview.

Neither the reductionistic sciences nor the complexity sciences are completely right or completely wrong in their understandings of how the world works. Their principles and laws just work in different circumstances and apply to different phenomena, sometimes related to the same event. For example, let's consider the extremely rare occurrence of a large meteor impact. If such an event were to become imminent, our understanding of the principles and the laws of physics would allow us to pinpoint the precise date of the impact years in advance. We would also be able to accurately predict the sequence of natural events that would unfold around the planet from the moment of the meteor strike to the subsequent resulting volcanic explosion hours later at the exact opposite end of the globe. The physical events associated with a large meteor impact follow deterministic laws that are highly precise and predictable.

What happens to life on the planet after impact is not so certain. While we know that anywhere from 50 to 90 percent of the world's species would become extinct and that, after thousands of years, new species would begin to emerge when the effects of the impact had dissipated, we cannot predict with any degree of precision what exact species would evolve in the reemergence of life on the planet. This is because the biological events associated with the development of new species follow probabilistic laws that are variable and evolutionary.

As our scientific knowledge continues to expand, we are learning that the laws of nature fall into at least two different paradigms and that these paradigms work very differently from each other. Thus, in the world of science, there is no single "theory of everything," which means that there is no one consistent set of natural laws that explains how the universe works. The laws that apply depend upon the phenomena of our investigation. If we are studying the solar system, we find a universe that is highly stable and predictable with properties, such as gravity, that reflect the workings of precise deterministic linear relationships that behave consistently, regardless of time and space. Thus, a plate that drops from a table in 17th century England falls at the same rate and hits the floor in the same amount of time as a plate that falls from a table in 21st century Japan. On the other hand, if we are studying cloud formations, we find a milieu that is variable and changing and that reflects the workings of adaptable self-organizing relationships where similar combinations of cloud cells behave differently depending upon their interactions with their environments. That's why weather forecasts are always presented as probabilities.

For the last 150 years, the machine mindset has assumed a socioe-conomic world that follows the laws and principles of reductionistic science. Because the primary task of the Industrial Age business has been to leverage machines and to maintain stability, the mechanistic paradigm of classical physics worked. However, as we transition into the Digital Age and as the primary task of business shifts to leveraging networks and managing innovation, executives will need to come to terms with the new reality that the mechanistic assumptions of an outdated mindset no longer fit today's business challenges. If they are to successfully manage large organizations in the new economy, today's managers need to master the insights from a new worldview more consistent with the principles and laws of an entirely different scientific paradigm.

TWO TYPES OF COMPLEX SYSTEMS

The basic difference between these two paradigms is that the components of the reductionistic sciences operate in complex stable systems while the phenomena of the complexity sciences operate in complex adaptive systems. A complex stable system is a closed system where the key to stability is to master all the mechanical details that need to come together to produce equilibrium. Thus, when building or flying airplanes, a comprehensive knowledge of all the detailed mechanical requirements for maintaining stable flight within a closed system structure is very appropriate. However, our understanding of how to operate complex stable systems has not only shaped the way we build and fly planes, but for well over a century, it has also influenced the way we have managed large organizations. The machine mindset assumes that business organizations are closed systems and that the fundamental job of management is to maintain the equilibrium of the company. Thus, traditional management structures assume that work can be subdivided into departments and that the way to manage complexity is to establish global control systems to centrally manage all the details. Accordingly, these systems are designed to provide regulatory feedback so that managers, like engineers and pilots, can apply immediate corrective action to restore balance.

A complex adaptive system, on the other hand, is an open system where self-managing agents, following the same set of simple nonlinear rules, create complex orderly patterns through an iterative interactive process among themselves and with the environment. These systems operate by generating evolutionary feedback to identify when it is time to make a change so they can successfully adapt to their changing circumstances. The human brain, cloud formations, colonies of ants, and flocks of birds are all examples of complex adaptive systems. A common attribute of these systems is that they do not rely on centralized control structures for accomplishing order, but rather depend upon the cooperative behavior of the interactive self-organizing agents to evolve high-order forms that no single agent could accomplish on its own.[2]

The Internet is another example of a complex adaptive system. There is no boss of the Internet or predetermined hierarchy to govern the collective behavior of the individual agents. Users are free to post pages and to link their websites with other pages to produce a highly effective and indispensible mosaic.

Because the horizontal business alliances of the Digital Age are far more likely to be open systems, a management model that relies exclusively on regulatory feedback to maintain the equilibrium of the established ways will not get the job done when managing innovation is the central business issue. Being innovative means knowing when to change and calls for the evolutionary feedback characteristic of complex adaptive systems.

COMPLEX ADAPTIVE SYSTEMS

Business sustainability in the fast-paced Digital Age calls for a new organizational paradigm. With their natural affinity for equilibrium and the status quo, hierarchical bureaucracies are ill-equipped to handle the issues of adaptation that inevitably accompany an accelerating pace of change. This is because, in fast changing times, business models can be turned upside down or, in some instances, can become quickly obsolete.

For example, have you noticed that people under 35 are far less likely to wear wristwatches than those of us who were born before the mid-1970's? When you live in a networked world, as the millennials do, the time is always available on your ever-present cell phone. Why would you need a separate timepiece? For decades, even though changes in style and technology required watchmakers to morph their products from mechanical jewel pieces to electronic digital devices, they could rely, until very recently, on the basic and stable premise of their century-old business model: People will always need a timepiece on their wrists. However, if watchmakers are going to sustain their businesses in the new networked world, they may have to reinvent their fundamental business model because their enduring standard could quickly become obsolete. To do this, they will probably also need to adopt a new organizational paradigm that better aligns with the reality that managing at the speed of change is only possible when your management model resembles a complex adaptive system.

Melanie Mitchell, in her excellent overview *Complexity: A Guided Tour*, defines a complex adaptive system as, "a system in which large networks of components with no central control and simple rules of operation give rise to complex collective behavior, sophisticated information processing, and adaptation via learning or evolution."[3]

Because the absence of central control is a pre-requisite for optimizing the performance of networks, pre-determined top-down hierarchies do not align well with complex adaptive systems. While it may be difficult for traditional leaders to let go of the status and the social power that comes with hierarchical positions, the sudden emergence of the Digital Age has redefined how power works in the most effective businesses. When the locus of power shifts from being in control to being connected, self-organized systems are far more effective than hierarchies.

Complex adaptive systems share three common organizing principles. The first is that intelligence resides in the whole system. This means that, while different agents may hold specific knowledge or differing interpretations of a common reality, no one agent is capable of processing all the information within the system. Self-organizing systems produce intelligence only when they have the capacity to process the diversity of knowledge that resides within the whole system. Thus, organizations are most intelligent when they have a rich diversity of perspectives and the means to access the collective intelligence derived from all the different points of view. This is in stark contrast to the conventional belief that the smartest organizations are those that identify the brightest among them and leverage their individual intelligence by giving them the power to define organizational thinking and to direct the activities of the many workers.

Gaining access to collective intelligence requires a sophisticated information processing capacity. In addition to the usual electronic information technology systems that all companies maintain, effective self-organization is only possible when businesses also have the ability to process the abundance of human intelligence distributed throughout the organization. This means that companies need to integrate social networking technology into their organizational processes as well as to embrace new forms of face-to-face meeting technologies, such as Work-Thrus, Work-Outs, and Open Space meetings. In most hierarchical organizations, this human dimension of information processing is generally lacking. However, as more executives come to appreciate that Digital Age businesses are essentially information processing networks, they will quickly learn that any company that cannot effectively process the full scale of its human intelligence is operating with a severe limitation. Margaret Wheatley wisely observes that "the greater the ability to process information, the greater the level of intelligence."[4] And in the wiki world, intelligence is the distinguishing competitive advantage.

The second organizing principle of complex adaptive systems is that simple rules guide complex collective behavior. This most important premise is completely counterintuitive to conventional wisdom. We usually think that complex structures will only work if we have detailed blue prints or a comprehensive set of rules and regulations. While this is usually true for mechanical tasks, it is not the way that biology works. In the organic world, the secret to the effective execution of complex tasks is that order is created by the collaborative application of a few simple rules rather than by compliance with a complex set of controls.

For example, James Surowiecki, in *The Wisdom of Crowds*, describes how a flock of birds accomplishes its group journey by creating a well-ordered formation that emerges from each of the birds following a set of four rules: 1) stay as close to the middle as possible; 2) stay two to three body lengths away from your neighbor; 3) do not bump into another bird; and 4) if a hawk dives at you, get out of the way.[5] By following this simple set of rules, the flock is able to self-organize its journey, reach its destination, and handle any predators it encounters along the way. There's no need for a dominant leader directing the activities of the flock when collaborative focus around a simple set of rules does a better job.

The self-organized flight of birds is just one of many examples from nature of how complex orderly structures emerge from a few simple rules and cooperative autonomous interactions. The high-order functionality of these complex adaptive systems clearly demonstrates that consistent execution does not necessarily require elaborate control structures. There are often circumstances where consistency is better served through the collaborative actions of self-organizing independent agents following a simple set of rules. Thus, one of the distinguishing features of complex adaptive systems is that responsibility for control and coordination rests with each of the individual agents rather than with one central executive.[6]

The third principle of self-organizing systems is that order emerges from the interaction of independent agents. In the organic world, there are no blue prints. Order is not preordained before the work begins, but rather emerges through an iterative process among the agents and their environment. Because organic processes are evolutionary, we can't know the result until it occurs. This is completely contrary to all the conventional wisdom about the importance of detailed planning for the consistent accomplishment of results. The notion that a large organization would approach an important initiative without a specific plan, and instead, let the results be defined by the interaction of the workers is completely contrary to a hundred years of accepted management practice. But this notion is precisely the secret behind the incredible effectiveness of Work-Thrus.

Work-Thrus incorporate all three of the organizing principles of complex adaptive systems. By assembling 25 – 50 people who represent a microcosm of the business, we embrace the notion that intelligence resides in the whole system, and we continually discover that there is nothing as powerful as getting everybody in the same room at the same time. The four cardinal rules for facilitating Work-Thrus, outlined in Chapter 7, effectively guide the complex collective behavior of our meeting process, enabling us to work through divisive and contentious issues with remarkable speed. Thus, within the span of two or three days, we are able access the rich reservoir of an organization's collective knowledge because we facilitate an emerging order using a process that cultivates dialogue and consensus rather than relying on the usual argumentative practices of supposedly healthy debates. By embracing a discipline where all voices are heard, where we have the capacity to quickly integrate differing ideas, and where the framework for action reflects a common ground of the best of everyone's thinking, we create a quick start to support the further iterations necessary to achieve the best solution possible. Unless companies have processes that recognize that the best order doesn't come from the a priori vision of the brightest among us, but rather emerges from the collaborative collective action of independent agents, they will be incapable of innovating at the speed of change.

CONTROL

Adopting the three organizing principles of complex adaptive systems as the foundation for building a management discipline is counterintuitive, incredibly uncomfortable, and just plain scary for leaders with long histories of managing by control. I can attest to this from personal experience. My own transformation from a hierarchical manager to a wiki-leader happened when I was suddenly given responsibility for an operation that needed quick improvement. As I surveyed the business and assessed what was working and not working, I quickly came to the conclusion that the primary root of the operational problems was the misplaced use of a hierarchical management model in a complex business alliance. I wasn't sure exactly what we needed to do differently, but I knew we had to make a dramatic change because the one thing that I knew for certain was that the continued use of a vertical management model in a horizontal business alliance was a guaranteed formula for failure.

Thus began a very personal business journey where I discovered that, in fast changing times, managing by control is an illusion and that the only way to drive consistency in a knowledge economy is to have the ability to quickly build a broad-based shared understanding among all the business partners. However, this was not as easy as it sounds, especially in the beginning. Before I could grow comfortable with using shared understanding to drive results, I had to first learn how to give up control. And that was hard in a business with a multitude of details. While it may be an illusion, there is a deeply shared belief among managers that strong control is the only way to stay on top of complex details.

To continue to maintain a belief in leading by control is to ignore the reality that the current volume of details in large organizations today is already beyond the capacities of traditional systems of central control. The only way for large organizations to avoid drowning in an ever-expanding ocean of details is to cultivate a common perspective across all the managers and workers so corporations are able to tap into and leverage their collective intelligence in real time. As the details of Digital Age businesses become seemingly infinite, corporations will be required to have competent processes for quickly and intelligently sorting through complexity, interpreting reality, and identifying the simple drivers of market success. These few drivers become the simple rules that allow large companies to behave as complex adaptive systems and successfully navigate the vast ocean of business details. While it may seem counterintuitive, simple rules actually do create a much higher order of control than the elaborate collections of controls so typical of the command-and-control organization.

Peter Drucker makes the point that we should not confuse the words "controls" and "control" because they have entirely different meanings.[7] Drucker notes that controls are analytical and provide information about past events, whereas control is normative and focused on future direction. This is an important distinction because, when the world is stable, the past can serve as a proxy for the future, and therefore, systems of intricate controls can provide reliable assurances about the state of organizational control. However, in fast-changing times, the future is likely to be very different from the past, and systems of controls can actually weaken the overall state of control when change and adaptation are critical to future market success. In that case, control is better served by a clear focus on what's most important that is reflected in a simple shared understanding that permeates the organization and helps to drive consistent and responsive adaptation to changing circumstances. The texture of control in complex adaptive systems is fundamentally different from the fabric of practice in complex stable systems.

This is not to imply that measurement of past events and details is not important. Quite the contrary, historical measures are incredibly useful because they provide essential facts that the workers can draw upon to bridge the inevitable anomalies between past circumstances and future expectations as they serve customers and execute day-to-day business processes in times of great change. What we are saying is that management's primary focus is always the future and never the past and that, when the past is no longer a proxy for the future, managers should stop monitoring the myriad of details as their primary strategy for fostering control in the organization. The details should be left to the people who are closet to the customers, more familiar with the business processes, and are, thus, also in the best position to execute quick and intelligent responses to changing conditions.

It's an uncomfortable, yet true, paradox: The most effective way for executives to assure that their organizations remain under control is to give up the illusion that they can exercise personal control over the details of the work. For leaders schooled in the traditional ways of managing, this is a difficult pill to swallow because they are certain that, without their steady hands controlling the levers of the business, their organizations would fall into a permanent state of chaos. However, in actuality, their foregone conclusion is a misconception of their own creation because it turns out that a little chaos is not necessarily a bad thing.

EMBRACING CHAOS

Chaos is an important ingredient in the emerging order of complex adaptive systems. Disorder and ambiguity are necessary conditions for creativity and evolution. Chaos, in and of itself, is not destructive. It is the inability to effectively process chaos that can bring about the demise of organizations and institutions, especially in fast changing times. The reason that most executives fear that giving up control will create permanent confusion is because they know that their organizations do not have the processes to discover the emerging order resident in the chaos. Without processes such as Work-Thrus or wiki pages, then it is true that chaos can be a permanent state. However, when businesses have the capability to discover the emerging order in the disruption and the confusion of wide differences, chaos becomes a competitive asset and the resulting collective intelligence unveils a higher order and enables unprecedented innovation and efficiency. This is the secret behind the remarkable growth of Wikipedia. It also explains why we are having so much trouble with health care reform.

The recent health care debate did not work very well because it was precisely that – a debate. Debates are about who's right and who's wrong, and they tend to further reinforce the entrenched positions of widely disparate views, making the discovery of common ground almost impossible. Advocates become riveted on taking control of the message so they can advance their point of view, even if it means imposing their thinking on those who disagree. When one side is able to control the debate and exert its will, there are usually winners and losers. That's because these verbal jousts often enable coercion by either the majority or the powerful. In those instances where debates are able to bring together all sides, it's usually because none of the parties could amass either the majority or the power to get its way, so both sides are forced by circumstances to agree to a compromise that represents nothing more than a least common denominator solution.

It is often said that a good compromise is one in which everyone walks away unhappy, and when debate is the primary process for bringing closure to different opinions, that's usually the best that anyone can hope for. The problem with debates is that they are fundamentally about getting control, and thus, are poor processes for creating the large consensus necessary for discovering the best or the most innovative solutions.

Although the vast majority of Americans agree that the current health care system needs fixing, Congress has had great difficulty in bringing real closure to this issue because we do not have an effective process for discovering the emerging order resident in the diversity of opinions across the American people. Without such a process, it is impossible to create a meaningful consensus around an issue that deeply and personally touches everyone's life.

Given the ingrained culture of debate, power, and control inside the Beltway, if we are to change the way we process chaos on important national issues, the leadership may need to come from unusual places such as social networks or wiki pages creating a collective mosaic or from trusted private citizens sponsoring an innovative collaboration process to help us access our collective wisdom. If we want to create a future healthcare system that's under control, we have to give up the notion that we can control the outcome. The irony is that those who attempt to avoid the confusion by wrestling control and dictating a predetermined order inevitably create the very state of permanent chaos that they so loathe. As we've discussed earlier, every major initiative has two basic phases, order and chaos. Our only choice is the sequence. Why would anyone choose chaos last?

TRANSPARENCY

When dealing with human relationships, an important lesson we learn from the complexity sciences is that giving up control and embracing chaos often leads to a more effective state of control. By building a shared understanding and then delegating the exercise of control to independent agents whose actions are guided by the simple rules of a collective consensus, companies are not only more responsive to changing circumstances, but they are actually more controlled at the same time. The degree of transparency needed to build an effective shared understanding provides collaborative organizations with a much higher order control system than is ever possible in bureaucratic hierarchies.

Transparency is the most effective control system because when everyone knows everything, there are no secrets. Companies with high levels of freedom of information and freedom of action have more resources available to them to assure that the business remains under control. As a result, problems don't fester, innovation is not muted, and quality is continually improved. This explains why wiki-management businesses, such as W.L. Gore and Associates, are so much better controlled than their command-and-control counterparts. The level of transparency needed to make Gore's consensus management work eliminates the hidden agendas and the institutional ignorance that plagues organizations when secrets prevail.

Traditional organizations have lots of secrets. With work subdivided among departments and directed by managers who are often engaged in some form of "turf battle," it is not surprising that information does not flow freely and that many workers are unaware of what people do outside their departments. Sometimes the secrets are intentional, such as when information is shared on a "need to know" basis or even deliberately withheld. More often than not, most corporate secrets are the unintentional consequences of the functional fragmentation of work. Whatever the reason, hierarchical organizations breed secrets. And that explains why they need elaborate control systems.

When secrets prevail, there is little or no shared understanding among either the managers or the workers to guide consistent delivery of customer value. Worse yet, without the transparency that naturally accompanies shared understanding, there could be plenty of opportunities for greedy or malicious employees to defraud the company. To protect themselves from the potential adverse consequences of bureaucratic secrets, hierarchical organizations promulgate a continuous stream of rules and regulations and establish complex control structures based on checks and balances. These structures rely upon armies of supervisors and auditors to assure that everyone is following the rules and that people are not using their secrets to inappropriately enrich themselves. The theory is that, if everyone has someone to watch over him, the risks associated with the inevitable secrets in bureaucracies will be mitigated and the business will be under control. The unfortunate irony, however, is that often the application of complex rules and regulations only slows things down, creates confusion, and actually weakens control. The U.S. Tax Code is a perfect example.

The only way that the increasing number of Digital Age business alliances can remain consistently under control is by moving away from centralized authority to decentralized transparency. This means that pertinent business knowledge needs to be freely shared among the partners and that all related data and metrics have to be continually available to everyone. It also means that the individuals in the partnership must also be available to each other. Transparency isn't just about everybody knowing everything. It also means that everybody is available to everyone. Without both of these dimensions, true transparency is not possible.

Transparency is the new currency of business, especially among business alliances. The sophisticated collaboration structures that are essential for horizontal business arrangements are impossible without a high order transparency based on trust and freedom of information. In addition to sharing previously proprietary intelligence such as financial data, business plans, and market analyses, anyone working in a collaborative business partnership must also have the ability to independently verify this information at all times. Stephen M. R. Covey, in *The Speed of Trust*, makes the point that transparency is "about being real and genuine and telling the truth in a way that people can verify."[8]

When companies have the benefit of high order transparency, executives do not have to depend upon the representations of supervisors or auditors to assure the business is running smoothly. They can take comfort in the fact that when everyone has access to everything, if there's something that they need to know, they will find out sooner rather than later because when everyone is available to everybody, there are no secrets.

AN ENCYCLOPEDIA BUILT ON TRANSPARENCY

In the mid-1990's Ward Cunningham noticed that software engineers liked to rely on tried and tested methods to streamline their work whenever possible. Writing computer programs is cumbersome and tedious, so proven routines that save both time and effort can be very valuable to overworked computer programmers. Because at the time there was no practical way for engineers to share their methods, the typical software specialist was limited to the knowledge in his head or the routines stored in the company's systems library. Cunningham felt that there needed to be a way for individual programmers to pool their knowledge and create common staples for the software community. So, on March 25, 1995, Cunningham turned his idea into an innovative software program and launched the Wiki-WikiWeb site.[9]

The breakthrough concept behind Cunningham's innovation was the then radical practice of allowing any coder to edit any page on the site. WikiWikiWeb was open to all who wanted to contribute, and to encourage participation, the coders were not required to have either an account or a password. The "wiki," as it came to be known among its early aficionados, was designed to be a transparent dialogue where software engineers could leverage their collective knowledge. To help facilitate a cohesive conversation, each wiki page had the ability to record and retain every edit so that anyone accessing the site could see the iterative development of the software concepts. This unusual proclivity for transparency caught the attention of computer technicians who quickly flocked to the new site.

Cunningham was gratified that the software community so readily accepted his wiki concept. Little did he realize at the time, however, that a chance conversation during a dinner meeting between two colleagues would soon extend the popularity of Cunningham's innovation far beyond even his wildest imagination. A much larger world than the tight community of software specialists was about to discover the incredible power and speed of transparency.

When Larry Sanger met up his with his old friend Ben Kovitz on January 2, 2001, he had a lot on his mind.[10] It had been almost a year since Sanger had come to San Diego to work for Jimmy Wales as the editor in chief for Nupedia, a start up online encyclopedia. Wales' vision for the new venture was to use the power of the Internet to solicit volunteers who would contribute articles to build a free encyclopedia. However, by the end of 2000, the seven-step peer review process that Sanger and his academic advisors had designed had only produced a handful of articles. At this glacial rate, Wales and Sanger were both concerned about the viability of their ambitious project.

As Kovitz empathized with Nupedia's predicament, he urged Sanger to take a look at WikiWikiWeb.[11] Given its ease and transparency, he suggested that the wiki page just might be the solution for how large numbers of volunteers could produce and edit a high volume of encyclopedia articles. For Sanger, this was one of those moments where "the light bulb goes on." Kovitz's suggestion was a complete paradigm shift in the way encyclopedias could be built. Up until this point, Sanger's management model for building Nupedia was based on conventional protocols where articles go through a sequential series of reviews by a hierarchy of experts. In that "light bulb" moment, it became very clear to Sanger that the fundamental obstacle to Nupedia's sustainability was its seven-step closed system review process. He realized that, if the online encyclopedia was to succeed, it had to become an open system with the capability for real-time editing steered by the collective wisdom of the masses rather than the conventional wisdom of the experts.

Sanger enthusiastically shared his insights with Wales, who quickly recognized how an open system approach might solve the online encyclopedia's problems. Thus, on January 10, 2001, Wales added wiki software to the Nupedia web site.[12] However, not everyone in the Nupedia organization was as enthusiastic as Sanger and Wales. The academic experts were vigorously opposed to the notion that the masses could provide any value to a scholarly pursuit. They were professionals, and they were adamant that a collaboration with the crowd could never meet their high quality standards. Consequently, just five days later, on January 15, 2001, Wales removed the wiki software from Nupedia and launched a second independent project, which Sanger dubbed Wikipedia.[13]

We all know what happened from there. The meteoric growth of Wikipedia is well documented, and most of us have never heard of Nupedia. While the experts continue to debate the quality of the online encyclopedia, all of us are amazed that the world's largest and most widely used reference work continues to be built by a self-organized collaboration of the masses.

Wikipedia works so well because it follows the three common organizing principles of complex adaptive systems. It's fundamental premise is that intelligence resides in the whole system. Wikipedia doesn't believe that the smartest organization is the one with the smartest individuals – that was the Nupedia model and it didn't work. Wikipedia understands that the smartest organization is the one that has quick access to its collective knowledge, and thanks to the wiki page, it has the capacity to tap into the wisdom of the crowd at any moment of any day.

From the very beginning, Wikipedia has used just four simple rules to guide the complex collective effort of building an online encyclopedia for the planet. The first and most important of these rules is that all articles will present a neutral point of view. This means that there can only be one rendition of every article and that proponents of differing factions have to dialogue to form a consensus. As we know only too well from the dueling channels on cable television, there's limited value in a medium that fosters entrenched positions. Collective knowledge is only possible when there is a forum for discovering the common ground among differing points of view.

The second rule is that all content on Wikipedia has to be referenced to a published reliable source. Participants are required to list citations in their articles so that readers can independently verify the information. This leads to the third rule: Wikipedia does not publish original research. This policy preserves Wikipedia's core mission as an encyclopedia. Professional journals are the place for original research.

The last rule is that participants should assume good faith when working with other Wikipedians. Despite a few rare, but well-publicized, instances of vandalism on the site, this rule has worked exceedingly well. That's because the extensive ability to verify information available to everyone in highly transparent environments naturally engenders trust.

Finally, most of us continue to be incredulous by Wikipedia's dramatic affirmation of the power of the third organizing principle of complex adaptive systems. It's just as true for humans as it is for colonies of ants or flocks of birds: Order can emerge from the interactions of independent agents. Wikipedia provides compelling evidence that, when large organizations have access to collective knowledge, they need neither bosses nor experts to guide the work. In fact, they will produce a much higher order far more efficiently if the collective effort is guided by self-applied simple rules rather than by bosses and experts. Although it may feel counterintuitive, the experiences of Wikipedia, as well as Google and Gore & Associates, are challenging the conventional belief that reliance on self-directed teams in large organizations is a formula for disaster. For each of these organizations, the secret to their remarkable success has been their competency in applying the three organizing principles of complex adaptive systems. When business leaders have access to collective knowledge along with the ability to build a shared understanding around the few drivers of success, they enable self–organized networks of highly skilled professionals to achieve extraordinary performance.

Chapter 11

THE FOURTH RESPONSIBILITY:
FOCUSED MEASURES

In order to thrive – not just survive – and move to a higher level of performance, organizations need to focus on one or more critical measures that matter most, and companies need to focus everybody's attention on those measures.

- Dean R. Spitzer
Transforming Performance Measurement[1]

A flock of birds migrating a long distance doesn't need to figure out the simple rules of flight that guide how they organize themselves to accomplish the goals of reaching their destination and getting every bird there safely. Both the rules and the goals are genetically hard-wired. Migrating birds do not have to consciously choose to focus their efforts; nature provides the focus for them. When it comes to people in large organizations, it's a different story. We are hard-wired with neither goals nor simple rules. Mother nature does not provide us with focus when we gather together to do work. We have to choose our own goals and we are responsible for formulating the rules we will use to organize ourselves. Given the Digital Age's accelerating pace of change, maintaining effective focus will call for new ways of thinking and acting about corporate goals and rules that will cause us to rethink the common practices of traditional hierarchical organizations.

Most corporations today do not have a single integrated measurement system. The metrics in the typical business is an ad hoc collection of disconnected functional measures that, unfortunately, often work at cross-purposes. Consequently, the vast majority of workers cannot list the top corporate goals and priorities. They know what their tasks and assignments are, but they typically cannot tell you how their work connects to the larger corporate effort. Without a shared understanding of the key priorities, ad hoc metrics tend to produce a cacophony of interpretations about what is important for the business.

An unfortunate consequence of the lack of clear measures of success is that many of today's knowledge workers are disengaged and underutilized. This is a confusing state of affairs for the executive leaders who feel that they have made a substantial effort to effectively communicate the company's top priorities through various communiqués and corporate forums. What these leaders fail to grasp is that knowledge workers understand and engage with goals only when they are involved in their creation. It is then that they are able to see how their contributions connect with the work of their colleagues and they are also able to judge for themselves whether or not the goals make sense. Until knowledge workers are able to personally make this judgment, they do not engage with the goals no matter how many times these priorities are broadcast in one-way communications. Unless organizations change their ways by using collective learning rather than central planning to set their goals and by building shared understanding rather than sending well-intentioned memos to solicit the workers' commitment to those objectives, they are likely to find themselves at a distinct competitive disadvantage in a new economy built on the efficiencies of mass collaboration.

FOCUS

In the wiki world, knowledge workers need a broad focus if they are to work effectively. This is a very different from the way things worked in the mass production enterprises of the Industrial Age. When the context of the organization was the assembly line, work could be fragmented and individualized performance goals could be established for each worker. The industrial workers didn't need to know or understand the corporate goals because their engagement around those measures wasn't necessary to the success of the enterprise. The only goals that the industrial worker needed to be concerned about were her individual performance expectations because her focus was to complete her tasks. However, defining the scope of work as the accomplishment of tasks is insufficient when the challenge of organizing large numbers of workers is to reap the efficiencies of mass collaboration. When the primary context of strategy is collective learning and the driver of execution is self-organization, everyone needs to know and understand the goals, and everyone needs to share a common focus.

One of the prime contributors to the pervasive lack of clarity in traditional organizations is that they often have too many goals at one time. When new opportunities are continually arising in a fast-changing world and when organizations have not yet developed the collective learning processes to effectively narrow their focus on the right opportunities, managers often give in to the temptation to add one more critical initiative to an already overflowing plate. However, the problem with continually taking on more projects as the primary strategy for managing the new pace of change is that the greater the number of critical priorities, the less likely that any one of the initiatives will be accomplished with excellence. In its research for its training program, *The Four Disciplines of Execution*, FranklinCovey has quantified the relationship between the number of priority goals and the probability of excellent achievement.[2] They found that the likelihood of achieving all goals with excellence falls below 50% when there are more than three top priorities, and once the number of goals exceeds ten, there is no chance that any of the goals will be achieved with excellence. In assessing these results, Stephen Covey concludes, "There's a key principle that many fail to understand about focusing an organization: People are naturally wired to focus on only one thing at a time (or at best very few) with excellence."[3]

The piling up of centrally planned initiatives is very problematic when organizations are trying to keep up with the challenges of managing in fast changing times. Traditional organizations come from a long and successful history where managing complexity was about the effective control of a multitude of details. In the closed systems of the assembly lines, things did work when each individual worker focused on and accomplished her tasks. However, in the wiki world, organizations are more likely to be open systems where fulfilling the business mission requires continual interaction and iteration with both workers and customers to create intelligence and to produce knowledge applications. In this context, managing complexity is less about the details and more about sorting through the multitudes of developments to determine which ones are inconsequential and which ones might reshape the market. In the new economy, business is about working smarter not harder. Consequently, a strategy that deals with change by dumping more priorities on the corporate plate, fragmenting the new work into another set of tasks, and focusing specific individuals on the new tasks is doomed to failure.

In today's dynamic business environment, organizations will not be able to manage at the pace of change unless they involve workers in the identification, selection, and evolution of the top priorities. By cultivating a common focus about what's most important, a company will provide its workers with the simple set of rules that they need to effectively self-organize their efforts and achieve consistent excellent results to remain competitive in the new world of mass collaboration. Otherwise the current state of too many strategic initiatives and too much confusion about company goals will only get worse. Without common focus, there's no way for either the managers or the workers to have the frame of reference needed to exercise intelligent judgment in sorting through the increasing number of details that are inevitable in fast-changing times.

Measurement is the way that organizations define what is most important to the business. A good measurement system should clearly spotlight the critical few actions that drive the company's success. That's because the primary purpose of measurement is to provide a common focus to enable performance. Once a mutual frame of reference is defined, measurement systems can be effectively integrated so that each person can connect her individual efforts to a clear set of shared goals.

In setting these common objectives, it's absolutely essential that the leaders choose the right goals. This is an important area where executives need to embrace the wisdom of slowing down to move fast. Getting the goals right only happens when leaders are committed to a bias for results over a bias for action. They need to take the time to first understand and then measure, and avoid the bravado of setting premature goals based on impulse. While it may appear courageous and decisive, bravado is nothing more than bold action without understanding. And without understanding, the leaders are more likely to target what's easy rather than what's important to measure.

The right goals are not derived from executive impulse but rather reflect what's most important to customers. As we've emphasized throughout this book, the starting point for sustainable businesses is customer values. Thus, the leader's challenge is to facilitate effective learning processes that can sift through the complexities of evolving markets to correctly discover what is most important to their chosen customers. Once there is a consensus around key customer values, these attributes are then translated into a simple set of meaningful measures to effectively guide the local behavior of the people who are closest to the consumers. Today's knowledge workers are capable of making local interdependent judgments once they have a simple set of measures that they can use to bridge the analytical facts of the past with the changing circumstances of the present to create a consistent future.

THE BALANCED SCORECARD

One of the most important contributions to the practice of business measurement is the recent development of the Balanced Scorecard by Robert Kaplan and David Norton.[4] This insightful and innovative tool is a practical application that demonstrates the power of focused measurement for translating strategy into effective action in fast-changing times. Kaplan and Norton's simplified measurement template is a response to the many bad habits that seem to plague most corporate measurement systems today.

A common habit we see among traditional organizations is the practice of maintaining massive information systems that quantify every piece of available data, regardless of its significance. The voluminous reports from these gigantic data libraries don't clarify; they overwhelm. While these systems do supply important information, what they don't provide is a perspective for understanding the interrelationships among critical variables. Without a clear framework for interpreting the data, organizations experience the insidious effects of information overload as managers and workers alike are unable to process the sheer volume of information before them, demonstrating that when your focus is on measuring everything, you actually measure nothing. Thus, this grand data gathering becomes practically useless because it provides little insight and yields minimal organizational value to mobilize organizations to effective action.

The Balanced Scorecard recognizes the power of simplicity for facilitating effectiveness across large organizations by stripping away the noise from the cacophony of massive information systems. The scorecard contains 12 – 20 carefully selected measures that track organizational performance across four balanced perspectives: financial, customer, internal business processes, and learning and growth.[5] These select measures represent the key indicators that are most important to the corporation's strategic success. Thus, the Balanced Scorecard is a one-page integrated picture of the business that enables all areas within a company to align their local activities with a common set of simple measures. These selected benchmarks also serve as the frame of reference for interpreting and understanding the significance and the interrelationship of the various data elements contained in an organization's information system. Large data systems become powerful and efficient tools when there is a common strategic perspective for processing the information.

The lack of a meaningful template of simple business measures leads traditional organizations into the habit of relying on financial statements as the basic management measurement tool. This is a very dangerous practice because, for the most part, financial statements are collections of outcome measures that are not actionable. Financial measures are like final scores in a sporting event. Once the contest is over, there's nothing that any of the players can do to change the outcome. Financial statements are poor management tools because by the time you get the measures, there's nothing that the executives can do to manage the numbers – at least not legally! Unfortunately, several well-publicized companies have gotten themselves into serious trouble because their executives attempted to manage the numbers when they failed to manage the business. When business leaders respond to poor financial results by illegally manipulating the financial statements, this desperate move is usually a clear sign that the organization lacks a meaningful measurement template for managing the business.

The Balanced Scorecard provides this template. Kaplan and Norton recognize that managers cannot directly manage to financial numbers. They can only impact the success of the business by delivering customer value and by maintaining state-of the-art business processes. Thus, the Balanced Scorecard reflects the reality that financial results measure how effective the organization is in aligning its business processes with customer value. If a company needs to improve its financial results, it needs to direct its efforts toward meeting customer value, improving internal business processes, and maintaining the baseline of learning and growth to keep up with fast-changing markets. The balanced perspectives of the four categories of key indicators in a simple comprehensive scorecard provide executives with a highly effective management tool for identifying and implementing timely adaptations before the final financial results are tallied.

Another habit that the Balanced Scorecard addresses is the tendency for managers to look at all metrics as characteristically the same. The Balanced Scorecard makes an important distinction between driver measures and outcome measures. Unfortunately, most managers in traditional organizations seem to be largely unaware of this distinction. As referenced above, outcome measures are lagging indicators that describe final results. Driver measures, on the other hand, are leading indicators that quantify the levels of performance of the key activities that strongly influence the ultimate outcomes. An effective Balanced Scorecard is a mixture of related leading and lagging indicators that reflect the fundamental strategy of the business. When properly constructed, the driver measures provide reliable and actionable information about how and if the expected outcomes are being achieved, while the outcome measures provide the data necessary to continually validate whether or not the observed relationships between driver and outcome measures continue to hold true.

One of the most important uses of the Balanced Scorecard is for the managers and the workers to collectively understand important, but not necessarily obvious, relationships among the data elements. For example, Kaplan and Norton cite a perceptive discovery by Rockwater Manufacturing Corporation in working with its scorecard. Rockwater's executives noticed a connection between two of its key measures: the number of days of accounts receivable and customer satisfaction. It seemed that whenever there was an increase in the receivables, there was a corresponding decrease in the measure of customer satisfaction. It turned out that this was not a coincidence. Many times customers will convey their dissatisfaction with a vendor's work by withholding final payment until the work is acceptably completed. Thus, Kaplan and Norton note that, "The solution for Rockwater's long closeout cycle did not lie with additional training, education, or even technology in the accounts receivable department. The solution had to come from greatly improved communication between Rockwater's on-site project manager and the customer's representative."[6]

The focused measures of the Balanced Scorecard highlighted an important lesson for the Rockwater executives. If they wanted to know if their customers were happy, they just needed to look at the level of their number of days of accounts receivable. In their case, it turned out that accounts receivable was a driver measure for the outcome of customer satisfaction. By becoming aware of this relationship, Rockwater was able to respond quickly at the first sign of customer dissatisfaction and prevent full-blown crises that could lead to the ultimate loss of valued customers and deterioration in market share. In addition, they were also able to monitor the ongoing metrics of these two measures to test the continued validity of the relationship. Quantitative relationships are not always permanent and can evolve over time. Having a useful tool to continually validate the company's assumptions about key business relationships is critical when organizations are complex adaptive systems.

This leads us to the final bad habit of traditional organizations, and that is their tendency to treat all negative numbers as indicators of poor performance. When this happens, the immediate reaction of both managers and workers to unfavorable data is to deny, downplay, or dismiss the numbers, if at all possible, because the individuals are concerned that the unwelcome metrics will reflect badly in their annual performance evaluations. With this mindset, negative numbers are always viewed as enemies and never as friends. Kaplan and Norton do not share this perspective and stress that, in approaching the metrics in a Balanced Scorecard, everyone in the organization should understand that this collection of focused measures is a learning tool and not a controlling mechanism.[7] In other words, the Balanced Scorecard is more interested in promoting shared understanding rather than control as the driver of consistency in responding to the challenges of today's evolving markets. In this context, adverse results are not necessarily indications of lack of compliance or poor performance, but may merely reflect that markets are shifting or customer values are evolving and that it is time to adapt to new business conditions.

If managers and workers are in denial about negative numbers out of concern for their individual performance, they are likely to miss important collective learnings that are best handled sooner rather than later if organizations are to remain competitive in evolving markets. The important lesson in Kaplan and Norton's timely and innovative contribution is that business metric systems should not be exclusively performance systems. Some measures should be collected, collated, and examined for the sole purpose of facilitating organizational collective learning about the brutal or not-so-brutal facts of market reality. This is one of the most important benefits of the Balanced Scorecard. Consistent with the simple rules of complex adaptive systems, the focused measures contained in the scorecard provide a powerful tool for guiding the organization in the present by monitoring the key drivers of future success as well as empowering the organization with a strategic template for recognizing when it's time to adapt to a new environment and reposition the business.

PROCESS-ORIENTED MEASURES

A commonly held maxim across almost all organizations is that "you get what you measure." Thus, if you want to be sure that something will be done, convert the action into a quantifiable measure and link an individual's compensation to the computed results. This maxim is firmly imbedded in the conventional performance evaluation practices of most companies. Typically, annual bonuses and merit salary increases for both managers and workers are tied to measurable goals and objectives specifically tailored for each individual. For the most part, the maxim is true. Quantifiable measures do serve as powerful incentives for shaping what workers do as well as what they don't do.

The conventional practices of the performance evaluation discipline trace their roots to the task-orientation of command-and-control management. In the mass production enterprises, execution excellence is about everyone performing her individual tasks as assigned by the supervisor. Consistent with the principles of the chain of command, each functional supervisor is responsible for establishing and monitoring the specific measurable goals for each individual reporting to her. In the early days of mass production, this approach to performance measurement worked because the tasks were fairly straightforward and the likelihood of consistent measures across related functions was therefore reasonably high. However, as we moved through the 20th century and work became more complex and interdependent with the steady shift from manual workers to knowledge workers, the measurement practices of independent functional supervisors became problematic as corporations were finding that different functions in common business processes were working toward differing, and sometimes incompatible goals. This "silo effect," as it came to be known, can be very disruptive when the focus of work shifts from mass production to mass collaboration.

If functional supervisors have the sovereign right to establish worker goals, the quantifiable measures are inevitably task-oriented. This often yields nothing more than a random assortment of well-performed individual tasks. Consequently, when the tasks of the various workers are not well aligned, the performance of a company's core business processes may be nowhere close to execution excellence. Tasks, in and of themselves, are not the indicators of effective execution because only a fully functioning business process delivers customer value. The performance of individual tasks is only meaningful when combined with the aligned and successful accomplishment of all the other tasks in a business process. In the wiki world, where organizations work for the customer and the context of business is mass collaboration, the focus of measurement needs to be on processes and not tasks.

CROSS-FUNCTIONAL GOALS

Process-oriented measures are inherently cross-functional. This is what we discovered as we transitioned the management of the Blue Cross Blue Shield Federal Employee Program (FEP) from its command-and-control roots to the wiki-management discipline. As our senior leadership team examined the performance evaluation discipline within our national office, we quickly realized that the way we were setting individual worker goals did not support the level of collaboration that we needed to effectively lead a business alliance of 39 independent organizations. The one thing that most caught our attention was the number of instances where individuals in different departments were working on the same process toward the same objective, but with different metrics to define success. This meant that everyone working on the same initiative was not working toward the same goal. Because in our organization, just as in most companies, the functional supervisors had the sovereign right to determine individual goals, there was no established practice for the managers to coordinate worker goals across departments. And so, somewhat to our surprise, we discovered that our individual performance goals were often ad hoc collections of uncoordinated and misaligned expectations of functional supervisors who did not share a common perspective. We also learned that our knowledge workers were keenly aware of the misalignments and felt that they should be more involved in the goal setting process because they were closer to the business processes than their bosses.

Accordingly, in an effort to transition from uncoordinated task-oriented measures to more integrated process-oriented benchmarks, we adopted what we called the "cross-functional goals" process. Before the beginning of each business year, a diverse team of managers and workers would gather in a series of meetings to identify the most important cross-functional goals and to propose the common metrics for the measurement of those objectives. The leader of this team would periodically meet with the senior leadership group to review and discuss the developing metrics proposal. Through a series of iterative discussions over several weeks, we would refine the goals and the measures until both the cross-functional and the senior leadership teams reached a consensus. Once common agreement was achieved, the only measures that could be used for the cross-functional goals in individual performance evaluations were the consensus metrics. Supervisors had no discretion over nor could they modify the metrics of the cross-functional goals. This way we assured that everyone working in the same business process was working toward the same result.

The were four conditions that served as the framework for the construction of our annual cross-functional goals: 1) only goals that involved at least two departments could be candidates, 2) the determination of the goals and measures was to be achieved through consensus, 3) closure on goals and measures was to be reached before the start of the business year, and 4) all goals and measures had to be either results-based or value-based. This last condition was especially important because it assured that the final list would consist of only process-oriented goals and measures.

Task-oriented goals are often quantified using activity-based metrics that call for the timely completion of a discrete task that is usually within the complete control of a particular individual. An example of an activity-based measure is the requirement to submit a department budget by a certain date. Thus, positive performance is measured by the completion of the activity, regardless of the content of the budget or its overall contribution to the strategic direction of the organization. Results-based or value-based measures, on the other hand, are almost always process-oriented goals that are outside the ability of any one individual to accomplish, and therefore, require collaboration among teams of workers to assure an effective business process or the delivery of customer value. A collective consensus that minimizes the impact of a five percent budget reduction would be an example of a results-oriented goal that is likely to be far more productive than an across-the-board arbitrary budget cut.

The consensus practice that we used in FEP to determine cross-functional goals was an important contribution to our transition to becoming a smarter and faster business. This practice encouraged us to collectively examine our evolving market reality as we added and deleted goals in response to a changing business environment. The iterative discussions among the cross-functional team, the dialogues around the proposed measures with the senior leadership team, and the commitment to determine goals and measures by consensus among all members of both teams reinforced deep collective learning and a powerful shared understanding among our managers and our workers about our most important goals. The common focus around a simple set of cross-functional goals significantly boosted our capacity as effective leaders of the FEP business alliance as, over a five-year period, we increased our market share by ten percentage points and, year after year, set new records in the operational performance indices across all the Blue Cross Blue Shield organizations in the FEP business alliance.

SUCCESS MEASURES

As part of our commitment to facilitate common focus, another discipline that we adopted at FEP was the practice of identifying the top 3 – 5 most important items. Whether we were considering the overall business or a particular initiative, we consistently identified the top 3 – 5 items that would make the difference in our performance. In any large business or in any major project, there are often hundreds, perhaps even thousands, of details that need to come together for success. And while it is true that the "devil is in the details" and successful performance of a business process is dependent on everything being done correctly, we discovered that the secret to accomplishing the many tasks was more about facilitating a common focus on the top 3 – 5 critical items and less about monitoring all the details. This is why the assignment for almost all small group exercises in Work-Thrus is to list the top 3 – 5 most important observations or concerns about the process, project or issue for discussion.

Not all details are equal. Some details are more important than others because there are always a handful of items in any project or initiative that are the critical hurdles on the path to success. Often many of these hurdles are not immediately obvious or even known at the start of a project. Organizational learning practices to collectively identify the top 3 – 5 items in a project often serve as catalysts to enlighten everyone throughout the company about what they didn't know that they didn't know. With a clear focus on what's most important, managers and workers together are able to successfully handle critical issues at the front-end rather than being surprised at the back-end, and they have a powerful frame of reference from which they can ably self-organize the remaining details.

Clear focus is what enables organizations to keep up with an accelerating pace of change. A shared understanding about the most important items serves the same purpose in organizations as the simple set of rules for a flock of birds. Thus, everyone in a company should be fully aware of what are the 3 – 5 most important measures of business success and they should be constantly aware of the current metrics for these parameters. If you were to walk into any traditional organization today and ask a sample of managers and workers what were their 3 – 5 most important success factors and how were they doing on these, how many of the individuals would be able to answer the questions? When organizations are structured for knowledge and speed, everyone knows the answers to these questions.

The top 3 – 5 most important measures of business success are never outcome measures such as market share or earnings per share; they are always driver measures because only driver measures are actionable. Unfortunately, most organizations do a better job of broadcasting their outcome measures than they do of discovering the critical few drivers of success.

The selection of the top few drivers is not an ad hoc process where choosing any 3 - 5 measures will do. Identifying these critical measures is another example of where it is essential that organizations slow down to move fast. More often than not, the discovery of an organization's critical few drivers is an iterative collective learning process that involves both the managers and the workers.

When we engaged in this discovery process at FEP, we identified four measures that were the clear drivers of either market share or profitability. If these measures were positive, we could be reasonably certain that the ultimate outcomes would be positive. Conversely, if these parameters turned negative, we had a learning tool that enabled us to proactively assess our processes and our environment to determine whether we needed to make operational or strategic adjustments in enough time to minimize the effects of the developments on our business outcomes. But most importantly, we had a clear focus for the self-organization of the efforts of the thousands of individuals among the 39 Blue Cross Blue Shield organizations participating in the FEP business alliance.

Discovering and building a shared understanding around the few drivers of success not only helped us to focus on the right things; it also guided us in doing things right because, when knowledge workers clearly understand what is most important, they are fully capable of making the connections between their tasks and the critical drivers to self-organize their work in real-time. In times of accelerating change, managers simply do not have the time to oversee all the details, as they could in the days of mass production

In today's mass collaboration businesses, the details are best left to the workers who are much closer to both the customers and the business processes. Managers are learning that monitoring all the details is counterproductive because micromanagers slow companies down and never move fast. When organizations are structured for knowledge and speed, managers slow down only to build consensus and shared understanding about the few drivers that serve as the simple rules that enable their businesses to move faster than the competition.

The tasks, responsibilities, and practices of effective executives in today's Digital Age are dramatically different from those that defined the job of their Industrial Age counterparts. When the fundamental work of the corporation is mass production, command-and-control practices based on central planning and elaborate controls work because then it is possible for management to assure the accomplishment of the multitude of tasks by distributing oversight of functional activities to a cadre of managers arrayed in a chain of command. In the traditional hierarchical organization, a focus on maintaining a centralized system of controls to monitor all the tasks for compliance with pre-determined standards is the basic management strategy for organizing the many activities of the large numbers of workers in complex stable systems.

However, when the fundamental work of the corporation is mass collaboration, wiki-management practices based on collective learning and shared understanding are critical for adapting to ever-changing business environments. Knowledge creation is now the fabric of work, and if corporations expect to keep up with the new economy's pace of change, it is input, rather than compliance, that they most need from today's knowledge workers. A shared understanding of the simple rules for market success discovered through collective learning processes that incorporate the insights of both managers and workers is now the key to effective execution. In the fast-changing times of the Digital Age, organizations are most efficient when large numbers of workers have the necessary tools to self-organize their work within a collaborative infrastructure. In the new wiki world, managers need to leave the control of the details to the workers and learn that the basic management strategy for organizing the many activities of large numbers of workers in complex adaptive systems is to focus on the few drivers to accomplish the many tasks.

Chapter 12

THE FIFTH RESPONSIBILITY: COLLABORATIVE COMMUNITY

Twenty years from now we will look back to this period of the early twenty-first century as a critical turning point in economic and social history. We will understand that we entered a new age, one based on new principles, world-views, and business models where the nature of the game was changed.

- Don Tapscott & Anthony D. Williams
Wikinomics[1]

For almost 50 years, we have known that participative management produces better results than traditional command-and-control practices. Beginning in the 1960's with Douglas McGregor's identification of Theory X and Theory Y and with Abraham Maslow's penetrating insights into the higher reaches of human nature, we have understood that, when managers involve employees in defining the work to be done, the workers are more engaged in their efforts and more committed to performance. Throughout the second half of the 20th century, McGregor's and Maslow's profound influence sparked a human relations movement to humanize the industrial workplace. Personnel departments were renamed Human Resources while the new discipline of organizational development was given a seat at the executive table. A new leadership industry was born to retrain legions of executives to enhance their "people skills." Management was "out" and leadership was "in" because the new ways of thinking were about leading people, not managing things. However, despite all the efforts and resources committed to retooling executives and humanizing the office, the new ways of thinking have not translated into new ways of acting. While the interpersonal skills of managers have improved over the last half-century, for the most part, the involvement of workers has been limited to selective consultation. When it comes to implementing the insights of the human relations movement, management's efforts have been far more about style than substance.

However, given the sudden arrival of the revolutionary technologies of the Digital Age, today's managers will not be able to meet the challenges of a new and very different economy unless they transform the substance of management. The recent onset of an accelerating pace of change, the new efficiencies of electronic networks, and the emergence of knowledge as an economic asset will inevitably bring about a change in the dominant management model for the very simple reason that hierarchical management will not work in the wiki world. The practicalities stemming from our newfound capacity for mass collaboration will compel organizations to do what the moral suasion from the insights of the human relations experts of the 1960's had only hoped to accomplish – to change both the style and the substance of management.

HORIZONTAL NETWORKS

Mass collaboration can take on many different forms. It is sometimes the individual contributions of a global corps of volunteers to produce a web-based encyclopedia for the planet. It can be a b-web where different independent companies, each retaining its own identity, come together in an internet business alliance to leverage their strengths in a common platform and where they are able to generate more business as partners than they could do separately. Mass collaboration can also be three geographically dispersed teams working together on a common project in shifts around the globe, giving new meaning to working 24/7. Or it can be a critical mass of managers and workers collaborating as a cross-functional team in a Work-Thru to identify breakthrough solutions to next generation business processes. What all these forms of mass collaboration have in common is the capacity to expand an organization's knowledge and to increase its speed through decentralization in a way that challenges the conventional wisdom of hierarchies.

Decentralization is a prerequisite for mass collaboration. As a result, if organizations want to compete in the inherently more dynamic and innovative wiki world, they will need their managers to abandon the comfort of their top-down structures and to learn new ways of acting if they expect to effectively tap into the expansive knowledge and the incredible speed of these different forms of horizontal networks.

As the Internet continues to flatten the world, the emerging capacity for mass collaboration will also flatten organizations and create new possibilities for business alliances as more companies discover that new ways of organizing large numbers of people is a competitive necessity if they are to take advantage of the remarkable speed and effectiveness of horizontal networks. The new technologies that now make mass collaboration possible will reshape all the accepted notions about how work gets done in large groups as more organizations discover that horizontal partnership is far faster, much smarter, and less costly than vertical integration.

One community of workers that fully appreciates the power of mass collaboration is the world's disease control scientists. When your mission is to guard the globe against epidemics, success is not measured in dollars and cents but rather in lives saved and deaths prevented. When your work issues are literally matters of life and death, there is no illusion that one single person can know it all, there's no place for heroes, and there's no time for bureaucracy. Disease control scientists know that collaboration is essential where speedy innovation is an imperative to ward off a potential global pandemic. In one 30-day period in the early spring of 2003, the world witnessed the remarkable efficiency of the mass collaboration of the world's community of scientists, but because they did their work so well, most of us barely noticed.

In late November 2002, scientists at Canada's Global Public Health Intelligence Network (GPHIN), while routinely monitoring Internet media, observed reports of a possible flu outbreak in China and forwarded this information to the World Health Organization (WHO).[2] In early December, the WHO requested a report from the Chinese authorities and was assured in the government's response that its investigation into the appearance of the virus and the number of cases identified were completely consistent with the seasonal patterns observed in previous years.[3] However, in February 2003, the Chinese Ministry of Health reversed itself and reported to the WHO that 305 people had been stricken with a severe respiratory disease, which had claimed the lives of five of the ill.[4] Over the next several weeks, the WHO tested several specimens in its laboratories and was able to conclusively rule out the influenza virus as the cause of the ailing patients' illness. By mid-March, the WHO was certain that they were dealing with an entirely new disease, which they named SARS, and they also knew that they needed to isolate the root cause to avoid a potential epidemic.

On March 17, 2003, the WHO initiated a global effort involving 11 research laboratories from countries around the world, which was called a "collaborative multicenter research project."[5] If the WHO was to prevent a potential pandemic, organizing their efforts around knowledge and speed by tapping into the collective wisdom of a collaborative community was a given. In daily conference calls, scientists around the globe shared their observations and analyses, debated the results, and explored future avenues for their research. Through these daily calls, using the data that they were continually passing back and forth among all the laboratories, they were able to learn quickly from each other, leverage each other's ideas, and aggregate their dispersed observations into a developing collective knowledge. Within a matter of days, scientists at both the Hong Kong University and the Centers for Disease Control in the United States had separately identified the possible culprit of the new disease, and, after further research in labs in Germany, the Netherlands, and Hong Kong, the scientists were certain that the identified coronavirus was indeed the cause of SARS.[6] After a mere 30 days from the start of the scientific collaboration, on April 16, 2003, the WHO was able to announce its crucial discovery to the world. The agency was then able to provide specific guidance for clinical treatment to health professionals and was also able to make recommendations to international travelers to prevent the spread of the disease.[7] The quick work of this collaborative community was so successful that, on July 5, 2003, the WHO confidently declared that the SARS outbreak had been contained.

We were fortunate that the WHO did not have direct authority over the international community of scientists. Otherwise, we might have seen a research command center rather than a collaborative multicenter research project. If the SARS research effort had been organized into a centralized bureaucratic structure, it most likely would have taken months instead of weeks to find the root cause of the new disease. Invariably, politics always finds its way into centralized structures and distracts an organization from its core purpose by slowing down the pursuit of truth to manage perceptions. Centralized bureaucracies sometimes put their interests in looking good ahead of getting it right. That is exactly what happened when the Chinese government encountered the early cases of SARS. The government, at first, downplayed the seriousness of the public health threat and characterized the early instances as nothing more than the flu. It is only after chatter on the Internet made the spinning of the story impossible that the

Chinese government finally came forward with the complete facts. While the government was focused on managing perceptions, precious time was wasted that could have been better used in pursuit of the analysis of the new disease's cause.

In a way, the mass collaboration effort began with the Web community that served as the catalyst for the eventual mobilization of the world's scientific community. The SARS experience shows that communities are far more effective than bureaucracies when it comes to managing reality. In the communities of horizontal networks, politics doesn't distract the members from their core purpose because all the voices are equal, no one is in charge, and everyone understands that nobody is smarter than everybody. No centralized organization, or even a single individual, could have confirmed that cause of SARS in only 30 days. Only a mass collaboration of self-organizing professionals can uncover the unknown with this kind of speed. At the end of the day, there were no individual heroes or self-promoting bosses in the SARS story. Perhaps that's why most of us barely remember the episode. However, there truly was a heroic effort – only this time the hero was a global team. Every one of the scientists in the collaboration is responsible for finding the cause of SARS. And the scientists are perfectly alright with that because they fully appreciate what most businesses will soon learn: A self-organizing team of collegial professionals collaborating in a horizontal network always works smarter and faster than traditional hierarchies and individual heroes.

OPEN SOURCE COMMUNITY

Mass collaboration is creating entirely new ways of working together that only 20 years ago would have stretched the limits of believability. Who would have imagined that you could build a successful computer operating system using only volunteers working without a plan, without assigned tasks, and even without pay – and that the product that these freelancers put together would be so good that the very company that had arguably given birth to the information technology industry would abandon its own proprietary offerings to become part of the online community? Yet that is the incredible story of Linux and the emerging power of open source technology.

In 1991, Linus Torvalds, a graduate student at the University of Helsinki, came up with an innovative idea for creating a new computer operating system. Relying on the efforts of volunteer programmers around the world, Torvalds would use the long-established Unix language as a model for a state-of-the-art system that he dubbed Linux. Because Torvalds knew that computer programmers are a unique breed of people who love to interact and impress each other with their knowledge, Torvalds posted his initial source code for Linux on an online bulletin board and invited other programmers to build upon his work. A handful of programmers responded almost immediately with substantial changes, and it wasn't long before others joined the effort, spawning over time a virtual collaborative community of software engineers bonded by their pride as innovators in the creation of a truly first-class product. As interest in the software continued to grow, Torvalds decided to make the operating system commercially available under a general public license so that anyone could use it for free as long as each agreed that any changes made to the program are in the public domain and available to everyone.[8]

Torvalds insistence that all contributions to Linux remain in a collective common is a radical departure from established thinking and turns conventional notions of ownership upside down. In both the Agrarian and the Industrial Ages, economic power was derived from owning critical economic assets. Thus, the more land the farmer owned or the bigger and better the factories of the industrialist, the more wealth they had. In the economies of both the land and the machine mindsets, wealth was about the accumulation of scarce resources and property rights. Over time, as we transitioned from the Agrarian Age to the Industrial Age, many of the assumptions and principles that defined our understanding of ownership and land rights shaped our concepts of the corporation and intellectual property rights.

The modern corporation is a legal invention designed to segregate the assets and liabilities of a company from those of its shareholders. Thus, in the eyes of the law, corporations are treated as separate "persons" who can buy, sell, and own property. Throughout the life of the Industrial Age corporation, ownership has been a pervasive prime value that manifests itself in a tenacious predilection for accumulation and control. This explains why vertical integration has been such a strong preference for traditional organizations and why managers often behave as if the resources entrusted to them – whether they're physical, financial, or human resources – are proprietary assets for use at their discretion.

Intellectual property rights began to take on greater importance in the later decades of the 20th century when knowledge work gradually displaced manufacturing as the principle focus of corporate activity. According to the prevailing belief among traditional executives, if knowledge is power, then the more knowledge the corporation owns, the greater its market power. Thus, as the proportion of goods sold dramatically shifted from hard goods to electronic software, we witnessed an intense race among a new generation of competitors who shared a belief that proprietary ownership of the next great computer application was the key to market success.

Torvalds, however, doesn't share this belief and breaks the mold by showing no interest in building a competitive product or in owning intellectual property. His labor of love is a collaborative effort that, at the same time, no one will own and everybody will own because it will never be proprietary, will always remain in the public domain, and will always be free. The surprising success of Linux demonstrates, once again, that knowledge is an abundant resource and the only way that it grows is by giving it away. Proprietary ownership of knowledge only diminishes its value. This means that as knowledge becomes more critical to business success and as more enterprises discover the power and efficiencies of open source platforms, traditional organizations will need to abandon long-established notions of ownership, especially when it comes to knowledge work and knowledge workers, if they hope to succeed in the new wiki world.

As the popularity of Linux began to resonate in the systems community, one traditional computer corporation recognized that it was time to make a radical change from its old ways of thinking. IBM had been playing catch-up in the PC market by attempting, with much cost and little success, to build its own proprietary operating system to compete with Microsoft's dominant Windows application. However, as a budding wiki-management organization, IBM was not blinded by misguided illusions of wishful strategic thinking. The brutal market reality was becoming quite clear to IBM's executives: Big Blue was too late to the market to expect to build its own commercial product, and sinking more money into this initiative was a guaranteed loser. Nevertheless, it was also clear that IBM's competitiveness in the computer services and solutions market was dependent upon its ability to provide affordable operating systems for those customers seeking alternatives. To solve its dilemma, IBM recognized that it would need to abandon its long-standing notions of proprietary ownership, take an unorthodox leap into the public domain of open source technology, and completely transform the way its programmers worked. Thus, recognizing the futility of its proprietary quest, IBM made a bold strategic move and joined the Linux community of volunteer programmers. In charting this course, IBM had no illusions that their size and market power would hold any weight in the open source community. As large and as powerful as IBM is, Big Blue understood that, in the Linux community, their programmers would have no special status, that they would be expected to participate in open platforms just as any other programmer, and, of course, that any work performed by IBM's programmers would stay in the public domain and would be available to anyone for free.

IBM's alliance with Linux is a win-win for both organizations. With the addition of a multitude of IBM software experts, Linux's programming efforts receive a boost valued at $100 million per year.[9] For its part, at only 20 percent of the cost of a proprietary offering, Big Blue is able to develop and distribute an operating system that is compatible with its other product lines at no additional charge to its customers.[10] But perhaps, the greatest value for IBM from its venture into the world of open source technology is its discovery of the power of mass collaboration as a competitive advantage. Because of its Linux experience, IBM has first-hand knowledge of how today's challenge of organizing the work of large numbers is less about bosses and work assignments inside the company and more about leveraging the global network of professionals outside the organization. IBM has a distinct competitive advantage because it now has the capacity to achieve consistent results based on shared understanding and self-organization rather then on control and hierarchies. This means that with its ability to leverage the network of the world's best programmers and with its capacity to benefit from the new efficiencies of mass collaboration, IBM is able to work smarter, faster, and cheaper than its competitors who continue to struggle with the old bureaucratic models of proprietary ownership.

IBM comes away from its Linux experience with a new appreciation that knowledge is far more powerful when it is shared than when it is owned. Unlike many of its competitors, IBM fully grasps that knowledge is an abundant resource that can only be accessed through collective learning partnerships with workers both inside and outside the organization. IBM has also learned that sharing knowledge in the public domain pays itself back many times in the creation of unique value that can be used to better position the company's distinct products and services for market success. But most importantly, because of its Linux experience, IBM has become proficient at the two new critical core competencies for business success in the Digital Age: collective learning and mass collaboration. And that is a big competitive advantage for Big Blue.

BOUNDARYLESS ENTERPRISES

Mass collaboration is the capacity for individuals or groups of individuals to leverage their intelligence and to work together through distributed networks to produce faster, smarter, and less costly results. Whether you're an individual, a department, a company, or even a nation, everything that you need to succeed in today's Digital Age is not contained within the boundaries of your current intelligence. There are and there always will be more smart people outside your organization than there are inside. Now that we have the capacity to easily connect with the world's brightest people, the smartest organizations are no longer those who accumulate the best talent within their corporate walls, but rather they are boundaryless enterprises, who through state-of-the-art systems and social technologies are able to continually expand the intelligence of the workers inside the organization by leveraging the networks of knowledge beyond their artificial borders. This is the powerful lesson that Goldcorp learned, as we discussed in Chapter 8, when it reached out to the world's geologists to locate its hidden treasures of gold. This is also an important principle behind the sustained success of one of the world's oldest corporations, General Electric.

One of Jack Welch's proudest accomplishments during his tenure as GE's CEO was the company's adoption of a way of acting that he called "boundarylessness."[11] This new way of acting is the complete opposite of the "not invented here" thinking that is so prevalent in traditional organizations. In embracing boundarylessness, GE actively acknowledged that there are indeed more smart people outside the organization and that, if somebody out there already has the knowledge or a practice that the company needs, there's no point in reinventing the wheel. Accordingly, GE not only rewarded individuals who invented things, but they also explicitly recognized people who found great ideas outside the company and shared them with everyone inside the organization.[12]

As we noted above, IBM has also discovered the value and the importance of breaking down barriers for both business survival and competitive advantage in the new economy. IBM learned the lesson of boundarylessness the hard way when it was forced to adopt entirely new ways of thinking and acting or risk its survival. Reaching beyond its boundaries by taking the leap into open source and leveraging the talent's of the world's best programmers is one of the ways that IBM sustains its incredible turnaround. Today IBM fully appreciates that boundarylessness is the strategy that will keep the company from the pitfalls of the insular bureaucratic thinking that almost brought about its demise.

What GE, IBM and Linux all have in common is that they each fully grasp the valuable lesson that every large organization will need to learn to sustain itself in the permanent whitewater of our fast changing times: Mass collaboration is the next great leap in business efficiency and to remain competitive in the wiki world, corporations will need to embrace boudarylessness and dramatically change the way they organize the work of large numbers of people.

There are four ingredients that are necessary if corporations want to realize the full benefits of collaborative communities, and as we will see, the bureaucratic nature of top-down central planning and the communication constraints of command-and-control hierarchies are completely misaligned with management's new prerequisites.

THE FIRST INGREDIENT: COMMON SPACE

Managers and workers need to have a space where they can periodically come together to freely express their ideas and get a first-hand sense of the state of the whole project or process. This common space is a virtual or physical "town hall" and can take many forms. Linux gathers its programmers in Web-based venues, whereas Toyota has developed sophisticated audio-visual conferencing technology to bring geographically dispersed people together. In the Blue Cross Blue Shield Federal Employee Program (FEP), we gathered managers and workers from across the nation into Town Hall Conference Calls or into large hotel rooms when we facilitated Work-Thrus. What's important is that everyone knows that there is a place where they can go to periodically connect with everyone else involved in a project. As mentioned previously, when you need to manage at the pace of change, there is nothing as powerful as getting everybody together in the same place at the same time. When everyone involved shares the same space, each person has the opportunity to integrate his observations, opinions, and concerns with those of his colleagues to create solutions that represent the best of everybody's ideas. Furthermore, by working together in common space, each individual is able to clearly see how his contribution fits into the larger picture, and as a benefit, becomes acutely aware of the critical importance of keeping everyone directly informed as issues or surprises arise so that they are nipped in the bud.

Common space replaces the chain of command as the new context for fundamental communication within the organization. If we are going to effectively leverage networks, everyone in the network needs to know everything. The idea that information is fragmented and distributed on a "need-to-know" basis makes no sense when the corporate charge is to manage at the pace of change. Periodically gathering everyone into a common space is one of the important ways that organizations practice slowing down to move fast. When companies have the capacity to bring everyone together in a common exchange, they are transformed into collaborative communities where individuals develop critically important cross-functional relationships, become connected to the strategic purpose of the work, and take personal responsibility for the execution of results.

We witnessed the amazing efficiency of using common space and building community when we successfully installed a new claims processing system, as we discussed in Chapter 9, among the 39 independent Blue Cross Blue Shield organizations participating in FEP. Once a week we gathered in two-hour Town Hall Conference Calls where anyone who wanted to participate was invited to openly discuss anything that had occurred with the project over the recent week. The early identification of issues, the development of efficient integrated solutions in the presence of everyone, and the shared understanding that evolved from these common space gatherings created a vibrant community where engaged individuals took personal responsibility for making sure that everything worked well on day one.

When working on large complex projects, periodically gathering everyone – or at least a critical mass of everyone – into common space is essential if you need to get it done fast and you need to get it done right the first time. The FEP systems experience demonstrates that the sharing of information that happens in the common space of collaborative communities is far more effective than the fragmented distri-

bution of information so typical of the chain of command in hierarchical bureaucracies.

THE SECOND INGREDIENT: OPEN CONVERSATIONS

Open conversations happen when everyone in the common space
is encouraged to freely express his ideas and when each person is willing to listen to what everyone has to say. Getting people to share their
opinions is usually not difficult – it's getting everyone to truly listen to
each other that is frequently the challenge. That is why so many of the
conversations that take place in traditional organizations tend to be
debates among dominant individuals who spend a great deal of time
telling you what they think and very little time listening to what others have to say. Unless you have both the freedom of expression and
everyone's willingness to listen in a spirit of dialogue, you don't have
open conversations. Consequently, no one's observations, opinions, or
concerns should be off-limits, and no one's thinking should be dis-
missed out of hand. In a fast changing world, there is no room for
censorship or the preservation of insular corporate points of view.

When the common space of mass collaboration is the Web, corporate censorship is impossible. Because there is no boss of the Internet,
conversations in cyberspace take place in a virtual dialogue that naturally encourages both the full expression and the full hearing of
everyone's thoughts and ideas. The egalitarian quality of virtual communities inherently promotes the integration of diverse observations
and the creation of breakthrough thinking. Without anyone to censor
the conversations or to ascribe whose ideas have more weight than
others, a geographically dispersed group of individuals, such as the
Linux programmers or the Wikipedia scribes, are able to build on
each other's contributions and quickly create knowledge that no one
of them could either do alone or centrally direct in the same amount
of time.

When the common space of mass collaboration is a physical location, such as a large hotel room, creating the conditions for open communications is more challenging and usually requires some level of
facilitation. When people are gathered in a common physical space,
having open conversations does not mean that anyone is free to say
whatever they want whenever they want or to engage in the patterns
of interrupting and talking over each other that are so common in the
typical corporate meeting. Again, conversations are open only when

people are both free to express themselves and are willing to listen in a spirit of dialogue. That is why in Work-Thrus, for example, when it is time for clarifying questions only, anyone is free to ask any clarifying question but is not free to express any opinion at that time. The protocol for clarifying questions assures that the presenters are being heard and not ignored. There will be other places and times in the Work-Thru for the free expression of other observations and concerns. Open conversations in common physical space are not free-for-alls but rather dialogues in which everyone can participate by observing protocols that foster both free expression and genuine listening. Accordingly, the leader's role in these meetings is not to influence the content of the discussion, but rather to be the guardian of the context of the conversation by assuring that everyone in the group adheres to a basic set of protocols to promote dialogue and collaboration. In the collaborative communities of wiki-management organizations, open conversations replace the scripted conversations so common in hierarchical bureaucracies.

THE THIRD INGREDIENT: CONSENSUS AGREEMENTS

Mass collaboration works best when conclusions about understanding what's important to customers or what's the best way to improve a business process are based on a broad consensus among managers, workers, suppliers, and if possible, customers. While the thought of building consensus across such a wide spectrum of stakeholders may appear dauntingly time-consuming and seem absolutely impossible, W.L. Gore's very successful use of self-organization is clear proof that broad consensus building is not only possible in large organizations, but is – quite contrary to conventional thinking – the secret to its consistent profitability.

When everyone's voice has been heard, people are more likely to agree with the consensus, even if it does not reflect their personal preferences. As a result, they are more likely to take willing responsibility for implementing the group consensus. This is especially true for knowledge workers because those few participants who might have preferred another approach are far more likely to accept a thoughtful consensus from among all the players than a discretionary directive from a lone decision maker disconnected from the day-to-day work. You may recall the difference of opinion in the Work-Thru, referenced in Chapter 7, between the representatives of the central processor of the health insurance product and those of the central processor for a proposed new dental product in Blue Cross Blue Shield FEP. The different advocates believed passionately that that their organizations should serve as the lead processor in coordinating benefits between the existing health and the proposed dental products. After a 45-minute small group exercise, it was obvious that there was a clear consensus across all the participants to use the health processor as the lead coordinator. Even though this was not the preference of the individuals participating from the dental processor, they readily accepted the collective wisdom of the group. Without the capability to achieve quick consensus within the context of the Work-Thru, the only ways to resolve the difference of opinion would have been through protracted negotiations or by an arbitrary decision, neither of which would have been as thoughtful or as willingly accepted as the consensus.

Some traditional managers may have difficulty making a commitment to managing by consensus because they don't believe that it's good business to turn their organizations into democracies. While W.L. Gore clearly demonstrates that large companies can be successful using a democratic organization model, embracing the wiki-management discipline does not require organizations to become democracies. GE, for example, uses its Work-Out process to bring people together into a common space for open conversations where the workers come to consensus agreements on recommendations for management. These recommendations are presented to GE's managers who must give on-the-spot yes-or-no decisions to at least 75 percent of the consensus recommendations. While decisions remain the prerogative of managers, they are guided by the consensus thinking of the workers. GE uses the collaborative communities of Work-Outs to make sure that bureaucracy does not get in the way of its agility to manage at the pace of change. Because GE has the protocols and the practices for quickly tapping into the collective wisdom of its workers, the managers have better ideas for making better decisions.

For the most part, workers are less concerned about who makes the decision than they are about implementing a good decision. When professionals are directed to do something that they are convinced will work, they are more than willing to follow through. Professionals are motivated by the satisfaction of getting the right things done. What most bothers workers, especially knowledge workers, is being told to do something that they know makes no sense, won't work, and will result in a great deal of time-consuming rework that could have been avoided if they only had been given a voice before the decision was made. Workers don't necessarily need to make the decision; they just need to have their voices heard and to know that their input actually counted when the managers came to their decision. By continually involving workers in consensus conversations at the front end, managers will have the advantage of the collective intelligence of the people who know the customers and the processes best when it comes time to make decisions. GE is not a democracy, but through its Work-Out process, it is able to build a quick consensus among its workers about the best ways for GE to work and to use that information to guide decision-making.

Even open source communities, such as Linux, aren't complete democracies. While the volunteers collaborate in cyberspace and develop a consensus product as they build upon each other's work, sometimes recurring conflicts among the programmers need to be resolved or sometimes different patches of the operating system need to be stitched together to complete the fabric of the overall product. In those instances, Linus Torvalds and a select core group will make decisions to resolve recurring conflicts and to preserve the integrity of the overall operating system.[13] What's different about Linux is that this type of central decision-making is the exception rather than the rule, and that these rare central decisions are always open for criticism, further discussion, and revision if Torvalds and his core group didn't get it right.

Although wiki-management organizations do not necessarily need to be democracies when it comes to making decisions, they understand that the leap in efficiencies made possible by the emergence of mass collaboration is only realized when the thinking that is the foundation for decision-making reflects the consensus agreements from the community of workers rather than the insular views of a bureaucratic elite.

THE FOURTH INGREDIENT: SELF-ORGANIZED WORK

In the wiki world, workers are not assigned tasks by bosses. Rather they decide among themselves what they will do and who will do it. Knowledge workers don't need to be told what to do or how to do their jobs because they know the content of their work far better than their managers. The efficiencies of mass collaboration are only possible when the workers organize their own work.

This is a dramatic departure from the traditional mass production enterprise of the Industrial Age. Then the bosses were the engineers of the assembly line and they did know the jobs better than the workers. Thus, they had the knowledge to effectively divide the labor into discrete task assignments among functionally segregated workers as well as the ability to monitor and control the performance of all the activities that needed to come together at the end of the assembly line process.

The task-orientation at the heart of traditional hierarchical management doesn't work in the new Digital Age. The efficiencies of mass collaboration are only possible when companies focus on business processes. Every worker needs to be familiar with the tasks and activities of everyone who is part of his business process so that he can recognize how changes in what he does affects the work of others and how the work of his colleagues impacts what he does. In process-oriented companies, workers are accountable for the accomplishment of results rather than merely for the completion of their tasks and they are accountable to each other rather than to a boss. This drives greater efficiency because, in today's businesses, it is the knowledge workers and the service workers who are often the first to observe changes in customer values or deficiencies in business processes. Workers who are responsible for self-organizing their own work will quickly find each other and agree on the necessary adjustments while the changes or the deficiencies are still small and manageable.

When workers are accountable for results and to each other and when they are able to act on their own consensus agreements, there's no finger pointing or playing the blame game that's so typical in task-oriented bureaucracies. If people are accountable only for their tasks and to their bosses, they can sit back and watch processes fall apart as long as their tasks are complete. However, when people are accountable for results and to each other, they all fail when the process breaks down and after-the-fact finger pointing becomes meaningless. In the wiki world, self-organized work is more effective than assignments by supervisors because knowledge workers are far more motivated by their standing with their professional peers than they are by pleasing the bosses. As a result, they are more willing to assume responsibility to make sure the overall process works.

The most difficult adjustment for organizations as they transition from hierarchical bureaucracies to collaborative communities will be coming to terms with the new reality that organizations no longer need bosses in order to be effective. It will be very hard for them to accept that the presence of bosses is actually is hindrance to the efficiencies possible with mass collaboration. However, Linux, Wikipedia, Google, W.L. Gore and the SARS research team are all examples of how organizations can become incredibly efficient when the role of the boss is diminished. In the collaborative communities of the wiki world, the leader's role is not to assign the work but to facilitate the collective learning and the shared understanding that the workers need to organize their own work so the organization can work smarter and faster than the competition.

A NEW CHALLENGE

In the later decades of the 20th century, the gradual increase in the number of knowledge workers coupled with the sudden appearance of an accelerating pace of change began to stretch the limits of the effectiveness of a century-old management discipline. Despite the pressures from these two emerging developments, corporate executives have been reluctant to relinquish the control and the authority that comes with management positions in command-and-control organizations. Until now, they have been able to handle the competitive challenges of an accelerating pace of change by working everyone harder – but not necessarily smarter – through staff reductions and increases to the workloads of the remaining workers. Managers have also been able to finesse the demands for involvement by the increasing number of knowledge workers by adopting participative management practices that require accommodations in style, but that leave the basic substance of hierarchical management unchanged. While these accommodations reflect the bosses' growing understanding that the workers own the critical knowledge asset, the managers have also been keenly aware that worker knowledge only has economic value when it is combined with other workers' knowledge, and until recently, the only place that workers could go to find other knowledge colleagues was in corporations. Thus, the bosses have been able to sustain their ingrained belief that the workers still need the corporation more than the corporation needs the workers.

Whatever comfort managers may feel in their ability thus far to hold onto their century-old management discipline, they will soon learn that they are acting with a false sense of security. The firm rooting of the Internet is the tipping point that is escalating the Digital Age and changing the work we do and the way we work. By making mass collaboration possible, the Web becomes the catalyst that transforms the economic value of worker knowledge and accelerates the pace of change to the point where continued use of strategies to work harder is ineffectual. The only effective strategy for working in today's faster-paced world is to work smarter. The Internet and mass collaboration are also providing knowledge workers with attractive – and oftentimes more productive — alternatives for combining their knowledge with others to create economic value. As these alternatives expand, it is becoming clearer that today the corporations need the workers more than the workers need the corporations. This will become even more evident as an increasing number of knowledge workers are able to become free agents working for several companies at once.

The shift from mass production to mass collaboration means that companies need to reach outside their organizations for a significant number of their workers if they are to remain competitive in the wiki world. They also need to work far smarter and far faster than they currently do today. A century-old management model structured around order and authority will not get the job done. The new world of mass collaboration means that the bosses have no choice but to accept that the successful enterprises of the Digital Age will be wiki-management organizations designed for knowledge and speed. These organizations will be substantially different from traditional hierarchical bureaucracies. In Digital Age organizations, there are no chains of command, central planning, or distributed task assignments. Wiki-management enterprises are collaborative communities of horizontal networks whose interactive foundations are common space, open conversations, consensus agreements, and self-organized work because, when the primary task of the corporation is to leverage the networks, organizing large numbers of workers is truly a completely new challenge.

EPILOGUE

Whether we like it or not, the world where most of us grew up is quickly fading away. We now live in a wiki world where the power of networks and the speed of mass collaboration are redefining every aspect of our social lives, especially the work we do and the way we work. We are indeed at a tipping point where traditional corporations and their leaders find themselves in an unprecedented business reality for which they are totally unprepared. Never before have executives been faced with the challenge of transitioning large organizations from one socioeconomic era to another. After all, large business organizations are themselves creations of the Industrial Age. And never before have leaders been called upon to completely overhaul their assumptions, values, and beliefs about the fundamental realities of how organizations work.

Whether or not today's leaders are up to the challenge will not matter. Those managers who cannot wean themselves from the machine mindset and its beliefs in central planning and chains of command will disrupt only their own individual organizations or, at most, their traditional industries. Their resistance will have no lasting imprint on the overall economy because new organizations, and in some cases successor industries, will quickly fill the void when recalcitrant companies go out of business. As we discussed earlier, the failure of recording industry executives to seize the opportunity to transform their mass production industry into a file-sharing empire has not stopped the inevitable evolution of recorded music.

There is little doubt that the Digital Revolution and mass collaboration will transform every existing industry. The only question is whether or not your organization is smart enough and fast enough to sustain itself in the new economy. And the answer to that question will depend on whether your current management remains entrenched in the ways of a century-old mindset or is capable of taking the next great leap in the efficiency of work.

The current corps of business leaders will be challenged in making this bounce because most of them are baby-boomers. Sometimes dubbed the "Me Generation," the confreres of this demographic cohort are known for two attributes that have served them well in the past but are handicaps for the future. They are vocal and they are dominant. Since the turbulent 1960's, boomers have been most attentive to making sure that their voices are heard and doing whatever it takes to get their way. If that means drowning out the voices of others to pursue what they believe to be right, then so be it. Perhaps this explains why many feel the civility in the halls of Congress today is at an historic low. Today's younger citizens, in particular, scratch their heads wondering why their elected boomer representatives continually talk past each other and can't seem to find a way to integrate the best of their ideas. Boomers in positions of power and authority haven't exactly been the poster children for collaboration.

The boomers, in their time, were arguably the most difficult generation of adolescents that any group of parents had to raise, and they probably consider themselves fortunate that their children were not as troublesome to them as they were to their parents. However, they might be surprised to learn that the generation gap between them and their children is much wider than the rift the boomers had with their parents. In fact, in true boomer fashion, today's middle-aged parents would vehemently object, boast of their fine parenting, and proudly point to the great relationships that they have with their young adult children. Unfortunately, the boomers are missing what is in plain sight.

Unlike the 1960's, today's generation gap is a silent rather than a vocal rebellion. While it is probably true that the relationships between today's millennials and their parents are much improved when compared with the progeny of prior generations, this does not translate to the larger society. While today's young adults do get along well their own parents, they are quite alienated from their parent's generation. We see this in the reluctance of the millennials to adapt to the ways of traditional hierarchical organizations.

What is most alarming about today's generation gap is that it is so very silent. When the boomers were younger, they were annoyingly vocal in their rebellion because they were determined to replace the decision makers of their parents' generation and change the world. Simply stated, their parents had something the boomers wanted: the power and authority to be in charge. The fact that today's younger adults are so silent in their rebellion means only one thing: the boomers don't have anything that the millennials want.

Today's young adults don't need to be in charge to change the world because they have already created their own world and live in a very different reality from their parents' generation. In their world, you don't have to be in charge to get things done; you just have to be connected. The millennials don't value the traditional power to command because they already know that they can accomplish much more through the power to collaborate. Thus, what we are witnessing is not so much a generation gap as it is a mindset gap. As we have noted on numerous occasions throughout this book, the boomers are the last generation of the machine mindset and are still living in a mass production world, while the millennials are the first generation of the network mindset and are firmly rooted in the new mass collaboration world.

Today's version of a generation gap will not resolve itself in the usual way with the younger generation acclimating to the dominant worldview of their elders. For all their bravado about changing the world, once the boomers secured the positions of social power and authority, they fell in line with the established ways of previous generations. This will not be the case for the millennials. Every new generation for the foreseeable future will be quickly socialized into the new ways of the network mindset. This means for the first time in over 100 years, it is the older and not the younger generation that needs to adapt to be aligned with society's dominant mindset. That is why today's generation gap is so silent. It turns out that this is not your usual youthful rebellion, but rather an inevitable evolution. The millennials don't have to make any noise to change the world. That's because they are able to see what most boomer bosses have yet to recognize: Somewhere in the last decade the world as we have known it has indeed ended. We are all now living in a wiki world.

Today's boomer executives do not have much time to close the mindset gap and learn the new skills and competencies of mass collaboration. For those bosses who are not convinced that they need to change, they only have to widen their sights to see whole industries that are struggling under the burden of obsolete management practices. Some highly visible examples include the American automotive industry, the recording industry, the financial services industry, and most recently the healthcare industry. Each of these once-great institutions is bearing the brunt of the consequences of centrally planned decision-making by an elite few. Sooner or later the boomers will have to come to terms with the new realities of mass collaboration: Nobody is smarter than everybody and self-organizing teams operating from a shared understanding always work smarter and faster than individual heroes and star performers.

While it certainly is possible for traditional companies and their leaders to make the leap to the new efficiencies of mass collaboration, so far the incidence of success has not been much better than the very small percentage of companies that Jim Collins and his researchers found were able to make the leap from good-to-great. If Collins is right in suggesting that good is the enemy of great, there is reason to be concerned whether today's corps of boomer bosses will recognize the need for change. After all, most companies today, despite the difficulties of the recent recession, are delivering the bottom line. Are these business leaders likely to repeat the mistakes of the recording industry executives who tried in vain to preserve their 20th century business model or will they show the foresight of a Jack Welch and radically transform their management practices to be better prepared for a much faster world? And, even if they recognize the need for change, will the boomer bosses have the strength and the courage to abdicate power and learn to trust the wisdom of the crowd? The sustainability of many companies may depend on the answers to these questions.

While learning the new ways of mass collaboration is indeed challenging, those who can make the leap will never look back. That's because when leaders discover the power and the speed of mass collaboration, they enable extraordinary performance. This was our experience in the Blue Cross Blue Shield Federal Employee Program (FEP), especially as we became proficient at facilitating Work-Thrus and Town Hall Conference Calls to access our collective knowledge and build a powerful shared understanding across large numbers of people. Our ability to build consensus among thousands of geographically dispersed workers provided us with an unprecedented capacity to work smarter and faster than was ever possible when we managed as bosses. We learned to appreciate that, if we were to successfully manage at the new pace of change, we had to accept the new realities of the redefined challenge for organizing the work of large numbers of people: We work for the customers and not the bosses; nobody is smarter than everybody; workers are partners and not subordinates, and focusing on the few critical drivers facilitates the accomplishment of all the tasks.

Of these new realities, the one that stood out the most, left the deepest impression upon us, and was consistently reinforced, especially when we facilitated Work-Thrus, was the clear fact that nobody is smarter than everybody. Having been raised in the firm belief that a single talented hero or an elite group of highly intelligent executives can lead organizations to greatness, we were consistently and pleasantly surprised to discover the untapped depth of knowledge that resided across all the managers and workers. Learning to leveraging this collective knowledge is what enabled us to make the leap to extraordinary performance and to become an incredibly effective organization.

The effective large organization is one of the most important human accomplishments. There are few greater satisfactions than being part of an effort that makes a contribution and a difference that no one of us could do alone. If we want of be part of something extraordinary, we usually need to partner and work with other people. Effective large organizations allow ordinary people to do extraordinary things.

According to Peter Drucker, the unique purpose of an organization is to make strength productive.[1] The wonderful thing about effective organizations is that we do not have to be individually perfect to succeed. We just have to be perfect together. The special power of organizations is that, when they work well, they render our weaknesses insignificant by combining only our strengths and creating collective excellence. Thus, the closest most of us ever get to perfection is when we work well together and mutually experience the benefits of each other's strengths.

That being said, just are there are no perfect people, there are no perfect organizations. Command-and-control organizations are not perfect and neither are their wiki-management successors. Each of these approaches has its strengths and its weaknesses, and all organizations have issues and challenges – that's just the nature of organizational work.

Although we have accented the weaknesses of command-and-control, there can be no doubt that over the course of the last century the large hierarchical organizations of mass production have greatly improved our lives. These organizations have made a dramatic contribution to our standard of living and our quality of life. The world of the early 21st century is a very different place thanks to the contributions of mass production companies over the last century, and despite their much-publicized imperfections, there are very few of us who would choose to return to the ways of the Agrarian Age. The ordinary people in Industrial Age corporations did indeed accomplish extraordinary things.

And although we have emphasized the strengths of the wiki-management organization, these companies are also only human and will have their fair share of problems and weaknesses. Just as mass production organizations have had to deal with the flaws of the bosses, mass collaboration enterprises will need to learn to handle the inevitable deficiencies of the facilitators.

Neither of these ways of organizing large numbers of people is inherently right or inherently wrong, they are simply right or wrong for different times. Given the nature of the work and the lower level of education of the average industrial worker in the late 19th century factories, self-organized work probably would have resulted in only chaos and confusion. Likewise, given the nature of work and the higher level of education of the average knowledge worker in the early 21st century, hierarchically organized work will not sustain companies in an economic world that values knowledge and speed. And, perhaps a hundred years from now neither command-and-control nor wiki-management will be the right fit for the next new socioeconomic era as the world transitions into a post-Digital Age era.

But for now, we are living and working in the new and unfamiliar Digital Age. Over the next decade or two, its network mindset will continue to reshape the ways of thinking and the ways of acting across all social institutions. Inevitably, wiki-management will replace command-and-control as the dominant management practice not because it's inherently better but because it's right for the times. That being said, command-and-control management will not disappear with the advent of the Digital Age any more than farming disappeared with the arrival of the Industrial Age. However, just as farming is no longer the primary occupation as it was in the 18th century, neither will command-and-control be the dominant practice as it was in the 20th century.

The rules of the game have changed. Those of you in leadership roles, especially those of you who are boomers, will need to make the leap to a new level of organizational excellence if you want to meet the new business challenge of the 21st century. This means resetting the ways you manage, the ways you meet, and the ways you measure. For those leaders who have the courage to reinvent their management identities by learning how to facilitate collective learning and shared understanding, you will be amazed to discover the astonishing organizational capacity that has been there all along. You will be pleasantly surprised by the incredible power of mass collaboration as you continually marvel at the outstanding results of ordinary people doing more extraordinary things than you ever thought was possible. Have the courage to make the leap, because whether we like it or not, the revolution is inevitable. The Digital Age is changing the work we do and the way we work. Welcome to the wiki world!

NOTES

CHAPTER 1

1 Gary Hamel, *The Future of Management*, (Boston, MA: Harvard Business School Press), 2007, 41.
2 Jim Collins, *Good to Great: Why Some Companies Make the Leap...and Others Don't*, (New York: HarperCollins), 2001, 41.
3 Ibid.
4 Don Tapscott and Anthony D. Williams, *Wikinomics: How Mass Collaboration Changes Everything*, (New York: Portfolio), 2006.
5 Martin A. Schwartzman, State of New York Insurance Department Report, "Empire HealthChoice, Inc D/B/A Empire Blue Cross and Blue Shield: Summary of Recovery Efforts Related to September 11, 2001 Destruction of the World Trade Center As of November 28, 2001," June 10, 2002, 7-8.
6 Ibid. 24-25.
7 Hamel, *The Future of Management*, 16.
8 Michael Hammer, *Beyond Reengineering: How the Process-Centered Organization Is Changing Our Work and Our Lives*, (New York: Harper Business), 1996, 97.
9 Michael Hammer and James Champy, *Reengineering the Corporation: A Manifesto For Business Revolution*, (New York: Harper Business), 1993.
10 Peter Senge, *The Fifth Discipline: The Art and Practice of the Learning Organization*, (New York: Doubleday/Currency), 1990.

CHAPTER 2

1 Peter F. Drucker, *Management Challenges for the 21st Century*, (New York: Harper Business), 1999, 139.

CHAPTER 3

1 Thomas L. Friedman, *The World is Flat: A Brief History of the Twenty-First Century*, (New York: Farrar, Straus, and Giroux), 2005, 8.
2 Ibid. 84-85.

3 Don Tapscott and Anthony D. Williams, *Wikinomics: How Mass Collaboration Changes Everything*, (New York: Portfolio), 2006, 18.
4 Elizabeth Haas Edersheim, *The Definitive Drucker*, (New York: McGraw Hill), 2007, 103.
5 Ibid. 83-85.

CHAPTER 4

1 William C. Taylor and Polly LaBarre, *Mavericks at Work: Why the Most Original Minds in Business Win*, (New York: Harper-Collins), 2006, 110.
2 Gary Hamel, *The Future of Management*, (Boston, MA: Harvard Business School Press), 2007, 16.
3 Jim Collins, *Good to Great: Why Some Companies Make the Leap...and Others Don't*, (New York: HarperCollins), 2001.
4 James C. Collins and Jerry I. Porras, *Built to Last: Successful Habits of Visionary Companies*, (New York: HarperCollins), 1994.
5 Collins, *Good to Great*, 6.
6 Ibid. 1.
7 Ibid. 12-13.

CHAPTER 5

1 W. Chan Kim and Renee Mauborgne, *Blue Ocean Strategy: How to Create Uncontested Market Space and Make the Competition Irrelevant*, (Boston, MA: Harvard Business School Press), 2005, 172.
2 Stephen R. Covey, *The 8th Habit: From Effectiveness to Greatness*, (New York: Free Press), 2004, 218.
3 Ibid.
4 Ibid. 274.
5 Elizabeth Hass Edersheim, *The Definitive Drucker*, (New York: McGraw Hill), 2007, 11.

CHAPTER 6

1 Michael Treacy and Fred Wiersema, *The Discipline of Market Leaders: Choose Your Customers, Narrow Your Focus, Dominate Your Market*, (Reading, MA: Addison-Wesley), 1995, 25.

2 William C. Taylor and Polly LaBarre, *Mavericks at Work: Why the Most Original Minds in Business Win*, (New York: Harper-Collins), 2006, 38.

3 Ibid.

4 Michael Hammer, *The Agenda: What Every Business Must Do to Dominate the Decade*, (New York: Crown Business), 2001,179.

5 Jeffrey K. Liker, *The Toyota Way: 14 Management Principles from the World's Greatest Manufacturer*, (New York: McGraw-Hill), 2004, 228-229.

6 Ibid. 229.

7 Ibid.

8 Ibid. 229-230.

9 Peter F. Drucker, *Management Challenges for the 21st Century*, (New York: HarperCollins), 1999, 28.

10 Brian Hiatt and Evan Serpick, "The Recording Industry's Decline," *RollingStone.com*, posted June 19, 2007, 2:29 pm.

11 Ibid.

12 Treacy and Wiersema, *The Discipline of Market Leaders*, xiv.

13 Ibid.

14 Taylor and LaBarre, *Mavericks at Work*, 184-185.

15 Ibid. 136.

16 Ibid.

17 Joseph A. Michelli, *The Starbucks Experience: 5 Principles for Turning Ordinary into Extraordinary*, (New York: McGraw-Hill), 2007, 20-21.

18 Ibid. 15.

19 Ibid. 7.

20 Thomas Friedman, *The World Is Flat: A Brief History of the Twenty-First Century*, (New York: Farrar, Straus, and Giroux), 2005, 436.

21 Stephen M. R. Covey, *The Speed of Trust: The One Thing That Changes Everything*, (New York: Free Press), 2006, 189.

22 Ram Charan, Know-How: *The 8 Skills That Separate People Who Perform from Those Who Don't*, (New York: Crown Business), 2007, 26.

23 Robert M. Schindler, "The Real Lesson of New Coke: The Value of Focus Groups for Predicting the Effects of Social Influence," *Marketing Research*, December 1992, 25.

24 Constance L. Hays, *The Real Thing: Truth and Power at the Coca Cola Company*, (New York: Random House), 2004, 120.

CHAPTER 7

[1] James Surowiecki, *The Wisdom of Crowds: Why the Many Are Smarter than the Few and How Collective Wisdom Shapes Business, Economies, Societies, and Nations*, (New York: Doubleday), 2004, xiv.

[2] Robert Slater, *Jack Welch and the GE Way*, (New York: McGraw Hill), 1999, 135-137.

[3] Jack Welch with John A. Byrne, *Jack: Straight From the Gut*, (New York: Warner Books), 2001, 182.

[4] Ibid. 182-183.

[5] Jack Welch with Suzy Welch, *Winning*, (New York: Harper Business), 2005, 56.

[6] Stephen R. Covey, *The 7 Habits of Highly Effective People*, (New York: Simon and Schuster), 1989.

[7] Linda Ellinor and Glenna Gerard, *Dialogue: Rediscovering the Transforming Power of Conversation*, (New York: John Wiley & Sons, Inc), 1998, 39.

CHAPTER 8

[1] Peter M. Senge, *The Fifth Discipline: The Art and Practice of the Learning Organization*, (New York: Doubleday/Currency), 1990, 10.

[2] Ed Michaels, Helen Handfield-Jones, and Beth Axelrod, *The War For Talent*, (Boston, MA: Harvard Business School Publishing), 2001.

[3] Malcolm Gladwell, "The Talent Myth," *New Yorker*, July 22, 2002, 29.

[4] Ibid. 32.

[5] James Surowiecki, *The Wisdom of Crowds: Why the Many Are Smarter than the Few and How Collective Wisdom Shapes Business, Economies, Societies, and Nations*, (New York: Doubleday), 2004.

[6] Ibid. 10.

[7] Ibid. xix.

[8] Ibid. 74.

[9] Gary Hamel, *The Future of Management*, (Boston, MA: Harvard Business School Publishing), 2007, 201.

[10] Don Tapscott and Anthony D. Williams, *Wikinomics: How Mass Collaboration Changes Everything*, (New York: Portfolio), 2006, p. 7.

11 William C. Taylor and Polly LaBarre, *Mavericks at Work: Why the Most Original Minds in Business Win*, (New York: Harper-Collins), 2006, 63-64.

12 Tapscott and Williams, *Wikinomics*, 9.

CHAPTER 9

1 Eugene Eric Kim, *eekim.com Wiki: Shared Understanding.*

2 Stephen R. Covey, *The Eighth Habit: From Effectiveness to Greatness*, (New York: Free Press), 2004, 218.

3 Lori L. Silverman, *Wake Me Up When the Data Is Over: How Organizations Use Storytelling to Drive Results*, (San Francisco, CA: Jossey-Bass), 2006, xxiii.

4 Ralph Welborn and Vince Kasten, *The Jericho Principle: How Companies Use Strategic Collaboration to Find New Sources of Value*, (Hoboken, NJ: John Wiley & Sons, Inc.), 2003, 122.

5 Ibid.

6 Gary Hamel, *The Future of Management*, (Boston, MA: Harvard Business School Publishing), 2007, 87.

7 Ibid. 88-89.

8 Alan Deutschman, "The Fabric of Creativity," *Fast Company*, December 2004, 54.

9 Hamel, *The Future of Management*, 91.

10 Malcolm Gladwell, *The Tipping Point: How Little Things Can Make a Big Difference*, (New York: Little, Brown, and Company), 2000, 186.

11 Hamel, *The Future of Management*, 93.

12 Deutschman, "The Fabric of Creativity," 54.

CHAPTER 10

1 Margaret J. Wheatley, *Leadership and the New Science: Discovering Order in a Chaotic World*, (San Francisco, CA: Berrett-Koehler Publishers, Inc.), 1999, 106.

2 Ronald E. Purser and Steven Cabana, *The Self-Managing Organization: How Leading Companies Are Transforming the Work of Teams for Real Impact*, (New York: Free Press), 1998, 14-15.

3 Melanie Mitchell, *Complexity: A Guided Tour*, (New York: Oxford University Press), 2009, 13.

4 Margaret J. Wheatley, *Leadership and the New Science*, 98.

5 James Surowiecki, *The Wisdom of Crowds: Why the Many Are Smarter than the Few and How Collective Wisdom Shapes Business, Economies, Societies, and Nations,* (New York: Doubleday), 2004, 101.

6 Purser and Cabana, *The Self-Managing Organization,* 147-148.

7 Peter F. Drucker, *Management: Tasks, Responsibilities, Practices,* (New York: Harper & Row), 1974, 494.

8 Stephen. M. R. Covey, *The Speed of Trust: The One Thing That Changes Everything,* (New York: Free Press), 2006, 153.

9 Andrew Lih, *The Wikipedia Revolution: How a Bunch of Nobodies Created the World's Greatest Encyclopedia,* (New York: Hyperion), 2009, 58.

10 Ibid. 43-44.

11 Ibid. 44.

12 Ibid. 61.

13 Ibid. 45, 64.

CHAPTER 11

1 Dean R. Spitzer, *Transforming Performance Measurement: Rethinking the Way We Measure and Drive Organizational Success,* (New York: AMACOM), 2007, 76.

2 FranklinCovey, *The Four Disciplines of Execution,* Participant's Course Manual, 2004, p. 10.

3 Stephen R. Covey, *The 8th Habit: From Effectiveness to Greatness,* (New York: Free Press), 2004, p. 281.

4 Robert S. Kaplan and David P. Norton, *The Balanced Scorecard: Translating Strategy into Action,* (Boston, MA: Harvard Business School Press), 1996.

5 Ibid. p. 2.

6 Ibid. pp. 94-95.

7 Ibid. p. 25.

CHAPTER 12

1 Don Tapscott and Anthony D. Williams, *Wikinomics: How Mass Collaboration Changes Everything,* (New York: Portfolio), 2006, 19.

2 David L. Heymann and Guenael Rodier, "Global Surveillance, National Surveillance, and SARS," *Emerging Infectious Disease - Medscape,* February 10, 2004.

3 Ibid.

4 James Surowiecki, *The Wisdom of Crowds: Why the Many Are Smarter Than the Few and How Collective Wisdom Shapes Business, Economies, Societies, and Nations*, (New York: Doubleday), 2004, 158.

5 Ibid. 159.

6 Ibid. 159-160.

7 Heymann and Rodier, "Global Surveillance, National Surveillance, and SARS."

8 Tapscott and Williams, *Wikinomics*. 24.

9 Ibid. 81.

10 Ibid.

11 Jack Welch with Suzy Welch, *Winning*, (New York: HarperCollins), 2005, 85.

12 Ibid.

13 Tapscott and Williams, *Wikinomics*, p. 280.

EPILOGUE

1 Peter Drucker, *People and Performance: The Best of Peter Drucker on Management*, (Boston, MA: Harvard Business School Publishing), 2007, 85.

CPSIA information can be obtained at www.ICGtesting.com
Printed in the USA
LVOW102138030213

318413LV00021B/531/P